D1303189

VOLUME

5

RENEWAL:
A TWENTY-YEAR
COMMITMENT

REPORT
OF THE ROYAL COMMISSION
ON ABORIGINAL PEOPLES

Canadian Cataloguing in Publication Data

Canada. Royal Commission on Aboriginal Peoples.
Report of the Royal Commission on Aboriginal Peoples.

Issued also in French under the title:
Rapport de la Commission royale sur les peuples autochtones.

Contents: v. 1. Looking forward, looking back –
v. 2. Restructuring the relationship –
v. 3. Gathering strength –
v. 4. Perspectives and realities –
v. 5. Renewal: a twenty-year commitment
ISBN 0-660-16413-2 (V. 1);
ISBN 0-660-16414-0 (V. 2);
ISBN 0-660-16415-9 (V. 3);
ISBN 0-660-16416-7 (V. 4);
ISBN 0-660-16417-5 (V. 5).
Cat. no. Z1-1991/1-1E (V. 1);
Cat. no. Z1-1991/1-2E (V. 2);
Cat. no. Z1-1991/1-3E (V. 3);
Cat. no. Z1-1991/1-4E (V. 4);
Cat. no. Z1-1991/1-5E (V. 5).

1. Native peoples – Canada.
2. Native peoples – Canada – Social conditions.
3. Native peoples – Canada – Economic conditions.
4. Native peoples – Canada – Politics and government.
I. Title.

E78.C2R46 1996   971'.00497   C96-980078-9

Available in Canada through
your local bookseller
or by mail from
Canada Communication Group – Publishing
Ottawa, Canada K1A 0S9

Cat. no. Z1-1991/1-5E
ISBN 0-660-16417-5

Cover: Elsie (Klengenberg) Anaginak, "Granny Teaches Grandchildren",
1992, stencil print on Arches paper, 56 x 43 centimetres.
Endpapers: Mireille Siouï, "Dans la maison d'Handiaouich, la petite tortue",
intaglio, watercolour on paper, 50 x 32.5 centimetres.
Courtesy: Departmental Library, Indian and Northern Affairs Canada.
Photograph facing page 1: Fred Cattroll.

Canada	Groupe
Communication	Communication
Group	Canada
Publishing	Édition

VOLUME

5

RENEWAL:
A TWENTY-YEAR
COMMITMENT

CONTENTS

A Note About Sources

Among the sources referred to in this report, readers will find mention of testimony given at the Commission's public hearings; briefs and submissions to the Commission; submissions from groups and organizations funded through the Intervener Participation Program; research studies conducted under the auspices of the Commission's research program; reports on the national round tables on Aboriginal issues organized by the Commission; and commentaries, special reports and research studies published by the Commission during its mandate. After the Commission completes its work, this information will be available in various forms from a number of sources.

This report, the commentaries and special reports, research studies, round table reports, and other publications released during the Commission's mandate will be available in Canada through local booksellers or by mail from

Canada Communication Group – Publishing
Ottawa, Ontario
K1A 0S9

A CD-ROM will be published following this report. It will contain the report, transcripts of the Commission's hearings and round tables, overviews of the four rounds of hearings, research studies, the round table reports, and the Commission's special reports and commentaries, together with an educators' resource guide. The CD-ROM will be available in libraries across the country through the government's depository services program and for purchase from

Canada Communication Group – Publishing
Ottawa, Ontario
K1A 0S9

Briefs and submissions to the Commission, as well as research studies not published in book or CD-ROM form, will be housed in the National Archives of Canada after the Commission completes its work.

A NOTE ABOUT TERMINOLOGY

The Commission uses the term *Aboriginal people* to refer to the indigenous inhabitants of Canada when we want to refer in a general manner to Inuit and to First Nations and Métis people or peoples, without regard to their separate origins and identities.

The term *Aboriginal peoples* refers to organic political and cultural entities that stem historically from the original peoples of North America, rather than collections of individuals united by so-called 'racial' characteristics. The term includes the Indian, Inuit and Métis peoples of Canada (see section 35(2) of the *Constitution Act, 1982*).

Aboriginal people (in the singular) means the individuals belonging to the political and cultural entities known as 'Aboriginal peoples'.

The term *Aboriginal nations* overlaps with the term Aboriginal peoples but also has a more specific usage. The Commission's use of the term nation is discussed in some detail in Volume 2, Chapter 3, where it is defined as a sizeable body of Aboriginal people with a shared sense of national identity that constitutes the predominant population in a certain territory or collection of territories.

The Commission distinguishes between local communities and nations. We use terms such as *a First Nation community* and *a Métis community* to refer to a relatively small group of Aboriginal people residing in a single locality and forming part of a larger Aboriginal nation or people. Despite the name, a First Nation community would not normally constitute an Aboriginal nation in the sense that the Commission defined the term above. Rather, most (but not all) Aboriginal nations are composed of a number of communities.

Our use of the term *Métis* is consistent with our conception of *Aboriginal peoples* as described above. We refer to the *Métis* as distinct Aboriginal peoples whose early ancestors were of mixed heritage (First Nations, or Inuit in the case of the Labrador Métis, and European) and who associate themselves with a culture that is distinctly Métis. The more specific term *Métis Nation* is used to refer to Métis people who identify themselves as a nation with historical roots in the Canadian west. Our use of the terms *Métis* and *Métis Nation* is discussed in some detail in Volume 4, Chapter 5.

Following accepted practice and as a general rule, the term *Inuit* replaces the term *Eskimo*. As well, the term *First Nation* replaces the term *Indian*. However, where the subject of discussion is a specific historical or contemporary nation, we use the name of that nation (e.g., Mi'kmaq, Dene, Mohawk). Often more than one spelling is considered acceptable for these nations. We try to use the name preferred by particular nations or communities, many of whom now use their traditional names. Where necessary, we add the more familiar or generic name in parentheses – for example, Siksika (Blackfoot).

Terms such as *Eskimo* and *Indian* continue to be used in at least three contexts:

1. where such terms are used in quotations from other sources;
2. where *Indian* or *Eskimo* is the term used in legislation or policy, and hence in discussions concerning such legislation or policy (e.g., the *Indian Act*; the Eskimo Loan Fund); and
3. where the term continues to be used to describe different categories of persons in statistical tables and related discussions, usually involving data from Statistics Canada or the Department of Indian Affairs and Northern Development (e.g., status Indians on-reserve, registered Indians).

1

Laying the Foundations of a Renewed Relationship

In this report we have made recommendations affecting virtually every aspect of Aboriginal people's lives. We have sought to grapple with entrenched economic and social problems in Aboriginal communities while also seeking to transform the relationship between Aboriginal nations and Canadian governments. Each problem addressed would be difficult to resolve on its own; the problems are rendered more challenging by their interdependence. The scale and complexity of the task is daunting. Implementation will be much easier, however, if the essential themes of this report are kept in view. If one theme dominates our recommendations, it is that Aboriginal peoples must have room to exercise their autonomy and structure their own solutions. The pattern of debilitating and discriminatory paternalism that has characterized federal policy for the past 150 years must end. Aboriginal people cannot flourish if they are treated as wards, incapable of controlling their own destiny.

We advocate recognition of Aboriginal nations within Canada as political entities through which Aboriginal people can express their distinctive identity within the context of their Canadian citizenship. Aboriginal people do not have to surrender their identity to accomplish those goals. Non-Aboriginal Canadians cherish their identity as Newfoundlanders or Albertans, for instance, and still remain strongly committed to Canada.

At the heart of our recommendations is recognition that Aboriginal peoples *are* peoples, that they form collectivities of unique character, and that they have a right of governmental autonomy. Aboriginal peoples have preserved their identities under adverse conditions. They have safeguarded their traditions during many decades when non-Aboriginal officials attempted to regulate every aspect of their lives. They are entitled to control matters important to their nations without intrusive interference. This authority is not something bestowed by other governments. It is inherent in their identity as peoples. But to be fully effective, their authority must be recognized by other governments.

1. A New Beginning

The rebalancing of political and economic power between Aboriginal nations and other Canadian governments represents the core of the hundreds of recommendations contained in this report. Unless accompanied by a rebalancing of power, no progress can be made on other fronts without perpetuating the status quo. The effects of the past will not be undone overnight. The essential themes that underpin our recommendations and can assure the rebuilding of Aboriginal life in Canada are as follows.

First, Aboriginal nations have to be reconstituted.

Nations have been divided by policy and legislation. The basic unit of government in First Nations today is the band, a creation of the *Indian Act*. A band usually includes only a portion of a nation; First Nations people who lost status or did not qualify for status under the *Indian Act* have been excluded from their communities. As a result, bands are usually too small for effective self-government.

The situation is worse for Métis people, who have experienced very limited political recognition. Only Inuit are well advanced in the process of political reform. There must be latitude for Aboriginal people to reconstitute broader affiliations. We propose a process through which Aboriginal communities join together in new institutions to seek recognition of their status as modern nations.

Second, a process must be established for the assumption of powers by Aboriginal nations.

A definition of powers and mechanisms of transfer from other orders of government must be put in place. We recommend that this be undertaken in two phases: a recognition period in which Aboriginal governments exercise core power on their present territory, and a subsequent treaty process in which full Aboriginal jurisdiction on an expanded land base is negotiated with other Canadian governments. We expect that Aboriginal nations will exercise their powers incrementally as they develop expertise and gain experience. They will, however, have the right to exercise those powers and will control the pace of their own political development.

Third, there must be a fundamental reallocation of lands and resources.

We documented in Volume 2, Chapter 4 how Aboriginal peoples have been systematically dispossessed of their lands, not just in the first rush of settlement but continuing with the erosion of reserves, the elimination of hunting and fishing rights, and interference with other traditional uses of lands and resources.

As a matter of elementary justice, the spirit and intent of historical treaties with respect to sharing lands and resources have to be honoured. It is a matter of Canadians keeping their word, of fulfilling the commitments on which Canada was founded. But it is also critical for the future of Aboriginal nations, which cannot survive if they remain without resources, excluded from the bounty of the land and confined to parcels left over from settlement. Aboriginal people do not expect to obtain full restitution: they do not want to push non-Aboriginal Canadians into the sea or deprive them of their backyards, as the recent history of land claims settlements makes clear. But they do expect to be dealt with fairly, in a manner that recognizes their relationship to the land and their right to share in its resources, and in a way that respects the solemn agreements enshrined in the treaties.

Fourth, Aboriginal people need education and crucial skills for governance and economic self-reliance.

Poverty and neglect have resulted in lower educational attainment and a lack of certain essential skills. The absence of employment opportunities destroys incentive and fuels hopelessness among youth. The move toward collective self-reliance will counter this. Aboriginal people will see that they have an opportunity to shape their destinies and will have reason to apply themselves at school, to go to college or university, or to learn a trade. Educational reforms are not a prerequisite for self-government; the two go hand in hand. Measures must be taken immediately to bridge the gap between current educational attainment and community needs.

Finally, economic development must be addressed if the poverty and despondency of lives defined by unemployment and welfare are to change.

As we will see in the next chapter, the total annual cost to Canadian society of Aboriginal people's economic marginalization amounts to one per cent of the gross national product. There is every reason to believe that with access to resources, to development capital and to appropriate skills, Aboriginal people can participate successfully in the globally oriented southern market economy and in the increasingly self-reliant mixed economy of northern communities.

These principles are central to implementation of our recommendations. Let us explore how these tasks can be carried out.

Canadians have shared a long and sometimes troubled history. Things have happened that are painful to recount and are deplored by the great majority of Canadians. Many of these events were the result of greed or ill will; others were the product of ignorance, misguided intentions or a lack of concern for peoples already at the edge of Canadian society. They have left their legacy in the social and economic conditions of Aboriginal communities and in the distrust and betrayal felt by Aboriginal people. A sense of profound injustice and pain was expressed in testimony before this Commission. The damage is real and will take time to heal. That history of hurt has to be reckoned with in creating a new relationship. We are not suggesting that we dwell on the past. Aboriginal people, like others in Canada, want to put the events of the past behind them and work toward a stronger and healthier future. To do that two things must happen.

First, there has to be a sincere acknowledgement by non-Aboriginal people of the injustices of the past. Widespread ignorance of the history of dispossession has made it increasingly difficult for non-Aboriginal people to admit the need for restitution. Unfortunately, as Aboriginal people have gained strength in the struggle for their rights there has been a rising tide of opposition among non-Aboriginal people with an interest in maintaining the status quo. Their watchword is 'equality': everyone should be treated the same, regardless of deprivation and disadvantage or the origins of these conditions. Acknowledgement and a genuine desire to make reparations are essential prerequisites of a renewed relationship of fairness and mutual respect.

Second, there must be a profound and unambiguous commitment to establishing a new relationship for the future. High-minded policy statements and piecemeal reforms, however meritorious, will not fulfil that commitment. Symbolism is important, however. The new relationship should be heralded by a symbolic step to demonstrate that a lasting commitment has been made. For this reason we recommend that the Sovereign issue a Royal Proclamation to signal the new beginning at a special gathering called for the purpose. The proclamation would set out the principal elements of the new relationship and outline its central institutions. It would be complemented by legislation defining those institutions in detail. This step would not settle all outstanding issues – that will take many years of negotiation and adjustment – but it would create a framework of principle, procedures and institutions for accomplishing change. It would establish a clear goal and the means for Aboriginal and non-Aboriginal people and nations to work toward the goal. It would celebrate the new beginning. We would expect that consultations on a Royal Proclamation and companion legislation could begin within six months of the release of this report.

2. THE PROCLAMATION AND COMPANION LEGISLATION

A preamble would express the desire for a new beginning. The government of the day will determine the wording, but we would expect the preamble to express certain perspectives and intentions.

It would invoke the *Royal Proclamation of 1763*, the proclamation that codified and affirmed the British Crown's recognition of Aboriginal title and governance. The new proclamation would confirm the principles of that foundation document. It would symbolize Canadians' rededication to mutual respect and trust in the tradition of the *Royal Proclamation of 1763*.

The new proclamation would acknowledge, in general terms, the injustices of the past, especially those associated with the paternalism and disrespect that characterized the period following the decline of the fur trade when Aboriginal title was ignored, treaty rights were undermined and the *Indian Act* was imposed.

The preamble might express profound regret for the harm caused Aboriginal peoples by policies that deprived them of their lands and that interfered, sometimes brutally, with family relationships, spiritual practices, customary ceremonies, structures of authority and governance, and traditional relationship with the land. It could acknowledge that wrongs were committed, often as a result of stereotypical attitudes that we now recognize as racist, and that Aboriginal peoples are still living with the consequences of those policies. The history of relations between Aboriginal and non-Aboriginal people was not unremittingly negative. There were many instances when individuals acted with wisdom and respect and where cross-cultural interaction was positive. But the profoundly harmful elements of the past must be acknowledged as a way of putting them behind us, as a means of reconciliation. The preamble could express the government's will henceforth to place its relationship with Aboriginal peoples on a proper footing, and it could express the hope that an honest acknowledgement of past wrongs will break the cycle of guilt and blame and free both sides to embrace a shared future with trust in each other.

The preamble should make clear the foundational principles of that new relationship. These include, above all, recognition that Aboriginal peoples have a right to fashion their own destiny and control their own governments, lands and resources. They constitute nations, with an inherent right of self-government. The federal Crown should undertake to deal with them as such. This would pave the way for genuine reconciliation and enable Aboriginal people to embrace with confidence dual citizenship in an Aboriginal nation and in Canada.

2.1 Recognition of Nations

A crucial first component of the renewed relationship will be nation rebuilding and nation recognition. All our recommendations for governance, treaty processes, and lands and resources are based on the nation as the basic political unit of Aboriginal peoples. Only nations have a right of self-determination. Only at the nation level will Aboriginal people have the numbers necessary to exercise a broad governance mandate and to supply a large pool of expertise. At the nation level they can develop institutions that are stable and independent of personality. Only with nationhood can Aboriginal peoples recapture the broad sense of solidarity that predated the relocations and divisions of the *Indian Act* era. We do not mean to suggest that community-level institutions are irrelevant. On the contrary, some activities are best located at the community level, and some Aboriginal peoples will adopt decentralized governing structures as a result.

The composition of nations will not always be straightforward. For some, the nation already exists. For others, nation institutions will emerge through a process of negotiation, political debate, and perhaps even trial and error. The majority of existing Indian governments are based on *Indian Act* bands, and reintegration of excluded citizens will be an important issue for them. Virtually all Aboriginal nations will have to go through a process of constitutional development before election procedures, mechanisms for ensuring accountability and decision-making processes can be put in place.

After an Aboriginal nation has been reconstituted, it can exercise self-government on its existing territory in core areas of jurisdiction and seek formal recognition from the governor in council for nation status and a formal agreement with the federal and provincial or territorial governments. The agreement would spell out core powers the Aboriginal government will exercise and provide financial resources to carry out those responsibilities. The nation would be the appropriate party to the subsequent treaty process that would establish the full scope of its jurisdiction, the nature of its fiscal and other relationships to governments, and the boundaries of its lands. Eventual adherence to the treaty resulting from this process would signal the nation's full and free participation in the Canadian federation.

Recognition would be the responsibility of the governor in council through a procedure set out in the Aboriginal Nations Recognition and Government Act we propose. The primary determination of whether a community satisfied the criteria would be entrusted to a panel established under the Aboriginal Lands and Treaties Tribunal. The panel would convey its evaluation to the governor in council who, although not bound to follow the panel recommendation, would have to give reasons for departing from them. The process would provide an orderly means of recognition in a manner functionally analogous to what occurs when countries seek recognition at the international level.

The process may work somewhat differently for Inuit. They have already begun to coalesce into four nation groups: Inuvialuit, and Inuit of Nunavut, Nunavik and Labrador. To some degree these groupings already have stable internal structures. Inuit have already opted for the exercise of government powers through mechanisms of public government. Thus, the system of recognition described here would be implemented in a different manner for them. Flexibility would also be needed in terminology to take account of Inuit and Métis traditions. Inuit collectivities might be termed 'peoples', for example (or another term acceptable to them), rather than 'nations'. Arrangements between Métis people or Inuit and governments might be settled through 'agreements', 'accords' or 'compacts' rather than 'treaties'.

These are the basic contours of the recognition process we propose. Because the transition to nation government is fundamental to the new relationship we envisage, the principles and means of recognition should form a basic element of the Royal Proclamation and its companion legislation.

The companion legislation would specify the criteria of nationhood, establish procedures, and set out the consequences of recognition. It would also provide for assistance to Aboriginal nations engaged in the process of nation-building, which might take the form of technical support, funding, and mediation services. The specific elements of the nation rebuilding and recognition process are described in detail in Volume 2, Chapter 3.

2.2 The Treaty Process

The Royal Proclamation and companion legislation would also lay the foundation for the treaty process. Negotiation would be triggered by a request by a recognized Aboriginal nation. That request might concern any of a range of matters falling within the scope of the process, such as the nation's desire to exercise powers beyond the core responsibilities of self-government, the nation's desire to achieve full implementation of an existing treaty, or the nation's wish to resolve a land claim. The request for negotiation would impose a clear obligation on all parties to negotiate in good faith, prompt the establishment of a regional treaty commission (if one did not exist), and give the nation and non-Aboriginal governments access to the research, mediation and other services of the relevant treaty commission.

We propose provincial and territorial involvement in all phases of the treaty negotiation process. Land settlements, the redistribution of government responsibilities, and co-management schemes all require provincial involvement. The provinces and territories cannot be indifferent about their obligations to Aboriginal peoples. In our view, they also have a fiduciary responsibility. As the principal beneficiaries of Aboriginal peoples' land losses resulting from disregard of treaties or failure to conclude them, they have a legal and moral obligation to participate in creating a new or renewed treaty relationship. We therefore propose formal consultations and negotiations between Aboriginal peoples' representatives and federal, provincial and territorial governments through the development of a Canada-wide framework agreement.

We should make absolutely clear, however, that the federal government does not need the support of all the provinces to take action on Aboriginal issues. Under section 91(24) of the *Constitution Act, 1867*, Parliament has primary jurisdiction with respect to Aboriginal peoples. The federal government cannot, consistent with its fiduciary obligation, sit on its hands in its own jurisdiction while treaties are broken, Aboriginal autonomy is undermined, and Aboriginal lands are destroyed.

The policies and instruments proposed for adoption in the Royal Proclamation and its companion legislation can be established by the federal government acting alone if necessary under section 91(24). The recognition process lies entirely within federal responsibility and can be implemented fully by the federal government. Many matters covered by the treaty process also fall within federal jurisdiction. If some provinces and territories refuse to participate, the federal government should move forward with the others, leaving it to subsequent persuasion or the courts to complete the circle.

We wish to emphasize again that our preference is for co-operative action by all governments in Canada. This is in the interests of the governments themselves, as issues that long have festered will be resolved expeditiously and in a spirit of goodwill, and settlements will be reached that work with, rather than against, provincial priorities. But the frustration of Aboriginal peoples is substantial and justified. Federal action on matters of federal jurisdiction should not be postponed.

The new proclamation would set out the principles underlying the treaty process. These would include the government's commitment to respect and implement existing treaties in accord with their spirit and intent and its willingness to reconsider, in the light of oral evidence and in the modern context, issues on which there was clearly no agreement at the time historical treaties were negotiated. Throughout, the proclamation should make clear that with respect to both terminology and substance, treaty processes will be sufficiently flexible to accommodate the diverse traditions of Aboriginal peoples, including Inuit and Métis.

The proclamation would be complemented by legislation establishing the framework for the treaty process. An Aboriginal Treaty Implementation Act would provide the legislative framework under which regional treaty commissions would be established. It would lay out the general guidelines for negotiating the reallocation of lands and resources. An Aboriginal Lands and Treaties Tribunal Act would create a tribunal to deal with specific claims and assist treaty processes. Finally, legislation would establish a new Department of Aboriginal Relations within which a Crown Treaty Office would have principal responsibility for the federal government's participation in treaty renewal and treaty making. (See Volume 2, Chapters 2, 3 and 4 for details on these proposals.)

2.3 Lands and Resources

The treaty process would provide the essential framework for dealing with issues of lands and resources. The treaty commissions and the tribunal would be the primary institutions in that process.

In the Royal Proclamation, the federal government should indicate its acceptance of certain principles relating to Aboriginal title. The first would be that Aboriginal land rights do not need to be extinguished to achieve a settlement of land claims or to agree to or implement new treaties. A second would state the federal government's recognition that Aboriginal title is a real interest in land. The third principle would signal the government's intention to resolve land claims in a manner that reconciles the interests of the broader society with Aboriginal title. Our special report on extinguishment and our chapters on treaties and lands and resources in Volume 2 suggest how these principles might be implemented.[1]

The Royal Proclamation should state the government's commitment to resolve questions about the redistribution of lands and resources as expeditiously as possible. While Aboriginal nations can invoke the treaty process as a means of resolving virtually all claims through negotiations, certain claims that raise relatively defined issues might be submitted to the tribunal for binding determination. These are the claims roughly corresponding to today's 'specific claims', although we propose an expanded definition of this term. The process of resolving claims is very slow at present. The proclamation should announce the government's intention to vest adjudicative jurisdiction in the tribunal so as to speed up the process.

One of the most pressing issues regarding lands and resources is the availability of interim relief. Even with the reforms proposed here, it will take considerable time to resolve land claims. Meanwhile, lands subject to claims are being sold, trees are being harvested, game is being killed or driven out, and communities are living in poverty. It is crucial that there be some protection of Aboriginal interests while the treaty process is being pursued. We have recommended that the tribunal have authority to grant interim relief. We also recognize that provincial and territorial involvement is essential in the design of that relief and necessary if the tribunal is to have authority to grant it.

The best forms of interim relief combine a high degree of protection for a portion of the territory, institutions for the co-management of critical resources in the territory, and financing for Aboriginal people in the form of a share of resource revenues. This provides substantial protection without freezing development. Moreover, the experience of working together under interim relief measures often makes a settlement easier to obtain. We therefore propose that a strong effort be made, in the context of negotiating a Canada-wide framework agreement, to develop principles to govern interim relief agreements containing these elements. Each interim relief agreement would be the result of successful negotiations involving an Aboriginal nation, the federal government and the relevant province. It would provide a framework of relief that could then be applied by the tribunal.

Métis people have traditionally faced unique difficulties in pursuing recognition as Aboriginal peoples, their right to governance, and their own land base. The Royal Proclamation would be an appropriate place for the federal government to state its stance on these issues. This would include recognition under section 91(24) of the *Constitution Act, 1867*, plans to secure an adequate land base, measures to provide Métis hunting and fishing rights equivalent to those enjoyed by other Aboriginal peoples, and steps to obtain constitutional confirmation of the Alberta Métis settlements. (For further details, see Volume 4, Chapter 5.)

3. A Canada-Wide Framework Agreement

In our view, the elements of the Royal Proclamation and companion legislation can all be adopted by federal action alone. They would signal the federal government's commitment to a profound transformation in relations between Aboriginal and non-Aboriginal people in Canada, and they would set in place the infrastructure to accomplish that transformation.

That said, our first preference is for co-operative, co-ordinated action by the government of Canada, the provinces and territories, and Aboriginal nations. To that end, we strongly recommend that as soon as possible after the release of this report, governments institute a framework for discussion of Aboriginal issues, with a view to establishing collaborative measures.

This kind of collaboration would be especially valuable in establishing the treaty process and the aspects of the process concerned with governance and land claims. We propose that first ministers and leaders of the national Aboriginal political organizations meet to review the principal recommendations of this report within six months of its release and establish a forum to develop a Canada-wide framework agreement. The work of that forum would be led by national Aboriginal organizations and ministers responsible for Aboriginal affairs. It would have a target date of the year 2000 to complete its work and would report annually to first ministers and national Aboriginal leaders.

Negotiations in the context of a framework agreement would focus on principles to govern land settlements, the recognition of legislative jurisdiction, fiscal arrangements and co-management on public lands, and interim relief agreements. The establishment of general principles to guide the treaty process by a Canada-wide framework agreement could make for more rapid progress in the settlement of claims.

If these consultations and negotiations are begun expeditiously, it may be possible to include some of their results in the Royal Proclamation and its companion legislation. Provinces that agree could enact legislation simultaneously to confer authority on the new institutions. Provinces could formally declare their support for the proclamation and their willingness to collaborate in achieving its aims.

RECOMMENDATION

The Commission recommends that

First Ministers
Meeting

5.1.1

First Ministers, territorial leaders and leaders of the national Aboriginal organizations meet within six months of the release of this report to

(a) review its principal recommendations;

(b) begin consultations on the drafting and enactment of a Royal Proclamation redefining the nature of the relationship between Aboriginal nations and Canadian governments; and

(c) establish a forum to create a Canada-Wide Framework Agreement.

4. GATHERING STRENGTH

4.1 Social Issues and Structural Change

The Royal Proclamation and its companion legislation focus on structural changes in the relationship between Aboriginal peoples and Canadian society. We assign priority to structural measures because of their capacity to set in train fundamental change in the social and economic conditions that have resisted reform over the past 25 years.

Redistributing power and resources and proclaiming a public commitment to change the relationship will open the door for Aboriginal people to take charge of their own future. Transforming life conditions will require sustained vision and energy over at least a generation. Aboriginal people must regain hope that fundamental change is attainable. To liberate the energies of Aboriginal and non-Aboriginal people alike, this hope must be nourished by visible progress in resolving pressing problems.

The assumption of responsibility by Aboriginal peoples does not mean abandoning Aboriginal people to work out their problems in isolation from each other, from Canadian governments, or from Canada's social and economic institutions. Just as we speak of Aboriginal people becoming full-fledged partners in Confederation, we also urge partnerships to address social and economic problems.

Throughout our report we propose how the energy of Aboriginal people can converge with government action to create a better future for all. We make recommendations to address past injuries and generate trust, to revitalize Aboriginal economies, to restore individuals, families and communities to health, to make the investment necessary to create safe and healthy housing and useful community services, to provide effective and culturally appropriate education, and to sustain Aboriginal identity and languages as a dimension of public life in Canada. The changes we propose are wide-ranging, interrelated and important; they are the measures that will enable Aboriginal people effectively to occupy the roles envisioned in this restructured relationship. The questions that remain are how to set priorities and how to gauge the level of investment required.

4.2 Four Dimensions of Social Change

In Chapter 3 of this volume we propose a level of financial commitment to support substantial change in political, economic and social realities. The amount we recommend will require choices to be made. Establishing priorities for the use of financial resources must be done by the Aboriginal people whose lives are directly affected, in consultation with federal, provincial and territorial governments. Those governments will retain much of the jurisdictional and fiscal responsibility in the years when the recommendations are first implemented. In setting priorities for implementation, careful attention will have to be paid to the interdependence of recommendations and the need to support change in one area with complementary action elsewhere.

We see four major dimensions for social, economic and cultural initiatives:

- healing of individuals, families, communities and nations;
- improving economic opportunity and living conditions in urban and rural Aboriginal communities;
- developing human resources; and
- developing Aboriginal institutions and adapting mainstream institutions.

Healing

Healing is a term used often by Aboriginal people to signify the restoration of physical, social, emotional and spiritual vitality in individuals and social systems. It implies the revitalization of their confidence in themselves, their communities and cultures, confidence that must be grounded in their daily lives.

Healing also has an intercultural meaning. Learning about and acknowledging the errors of the past, making restitution where possible, and correcting distortions of history are essential first steps in the process of healing between Aboriginal and non-Aboriginal people. In Volume 1 we recommended remedies for past injustices and neglect in residential schools, relocation policies, and the treatment of veterans. We also proposed a history of Aboriginal peoples to ensure that future generations of Canadians are better informed about the past and present role of Aboriginal nations in Canadian life.

Our recommendations in support of family life and for health and healing services adapted to the circumstances of Aboriginal people build on service systems in which substantial investment is already being made. Our recommendations focus on engaging Aboriginal people in the design, management and restructuring of services to make them more accessible and appropriate.

Healing also involves strategies to ensure people are no longer damaged in the formative years of their lives. In Volumes 2 and 3, we made recommendations relating to young children, noting the research in health sciences and education that documents the devastating effects of deprivation during the formative years. Our recommendations emphasize the importance of protecting children through culturally appropriate services, by attending to maternal and child health, by providing appropriate early childhood education, and by making high quality child care available, all with the objective of complementing the family's role in nurturing young children.

Child welfare and family services constitute an area of deep concern, especially among women in Aboriginal communities, and are of critical importance in addressing both justice and social issues. The measures we propose can involve large numbers of people in constructive activities that promote healing. Such activities foster the growth of local leadership and are matters on which Aboriginal people have taken significant and innovative steps in recent years, often transcending single communities.

Our recommendations on education are designed to remove the impediments to learning that result from discontinuity between the culture of the community and the culture of the school and to foster bicultural competence to allow Aboriginal youth to function effectively in Aboriginal and non-Aboriginal environments. Changes in curriculum and pedagogy are proposed to make education relevant to the tasks of consolidating an adult Aboriginal identity and bridging the divide between school and the workplace.

The work of healing is not confined to restoring balance and efficacy to Aboriginal individuals and families. Communities and nations are in need of healing too. Aboriginal traditions of mutual aid have been undermined by the loss of economic resources and the intervention of agencies and institutions that ignored the strengths of community systems and the authority of community customs.

Cultural revitalization is now being expressed not only in ceremonial practices but also in the development of community services rooted in traditional ethics of sharing and mutual responsibility. We are confident that reweaving the bonds of community and reinstating the ethic of communal responsibility will be enhanced by placing in Aboriginal hands authority for decisions about community services. Initially this authority is likely to be administrative, delivering services mandated by federal, provincial and territorial governments. As institutions of self-government are established, these services will be brought under the jurisdiction of Aboriginal nations and confederacies.

In Volume 2, Chapter 3, we discussed how trust and co-operation must be restored in nations whose members have been divided by geographical dispersion and categories of status defined by the *Indian Act*. Traditions of leadership, too, have been submerged or distorted by *Indian Act* impositions. Restoring nations to cohesion and efficacy is an extension of the healing process taking place at the individual and family level.

Our recommendations in Volume 3, Chapter 6 are directed to broadening the channels for affirming Aboriginal identity in Canadian life through support of Aboriginal participation in communications media and the arts. Preservation of Aboriginal languages and enhanced skills in communication, along with better intercultural relations, will contribute significantly to personal and collective healing and the rebuilding of nations.

Aboriginal people speaking at our hearings made it clear that healing is an Aboriginal responsibility. As expressed by Roy Fabian, executive director of the Hay River Treatment Centre in the Northwest Territories, "The whole process of healing is becoming responsible for ourselves." Chief Gordon Peters conveyed a similar view:

> Some call it healing; some call it regeneration. No matter what it is called, it is the same process – people taking control of their individual lives.

Chief Gordon Peters
Chiefs of Ontario
Toronto, Ontario, 18 November 1993*

Economic opportunity

Individual and community efforts to promote self-healing will be severely constrained unless there is complementary change in the economic opportunities available to Aboriginal people and a dramatic improvement in living conditions in Aboriginal communities. The second dimension of priorities for implementation therefore includes economic development, housing and community infrastructure.

Economic development can acquire considerable momentum as measures to achieve self-government and reallocate lands and resources are implemented, provided the tools of development are available. Next to lands and resources, the most critical tools are capital and skills. We propose that equity capital be made

---

* Transcripts of the Commission's hearing are cited with the speaker's name and affiliation, if any, and the location and date of the hearing. See *A Note About Sources* at the beginning of this volume for information about transcripts and other Commission publications.

available from federal and provincial governments at greatly enhanced levels through long-term development agreements with regional Aboriginal organizations, nations and confederacies, through a National Aboriginal Development Bank, and through private investment. The acquisition of management skills for various kinds of business enterprise is an important focus of our proposed human resources strategy in support of Aboriginal economies. A change in the way social assistance funds flow into Aboriginal communities could stimulate greater self-reliance by enabling these funds to be used to sustain traditional harvesting activities and to improve social and physical infrastructure.

A major initiative to upgrade housing and community infrastructure would also support the transition to self-government and enhance economic development, while countering significant threats to health and well-being. Clarifying the nature of ownership of residences on Aboriginal territory will improve incentives to maintain dwellings and invest in their improvement. In addition, adopting the principle that those who are able should pay for a portion of the cost of their housing will release resources, whether of federal and provincial governments or Aboriginal nations, to help those in greatest need. A housing initiative should be pursued immediately, and as nation governments are recognized they can take over institutions that manage and finance housing programs, provide technical skills in systems design, regulate standards, and maintain the housing stock.

Human resources

The third critical dimension of change is human resources development. Institutions of self-government, restructured human services, community infrastructure and revitalized Aboriginal economies need appropriately trained personnel. We propose a 10-year initiative to overcome barriers to Aboriginal participation in the labour force, building on experience gained in current training and employment development strategies. In Volume 3, Chapter 3, we recommend that the educational preparation of Aboriginal personnel to direct, plan and staff restructured health and human services should be a major policy emphasis. In our recommendations on adult and post-secondary education and education for self-government, we set out detailed strategies for reaching the twin objectives of an Aboriginal population knowledgeable in their culture and fully equipped to implement self-government, staff public services, sustain self-reliant economies, and engage freely in mainstream economic activities. (See Volume 2, Chapters 3 and 5, and Volume 3, Chapter 5.)

Education and training for Aboriginal governments and economies must achieve better integration between study and work through programs adapted to community realities, study and work placement combinations, scheduling to permit employed persons to enhance their qualifications, and access to training and education in or near Aboriginal communities.

Educational success will contribute to personal and communal healing, which in turn will result in more candidates presenting themselves for higher education. We therefore anticipate that a very substantial commitment to student support and innovative delivery of education services in First Nations, Inuit and Métis communities will be necessary well past the 20-year time frame for which we make fiscal projections in Chapter 3 of this volume. However, we also expect that educational outlays will begin to be offset by paybacks from increased employment and productivity by the end of the first decade of our social and economic strategy.

Institutional development

Institutional development is the fourth dimension of our recommendations for social, cultural and economic change. Aboriginal life is more complex than it was in the village and the hunting camp. In those contexts the family was the all-purpose mediator, teaching its members how to understand and respond to the world at large and interpreting to the community the contribution each member had to offer. Even in compact and isolated Aboriginal communities where intricate, layered kinship relations still prevail, Aboriginal people have turned to formal institutions to meet their needs for education, health care and political leadership, to give three examples.

Most contemporary institutions governing Aboriginal life are regulated by norms that originate outside Aboriginal communities. The services they offer are fragmented and sometimes overlapping. These services are extended or withheld from Aboriginal persons on the basis of status categories that are also determined by non-Aboriginal authorities. This results in a service deficiency affecting more than half of all Aboriginal people. In urban and rural off-reserve areas, Aboriginal people confront an array of services, scarcely any of which show even token acknowledgement of the varied cultures and needs of the people they are intended to serve.

We have concluded that in every sector of public life there is an urgent need to liberate Aboriginal initiative by making room for Aboriginal institutions. They should be part of education, health and social services, housing, communications and economic development, as well as the administration of government. As self-government is established, Aboriginal institutions will become instruments for meeting needs through self-determined means. They will be a primary place for innovation based on traditional knowledge and contemporary experience and judgement.

We have recommended support or reinstatement of sector-specific and regional organizations to pursue economic development. We have suggested the formation of new planning bodies or the designation of existing regional organizations to develop the integrated network of healing centres and lodges we propose. These organizations and institutions would precede nation rebuilding and self-government in many regions and should be structured to complement the development of nation structures. They need not be confined to serving a single nation.

Change is threatening because it means relinquishing practices that have become familiar and predictable, even if they are sometimes frustrating and painful. Progress in developing Aboriginal social and economic institutions can break habits of control and dependence. Effective institutions can function as a powerful stimulus to community revitalization and nation building.

4.3 Federal, Provincial and Territorial Contributions

It is essential that federal, provincial and territorial governments make firm commitments to support change in the four dimensions just outlined. The importance of commitment to the healing process in its many forms, to adapting the delivery of public services, to improving economic opportunity and living conditions, and to human resources development is already recognized to some degree by all governments. It is particularly important that governments make an early commitment to provide stable funding to Aboriginal institutions as they emerge from the planning process.

In Volume 4, Chapter 7, we set out an approach to apportioning financial obligations related to social expenditures. The jurisdictional debate between federal and provincial governments has seriously impeded the development of equitable and effective Aboriginal services. That debate must give way to decision and action.

At the start of this transition period, much of the jurisdiction and spending authority will continue to lie with federal, provincial and territorial governments. But the necessary initiatives will not be effective unless designed and implemented by Aboriginal people according to their priorities. Aboriginal people need to be able to direct resources to the areas where the need for social infrastructure is greatest.

We propose therefore that governments enter into multi-year planning and implementation processes on a provincial or regional basis with representatives of the Aboriginal nations of the area. Priority setting to address needs across the region might take up to two years. It could culminate in five-year funding agreements to permit stability of implementation. The creation of programs and institutions should be undertaken with the emerging nation structures in mind so that as nations are recognized, jurisdiction and resources could be assumed by the nation government with a minimum of friction.

5. Keeping Track of Progress

Ensuring that trust, once engendered, is honoured is a continuing responsibility, one that cannot be left to governments alone, buffeted as they are by the tide of events and transient priorities. The establishment of institutions to restructure the relationship through a Royal Proclamation and companion legislation should be accompanied by the creation of an equally vital institution to monitor progress toward self-government, an adequate land and resource base, and equality in social and economic well-being for Aboriginal peoples. This institution would assess the extent to which governments are honouring their commitments and the progress being achieved in implementing the recommendations of this Commission.

The value of the institution would lie in its independence and in its ability to focus the attention of legislators and governments on the continuing process of renewal. Monitoring is needed because the process will last not just years but several decades. Without regular review, the original objectives could too easily be forgotten or submerged in the preoccupations of the day. Monitoring is needed to help clarify issues that are complex and difficult to understand. Monitoring is a form of advocacy and also a vehicle for public education about changes taking place among Aboriginal peoples and in their communities. To achieve these objectives, we propose that the federal government establish an Aboriginal Peoples Review Commission that would be independent of government and report direct to Parliament.

A model for such a body already exists. The Office of the Commissioner of Official Languages was established to monitor compliance with the *Official Languages Act* following the 1967 report of the Royal Commission on Bilingualism and Biculturalism. The Commissioner of Official Languages is appointed by resolution of the Senate and House of Commons for a seven-year renewable term, and the act provides for the commissioner's independence from government. The commissioner reports annually to Parliament and has a close relationship with a joint committee of the Senate and the House of Commons. The commissioner deals mainly with individual complaints and reviews the application of the *Official Languages Act* in federal departments.

The mandate we propose for an Aboriginal peoples review commission would of necessity be broader, since it touches so many areas of Aboriginal life. We believe the commission should focus on the broad scope of change. Although accepting input from all sources, it should not deal with individual complaints. We envisage a commission established by Parliament and led by a chief commissioner, appointed for a fixed term by the Senate and House of Commons. The appointment process should include consultation with the national Aboriginal organizations and could be facilitated by an independent third party, such as a judge of the Supreme Court of Canada. Up to three part-time commissioners could be appointed to assist the chief commissioner. The independence of the commission's funding and staff must be assured. The chief commissioner should be Aboriginal, and most other commissioners and staff should also be Aboriginal.

The commission would report to Parliament annually on self-government, lands and resources, and the social and economic well-being of Aboriginal peoples. It would have the power to make special reports. Should an Aboriginal parliament be created, as we have recommended as an interim step toward creation of a House of First Peoples as a third chamber of Parliament, the commission would closely follow the work of that body.

The commission's mandate should be broad enough to include the activities of provincial and territorial governments within its review, although the commission would not be responsible to provincial and territorial legislatures. Its annual reports should provide the occasion for Parliament (and the provincial and territorial legislatures) to review Aboriginal issues regularly through committee hearings and debate.

Monitoring progress on the Aboriginal agenda without becoming unwieldy in staffing or budget will require an innovative approach. This might include co-operative arrangements with other organizations, such as the Aboriginal Justice Council recommended in our special report on criminal justice,[2] with Aboriginal and non-Aboriginal governments and with educational and research institutions. The commission's reports should aim to provide an overview of progress and shortcomings.

The commission would have the power to advise, to educate and, ideally, to persuade, but it would not have decision-making authority. Even if the commission develops credibility and public interest only slowly, its creation will be justified. Aboriginal peoples and Canadian governments will benefit from a regular assessment of what has been accomplished and what remains to be done – evaluation that has been lacking in the past. The commission's reports will motivate governments to move forward in fulfilling their promises to Aboriginal peoples. The review commission has the potential to be an important instrument for maintaining trust between governments and Aboriginal peoples.

RECOMMENDATIONS

The Commission recommends that

Aboriginal Peoples Review Commission

5.1.2

The government of Canada introduce legislation to establish an Aboriginal Peoples Review Commission that is independent of government, reports to Parliament and is headed by an Aboriginal chief commissioner.

5.1.3

The Aboriginal Peoples Review Commission regularly monitor progress being made

(a) by governments to honour and implement existing treaties;
(b) in achieving self-government and providing an adequate lands and resource base for Aboriginal peoples;
(c) in improving the social and economic well-being of Aboriginal people; and
(d) in honouring governments' commitments and implementing the recommendations of the Royal Commission on Aboriginal Peoples.

5.1.4

The Aboriginal Peoples Review Commission report annually to Parliament and that Parliament use the occasion of the annual report to address Aboriginal issues in committee hearings and debate.

5.1.5

Provincial and territorial governments co-operate with the commission in fulfilling its mandate and respond in their legislatures to the commission's annual assessment of progress.

5.1.6

Federal and provincial first ministers and territorial leaders meet at regular intervals with national Aboriginal representatives to assess implementation of reform measures and to raise public awareness of Aboriginal concerns.

6. AN INTERACTIVE STRATEGY

By now it will be clear that a fundamental combination of forces must be in place to make change possible. This no doubt motivated Chief Justice Brian Dickson to propose the extensive mandate of the Royal Commission on Aboriginal Peoples. Almost every aspect of the mandate interacts continuously with every other: measures for self-government have an impact on the administration of health and education, which bears directly on economic opportunity, which provides the means for good housing and financing social and cultural programs. A just reallocation of lands and resources has an impact on employment, on cultural and spiritual wholeness, and on the revenues needed for governance, education and social infrastructure.

Not all of our recommendations can be implemented simultaneously. Governments do not have the financial resources and Aboriginal nations do not have the human resources to absorb and manage simultaneous change on all fronts. But decisive intervention on many fronts at the same time is required to reap the benefits of the anticipated synergy.

We are convinced that our proposals will furnish the substance of political relations between Aboriginal people and Canadian society for the next two decades. With the adoption of the structural measures proposed in this chapter, a dramatic transformation will be set in motion. A profound, symbolic turning point in Aboriginal/non-Aboriginal relations will have been reached. The old relationship of paternalism and prejudice will have been rejected and, in its place, a foundation laid for a new partnership founded on responsibility and mutual respect.

The foundation would not be merely symbolic. The Royal Proclamation and companion legislation will establish the infrastructure for the new relationship. They will create the critical institutions for the shift to the nation as the basic unit of Aboriginal government and for structuring the negotiating process. They would signal a clear commitment to change, a commitment made all the more real by identifying clear pathways to change.

NOTES

1. See Royal Commission on Aboriginal Peoples (RCAP), *Treaty Making in the Spirit of Co-existence: An Alternative to Extinguishment* (Ottawa: Supply and Services, 1995); and Volume 2, Chapters 2 and 4.

2. RCAP, *Bridging the Cultural Divide: A Report on Aboriginal People and Criminal Justice in Canada* (Ottawa: Supply and Services, 1996).

2

Economic Disparities, Government Expenditures and the Cost of the Status Quo

In the first four volumes of this report we showed how inequitable and counter-productive the policies of dispossession and assimilation of Aboriginal peoples have been and remain. We discussed how these policies helped to create the conditions facing Aboriginal people today, and how changes in policies over the past several decades, while sometimes constructive, have not been sufficiently far-reaching to change the deplorable conditions in which many Aboriginal people live. This situation entails a considerable cost to Aboriginal people and to Canadians generally. In this chapter, we explore the nature and dimensions of that cost.

It is not difficult to find examples of government actions that have been costly to governments and to Aboriginal parties. Consider the years of prolonged negotiations and litigation sparked by the government's desire to circumscribe basic Aboriginal rights. (To cite just one example, during the 20 years it took to negotiate the Yukon comprehensive claim – with much of the delay resulting from shifting government policies and personnel – Yukon First Nations incurred a debt of $63 million. They should not have to bear the cost of government delay and confusion alone; the debt's repayment should be renegotiated.) Or think about the deterioration of publicly funded housing stocks on reserves, resulting largely from government's failure to construct houses to an adequate standard and ensure their maintenance. In this chapter, however, we focus on the cost of government actions that are perhaps not as obvious but are nonetheless substantial. We call them social costs, as they are borne collectively by all Canadians. We show that these costs will continue to be incurred year after year and will escalate as long as current policies are in place. Eliminating these costs through fundamental policy changes is a convincing argument for implementing the agenda proposed in this report.

Social costs fall into two broad categories: costs associated with the economic marginalization of Aboriginal people, and costs incurred as governments attempt to address social problems through remedial programs. As a group, Aboriginal people do not participate fully in the Canadian economy. They produce and earn less than an equivalent number of other Canadians. By any realistic standard, the contribution of Aboriginal people to the Canadian economy is much less than it could and should be. More than 150,000 Aboriginal adults do not know the satisfaction of earning an adequate income and being economically independent.[1] As a result, the wealth they could potentially produce is not being realized. The value of production and income forgone is a continuing cost that can never be recovered. We estimate that the cost of forgone production was $5.8 billion in 1996. Half the cost of forgone production is shifted to governments and thus is borne by all Canadians. Governments collect less tax revenue than they would if Aboriginal people earned adequate incomes, and they pay out more in social assistance, other income support payments, and housing subsidies.

The second category of social costs consists of the large amounts allocated to coping with social problems – in other words, the extra cost of government expenditures on remedial programs. If health and vitality were restored to Aboriginal communities, these expenditures could be reduced. We estimate that extra expenditures on remedial programs amounted to $1.7 billion in 1996.

Adding the two categories together, the total social cost of the status quo was $7.5 billion in 1996 – almost one per cent of the value of Canada's economic output as measured by the gross domestic product (GDP).[2] Again, although Aboriginal people bear a large part of the cost of the status quo, more than half the burden falls on Canadians generally through reduced government revenues and increased spending on social assistance, health care, child welfare, law enforcement and corrections and other remedial measures.

The social costs examined in this chapter are not one-time costs; they are incurred yearly and will likely increase unless fundamental changes are made. To demonstrate this, we examine the social and economic conditions that give rise to these costs and explore whether policies now in place have the capacity to change these conditions.

1. THE COST OF FORGONE PRODUCTION

Compared to other Canadians, Aboriginal people as a group participate in the economy at lower rates and therefore have lower incomes. The large majority of Aboriginal people would be better off if their economic potential were realized. In the following pages we explore that economic potential and what can be gained by realizing it.

TABLE 2.1
Selected Economic Indicators, 1991

	Aboriginal Rate[1]	Canadian Rate[2]
Earnings from employment per person age 15+	$9,140	$17,020
Labour force participation (% of population age 15+)	57.0%	67.9%
Unemployment rate (% of the labour force)	24.6%	10.2%
Earnings from employment per employed person[3]	$21,270	$27,880

Notes:
1. Adjusted Aboriginal population (see Volume 1, Chapter 2).
2. Includes all Canadians – Aboriginal and non-Aboriginal.
3. Income data are for 1990.

Source: Statistics Canada, "Labour Force Activity", catalogue no. 93-324, Table 1; "Profile of Canada's Aboriginal Population", 1991 Census, catalogue no. 94-325, Table 1; and Aboriginal peoples survey, custom tabulations.

To estimate the economic potential of Aboriginal people, we focus first on income from employment, using data from the 1991 census and Aboriginal peoples survey (APS) to estimate how much Aboriginal people would earn if they were employed more productively and in larger numbers. It seems reasonable to take earnings and production in the Canadian economy as a basis for estimating this potential; Aboriginal people and communities are part of the Canadian economy and can be expected to encounter similar economic opportunities and constraints. Of course, economic opportunity is not distributed evenly over Canada's large land mass, and we take this into account by adjusting our estimates for regional differences in economic opportunities. We then extend our analysis to include income from sources other than employment, including profits and investments. Finally, we estimate the cost of forgone production for 1996 and the related shortfall in employment.

Differences in economic outcomes between all Canadians and Aboriginal people are shown in Table 2.1. (In this chapter, data for Canada or 'all Canadians' include both Aboriginal and non-Aboriginal people.) There is a large gap in average earnings from employment (including self-employment) for persons aged 15 years and over. In 1990, Aboriginal people earned an average of $9,140, or 53.7 per cent of the Canadian average of $17,020. The difference is directly attributable to three factors: Aboriginal people participated in the labour force at a lower rate (57 per cent compared with 67.9 per cent); they experienced a higher unemployment rate (24.6 per cent compared with 10.2 per cent); and those who were employed earned less than employed Canadians ($21,270 compared with $27,880). The aggregate employment income for Aboriginal Canadians was $4.2

TABLE 2.2
Employment by Weeks Worked, 1990
(% of the population age 15+)

	Full-Time Employment		Part-Time Employment	
	Aboriginal People	All Canadians	Aboriginal People	All Canadians
1-26 weeks	14.2	8.4	7.6	5.8
26-48 weeks	9.5	10.7	2.5	3.5
49-52 weeks	20.5	36.9	2.9	4.7
Total	44.3	56.1	12.9	14.0

Source: Statistics Canada, "Educational Attainment and School Attendance", catalogue no. 93-328; and Aboriginal peoples survey, custom tabulations.

billion in 1991. An equivalent number of Canadians earned $7.8 billion from employment, or $3.6 billion more.

Differences in levels of employment are echoed in discrepancies in employment income. When we combine the labour force participation and unemployment rates presented in Table 2.1, we find that on average at any time in 1990, 43 per cent of Aboriginal persons aged 15 years and over was employed, compared to 61 per cent of all Canadians.[3]

To achieve parity with all Canadians in the rate of employment, 82,000 more Aboriginal people would have to have been employed. At Aboriginal people's earning rate in 1990, this extra employment would have brought in $1.8 billion in income and narrowed the earnings gap by almost half (48.6 per cent). If the level of earnings per employed Aboriginal person were raised to the overall Canadian level at the same time, the other half of the earnings gap (51.4 per cent) would be eliminated. The difference in the level of earnings per employed person is not as significant as the difference in the rate of employment. If employed Aboriginal persons had earned as much as employed Canadians earned on average in 1990, 36 per cent of the gap in earnings would have disappeared.

Differences in employment levels relate mainly to full-time, full-year jobs. Although Aboriginal people are well represented in employment involving up to 26 weeks of work in a year, only one-fifth of Aboriginal adults had a full-time, full-year job in 1990, compared to well over one-third of all Canadians (see Table 2.2). The shortage of full-time, full-year jobs applies to all Aboriginal groups, but is most acute for First Nations people living on-reserve. The disparities are somewhat smaller for women than for men.[4] Aboriginal women have been part of the trend of the last several decades toward greater labour market participation among women.

TABLE 2.3
Education and Employment Income, 1991

Highest Level of Education Completed	Aboriginal People* (% of population age 15 to 64)	All Canadians* (% of population age 15 to 64)	Average Employment Income Per Aboriginal Person ($000s)
Less than grade 9	25.4	11.8	12.7
Grades 9 to 13	32.2	22.8	15.3
High school diploma	12.9	21.3	19.4
College without certificate	8.0	6.2	15.8
College with certificate	14.2	17.9	20.5
University without degree	4.7	7.9	22.6
University with degree	2.6	12.2	33.6
Total	**100.0**	**100.0**	**17.8**

Note:

* Population age 15 to 64 no longer attending school full-time.

Source: Statistics Canada, "Educational Attainment and School Attendance", catalogue no. 93-328; and Aboriginal peoples survey, custom tabulations.

A person's level of education is closely related to the probability of finding employment and to employment income. In the case of Aboriginal people, less than half of those with a grade nine education or less were employed at any time in 1990, compared to more than 90 per cent of those with a university degree. Average employment income ranged from less than $13,000 for those with grade nine or less to more than $33,000 for those with a university degree. The gap in levels of education between Aboriginal people and all Canadians is illustrated in Table 2.3.

Using the data in Table 2.3, we calculated that 41.6 per cent of the $3.6 billion gap in employment income is associated with educational attainment.[5] This suggests that education is a major lever for improving economic outcomes for Aboriginal people. We know as well that such factors as ill health, disability and conflict with the law, although less significant, are also related to economic performance, and that improvement in these factors will also contribute to reducing the economic gap.

Opportunities for wealth creation are far from evenly distributed in Canada. In large areas of the country, including the mid- and far north where many Aboriginal people live, economic activity is limited and mainly resource-based. Regional economic disparities have persisted despite considerable efforts over several decades to reduce them. To reflect this diversity of economic oppor-

TABLE 2.4
Selected Economic Indicators for First Nations and Comparable Communities, 1986

	First Nations Communities	Comparable Communities	Canada
Labour force participation (% of population age 15+)	44.9	60.3	66.9
Unemployment rate (% of labour force)	33.3	14.9	12.0
Average income from employment, women ($000s)	3.3	4.4	7.3
Average income from employment, men ($000s)	6.5	12.8	17.9

Note: Data are for 1986 (the latest comprehensive data available). Comparable communities are communities located in the same geographic area as reserve communities (that is, in the same census sub-division or division), similar in population size, and organized as a municipality or village.

Source: DIAND, Community Comparison Project, unpublished.

tunity in our estimates, we took the location and size of Aboriginal communities into account and compared them with others of similar size and location.

As shown in Table 2.4, per capita income from employment in these more or less comparable communities is considerably less than the Canadian average; participation in the labour force is somewhat lower and unemployment is higher. Some of the First Nations communities are in urban areas and in regions with dynamic, high-performing economies, as are some of the comparable communities. Many First Nations communities, however, are small and remote from service centres (see Volume 2, Chapter 5). Even compared to similar communities, however, the economic performance of First Nations communities falls far short, particularly with respect to the level of employment. This illustrates the degree of exclusion of First Nations communities from the Canadian economy.

No similar comparison is available for other Aboriginal communities. Although some of these communities are small and remote, and may therefore have limited economic potential, many off-reserve Aboriginal people live in urban and metropolitan areas where they should have access to the same economic opportunities as most Canadians.[6] We believe, therefore, that the Canadian average is a good measure of the economic potential of Aboriginal people not living on reserves, with the exception of Inuit, who live mainly in small northern communities and whose income from employment is the second-lowest among Aboriginal groups, after that of Indian people living on-reserve. If we take com-

TABLE 2.5

Economic Indicators for Aboriginal People and All Canadians Age 15+, 1981 and 1991

	1981			1991		
	Aboriginal People	All Canadians	Gap	Aboriginal people	All Canadians	Gap
	1	2	2-1	1	2	2-1
Labour force participation rate	51.8	64.8	13.0	57.0	67.9	10.9
Unemployment rate	15.8	7.3	8.5	24.6	10.2	14.4
% with income less than $10,000	49.4	32.8	16.6	47.2	27.7	19.5
Average total income	$15,303	$23,119	$7,816	$14,561	$24,001	$9,440

Note: Figures for 'average total income' and '% with income less than $10,000' exclude persons reporting no income. Data are for 1980 and 1990, in 1990 constant dollars, and include income from all sources, not only employment earnings.

Source: Statistics Canada, "Canada's Aboriginal Population, 1981-1991: A Summary Report", research study prepared for the Royal Commission on Aboriginal Peoples [RCAP] (1995); data from the Housing, Family and Social Statistics Division, Statistics Canada, January 1995; Statistics Canada, "Labour Force Activity", 1991 Census, catalogue no. 93-324, Table 1; and 1991 Aboriginal peoples survey, custom tabulations. For information about research studies prepared for RCAP, see *A Note About Sources* at the beginning of this volume.

parable communities as the norm for First Nations people on-reserve and Inuit, and retain the Canadian average as the norm for other Aboriginal groups, the estimated potential employment income of Aboriginal people drops by $0.9 billion, from $7.8 billion to $6.9 billion, and the gap between Aboriginal people and all Canadians narrows from $3.6 billion to $2.7 billion.[7]

Employment earnings are only part of the income generated by economic activity. In 1990, earnings accounted for 61 per cent of the value of production (GDP), with the remainder made up of profits, capital consumption allowances and other, smaller income items.[8] To estimate the total economic gap between Aboriginal people and other Canadians, these other income items must also be taken into consideration. In the absence of data for Aboriginal people regarding these income items, we assumed that the composition of total income is the same for Aboriginal people as for all Canadians. Thus, in addition to a gap in employment income, there is also a gap of the same relative size in income from other sources. This leads to an estimate of $4.4 billion in 1990 for the gap in total income between Aboriginal people and an equivalent number of Canadians.[9]

We identified a lack of full-time, full-year jobs and lower levels of education as major factors in poor economic outcomes. We also showed that only a fraction

TABLE 2.6

Aboriginal and Canadian Populations Age 15+, Showing Percentage by Level of Education Attained, 1981 and 1991

	1981			1991		
	Aboriginal People 1	All Canadians 2	Gap 2-1	Aboriginal People 1	All Canadians 2	Gap 2-1
Elementary school	63.0	80.0	17.0	76.1	86.1	10.0
High school	29.1	52.1	23.0	42.5	61.8	19.3
Post-secondary certificate	8.9	13.7	4.8	13.3	15.8	2.5
Some university	6.7	16.0	9.3	8.6	20.8	12.2
University degree	2.0	8.0	6.0	3.0	11.4	8.4

Note: This table shows the number of individuals who have attained the level of education indicated, including individuals who have gone on to higher levels. Thus, in 1991, of the 76.1 per cent of Aboriginal people who completed elementary school, many have completed high school and a number have also gone on to study at colleges and universities. The category 'post-secondary certificate' includes those who may not have completed elementary school or high school.

Source: Statistics Canada, "Canada's Aboriginal Population 1981-1991: A Summary Report", research study prepared for RCAP; and data from the Housing, Family and Social Statistics Division, Statistics Canada, January 1995.

of the economic gap between Aboriginal people and Canadians is related to regional economic disparities, and we have reduced our estimate of the economic gap to eliminate this component. In Volume 2, Chapter 5 we presented a more complete analysis of the performance of Aboriginal economies. Besides the factors highlighted here, we discussed the disruption of traditional ways, dispossession from a rich land and resource base, and restrictions inherent in the *Indian Act*. The economic exclusion of Aboriginal people has had significant cumulative effects on individuals' employment skills, their incentive to pursue education and training, and the capacity of communities to engage in modern economic activity, and these too are obstacles to better economic performance.

Our analysis points to a number of deep-seated problems. The economic disadvantages facing Aboriginal people are not a passing phenomenon. In fact, disparities between Aboriginal and other Canadians are increasing, and they will likely continue to do so unless policies are radically altered. Between 1981 and 1991, the unemployment and income gaps widened (see Table 2.5). Aboriginal people in the labour market, whose numbers grew rapidly during that period, experienced much greater difficulty finding work. The unemployment rate soared, far outpacing the increase for Canadians generally, and the average income of Aboriginal people (adjusted for inflation) actually declined over the decade. Various factors contributed to these trends: a recession in the early 1990s, jobs lost in resource exploration and extraction activities in northern areas, and a decline in the price of fur.

With regard to education, some progress was made between 1981 and 1991. The proportion of the Aboriginal adult population with less than grade nine dropped from 37 to 24 per cent (see Table 2.6). High school completion rates rose from 29 to 42 per cent, and the proportion of post-secondary non-university certificate holders increased from nine to more than 13 per cent.

Educational attainment among Canadians generally also rose over the same period, but the disparities diminished in these three categories. As Table 2.6 shows, however, there is still a 10 per cent gap at the elementary level and a 19 per cent gap at the secondary level. Compared to Aboriginal adults, Canadian adults are still 1.5 times more likely to have completed high school.

The positive trends in high school education are related in part to policy initiatives such as greater Aboriginal control, more Aboriginal history and language in the curriculum, more schools in Aboriginal communities, and increasing the numbers of Aboriginal teachers. The positive trends may not continue, however, unless these kinds of reforms in education are extended and the social and economic prospects of children now in school improve.

Aboriginal people also made educational gains at the university level for the period 1981 to 1991, but the improvements were modest compared to those of Canadians generally. The gap in university participation and completion increased over the decade: by 1991 Canadian adults were 2.4 times more likely to have some university education and 3.8 times more likely to be a university graduate. Moreover, although Aboriginal participation in all forms of post-secondary education has been increasing, it remains significantly below general Canadian levels. Only when Aboriginal people begin to obtain college and university degrees at the same rate as all Canadians will we see the gap in educational attainment decline and ultimately disappear.

Deterioration in economic indicators for Aboriginal people in the 1980s appears to show that improvements in levels of educational attainment up to the high school level have not had much impact on economic outcomes. A much greater catch-up at all levels of schooling is required if greater employment and higher earnings are to be realized.

This brief review highlights how entrenched the economic disparities between Aboriginal people and Canadians generally are and how they increased during the 1980s. It is quite possible that during the 1990s, these disparities have continued to widen. A trend toward greater concentration of employment in low-wage jobs and a higher degree of marginalization has been observed in the economy as a whole. The rapid increase in federal social assistance expenditures from 1991-92 to 1995-96, as documented later in this chapter, suggests that conditions may have worsened in First Nations communities. Some improvements in the Canadian economy in general, and in some resource sectors in particular, might have tended to moderate the disparities, however. On balance, we can assume, without risk of exaggerating the economic gap facing Aboriginal people, that differences in income and employment between Aboriginal people and all Canadians have remained constant on a per capita basis since 1990. After adjusting for population and price changes, we calculate that the economic gap between Aboriginal people and an equivalent number of Canadians will reach $5.8 billion in 1996, compared with $4.4 billion six years earlier.[10] One-half of this gap is related to a gap in employment of 80,000 jobs.[11]

An economic gap of this size is not acceptable in Canada today. Our recommended strategies for change, discussed in Volume 2, Chapter 5 and elsewhere, present a major challenge to Canadians – Aboriginal and non-Aboriginal alike – and their governments. But we believe that success will follow implementation of the measures we propose. Avoiding the social costs of economic disparity and eliminating the economic disparities facing Aboriginal people is a viable and realistic policy objective.

First, we have no doubt that Aboriginal people will agree with the scope of development needed in their communities and on their traditional territories to create the jobs and incomes. We believe that Aboriginal people will seize economic opportunities and adapt to new economic realities, as they always have. Although Aboriginal people have a strong attachment to the land, and many wish to pursue traditional activities, they also want jobs that offer good incomes. They are not resigned to economic dependency. Experience has also shown that although Aboriginal people often resist development on their traditional lands, their attitude is different when they can control the negative effects of development and share in its benefits. Moreover, the two lifestyles – traditional activities and salaried employment – need not conflict. Many Aboriginal people combine traditional activities with salaried employment or commercial activity in different seasons and over the course of a lifetime.[12]

Second, we have been careful to base our estimate of economic potential on the actual performance of the Canadian economy. If Canadians in general can achieve a certain level of employment and productivity, so can Aboriginal people. In particular, our estimates take into account the diverse opportunities for wealth creation and differences in lifestyle across the country.[13] Aboriginal people can likely achieve the rates of employment and earnings we have estimated without massive migration to areas of greatest economic opportunity. We are not proposing that economically weaker regions of Canada catch up with wealthier areas; rather, we are suggesting that within each region and urban area, Aboriginal people should share more equitably in wealth-creation activities.

The rapid growth of the Aboriginal population will pose a challenge for the future. The Aboriginal population of working age is expected to expand by nearly 250,000 between 1996 and 2016, an increase of a 48.6 per cent in 20 years, compared with an expected 23.4 per cent increase for the same group in the Canadian population as a whole.[14] In the cities, Aboriginal people will compete for employment in growing job markets. In the resource-producing areas of Canada, employment may not expand enough to provide sufficient jobs for the growing Aboriginal and non-Aboriginal population. Aboriginal people will need a larger share of jobs in those regions. Other entrants to the labour market could find opportunities in parts of the country where more jobs can be created.

But there is reason to be optimistic about economic growth in the resource-producing areas if lands and resources are restored to Aboriginal peoples. Where land claims have been settled, Aboriginal people have taken control of resources and invested in their communities; regional economies have expanded, benefiting all who live there. In Volume 2, Chapter 4, we drew a comparison between the Cree people to the east and west of James Bay, and between Inuit in Nunavik and those in Labrador. Crees and Inuit in Quebec now have more economic tools at their disposal to improve their lot, and have used some of the proceeds of a land claims settlement to acquire and develop businesses. When Aboriginal people control resources and the businesses that exploit them, a larger part of the income generated is likely to remain in the region instead of being transferred to urban centres. The result is that more money is spent locally, and in turn more jobs and greater business activity are generated.

Some economic opportunities for Aboriginal people have not yet been widely recognized: Aboriginal communities can develop world markets for entirely new and unique products in cultural tourism, the arts, specialty foods, clothing, pharmaceuticals, sports and recreation, as well as in the construction and service industries. Many new jobs can be created as a result of an increase in two-way trade with neighbouring communities and wider outside markets. Given a growing land base and more investment funds from further claims settlements, coupled with self-government, a better-educated work force and healthy communities, there is a potential for a major turnaround in the economic fortunes of Aboriginal people.

To sum up, we conclude that under the right conditions, Aboriginal people could and would participate more fully in the broader Canadian economy. A failure to foster such conditions is causing a loss of production and income, conservatively estimated at $5.8 billion in 1996 and growing year by year. The cost of this missed opportunity is being borne by Aboriginal people and by all Canadians and can never be recovered.

2. GOVERNMENT EXPENDITURES: THE BURDEN OF REMEDIAL COSTS

The second major social cost associated with the current circumstances of Aboriginal people is government expenditures on remedial measures. First we review the growth and composition of federal expenditures on programs for Aboriginal people over the past 15 years. Next we examine total expenditures by federal, provincial, territorial and local governments relating to Aboriginal people and compare these with government expenditures for all Canadians.

2.1 Federal Expenditures on Targeted Programs

As Table 2.7 shows, in fiscal year 1995-96, the federal government intends to spend $6.2 billion on Aboriginal programs. More than two-thirds of this spending is administered by the Department of Indian Affairs and Northern Development (DIAND). Many of the most costly items include services that provincial governments provide to other Canadians: education, social assistance and social services, and health care. Also included are expenditures for municipal infrastructure in First Nations communities.

Over the 10 years from 1981-82 to 1991-92, federal expenditures on Aboriginal programs grew by 183 per cent; as a share of federal government spending (excluding debt charges), they increased from 2.9 to 3.7 per cent.[15] Adjusted for the effects of inflation, expenditures per Aboriginal person increased by 14 per cent.

By comparison, total per capita federal expenditures for the same period (excluding debt charges) increased by 3.8 per cent after inflation, and consolidated expenditures (excluding debt charges) by all levels of government increased by 12.4 per cent in real per capita terms. (Comparison with consolidated expenditures of three levels of government is meaningful since the bulk of federal spending on Aboriginal people is for services provided to all Canadians by provincial and municipal governments.) By this latter standard, then, federal spending on Aboriginal programs kept pace with changes in government spending generally.

Only a few federal programs are directed to all Aboriginal people. They include Pathways, Aboriginal Business Canada (formerly the Canadian Aboriginal Economic Development Strategy or CAEDS), and the Aboriginal programs of the Canada Mortgage and Housing Corporation (CMHC). Other federal spending generally relates to registered Indian people and Inuit. For the period 1981-82 to 1991-92, this latter category of spending increased by nine per cent on a real per capita basis. When expenditures are further narrowed to those directed to people living on reserves and Crown land and to Inuit (about three-quarters of the total), the real per capita growth rate is 16 per cent. The differences here arise mainly from differences in the rate of population growth.[16] These findings demonstrate that during the 1980s the federal government made financial resources available for a rapidly growing First Nations and Inuit population, with more or less the same rate of increase as for program spending by all Canadian governments combined.

Since 1991-92, federal expenditures on Aboriginal programs have continued to increase while overall spending has become increasingly subject to restraint. In 1995-96 federal spending on Aboriginal programs will be about $6.2 billion, an increase of 33 per cent over the 1991-92 level, while total federal

TABLE 2.7
Federal Expenditures on Programs Directed to Aboriginal People,
Selected Years ($ millions)

Department/Program	1981-82 Expenditures	1991-92 Expenditures	1995-96 Estimates
DIAND	1,252	3,412	4,493
Indian and Inuit Affairs	1,022	2,864	3,854
Self-Government	—	18	63
Claims	18	118	345
Economic Development	72	98	53
Lands, Revenues, Trusts	21	84	65
Education	307	846	1,153
Social Assistance and Social Services	221	731	1,108
Capital Facilities	240	623	756
Band Management	76	247	314
Program Management	50	45	42
Health Canada	174	639	995
Employment and Immigration (Training)	70	200	200
Canada Mortgage and Housing Corporation	77	240	305
Industry Canada (Business Development)	47	79	52
Solicitor General (Policing)	28	62	50
Other	4	42	107
Total	**1,652**	**4,674**	**6,202**
Real Per Capita Annual Growth		1.3%	3.4%

Notes: Data are for fiscal years beginning in April of the calendar year indicated. Expenditures listed in this table pertain only to programs directed specifically to Aboriginal people. Not included are federal expenditures on programs directed to the general population, a share of which relates to Aboriginal people. Expenditures on general programs are considered in the next subsection of this chapter.

Source: DIAND, *Growth in Federal Expenditures on Aboriginal Peoples* (Ottawa: Supply and Services, 1993); Canada, *1995-96 Estimates*; and calculations by RCAP.

expenditures (excluding debt charges) will revert to about their 1991-92 level. As a share of federal expenditures (excluding debt charges), Aboriginal program spending increased from 3.7 per cent in 1991-92 to 4.9 per cent in 1995-96. Compared with provincial and local government expenditures, federal Aboriginal program expenditures also have been growing rapidly in the past four years.

As Table 2.7 shows, the composition of government spending for the three periods 1981-82, 1991-92 and 1995-96 changed markedly in several respects. From 1981-82 to 1991-92, expenditures for most programs roughly tripled, with social development and health care expenditures increasing somewhat more rapidly and expenditures on education somewhat less so. Spending on claims increased more than sixfold over that 10-year period, but expenditures for economic development by DIAND and Industry Canada did not keep pace with these increases. Changes in federal spending for program management and band management reflect the devolution of program delivery from DIAND to First Nations communities.

Since 1991-92, spending has shifted as in the previous decade; aggregate expenditures have increased rapidly. Claims expenditures stand out because of the settlement of several comprehensive claims, the Saskatchewan Treaty Land Entitlement, and the increased budget allocation for specific claims. Economic development and, to a lesser degree, housing have taken the brunt of federal expenditure restraint. Spending on economic development by DIAND and Industry Canada declined sharply, and the Pathways budget for training remained unchanged. As for housing, the Rural and Native Housing Program was suspended in 1994, and CMHC stopped making commitments for new units under other off-reserve programs in April 1995. CMHC has also reduced by two-thirds the number of new dwellings to be built on-reserve. (New approaches to on-reserve housing, announced in July 1996, will be financed through reallocation within DIAND and CMHC budgets.) The increase in federal expenditures in the 1990s, as during the 1980s, is driven largely by an escalating need for basic services – education, health and social assistance – to a rapidly growing population that has become more economically dependent. Federal budgets for social assistance and health care services rose by more than 50 per cent in the past four years. A significant force behind this increase was the large number of Aboriginal youth who came of age in the last two years, swelling the ranks of the adult population. From 1991 to 1995, the Aboriginal population aged 15 years and older increased by 13.4 per cent – almost one per cent per year more rapidly than the Aboriginal population as a whole. The Indian Register indicates an even higher rate of growth for the adult population living on-reserve, where most federal spending is concentrated.

Some of these trends are reason for concern. We welcome the increased budgets for claims and the devolution of program delivery, as well as recent program enhancements in health care and social services. But we are disturbed by the evidence examined earlier in this chapter and by recent increases in federal government expenditures on social assistance, which indicate that the Aboriginal population is becoming more dependent on federal assistance. We are also concerned that expenditure reductions will diminish spending on services, such as social housing, that are vital to enable Aboriginal people to cope with deteriorating conditions in their communities. Worse, cutbacks in economic development programs and the levelling off of the training budget mean that less effort is being made to improve economic conditions for Aboriginal people. We fear that governments, facing further restraint, will not make the investments necessary to eradicate poverty among Aboriginal people and improve their living conditions.

2.2 Total Expenditures of All Governments

Let us now consider expenditures by provincial, territorial and local governments (see Table 2.8). All expenditure data and estimates discussed here are for fiscal year 1992-93; comprehensive data are essential for the analysis presented in this part of the chapter, and figures for 1992-93 were the most recent comprehensive data available at the time of writing.

A number of provincial programs for Aboriginal people are in place, but they tend to be small and short-lived compared with federal programs. Most provincial spending is in the form of general programs directed to a province's entire population. With few exceptions, the provinces do track program use by Aboriginal people. However, based on such information as we have been able to collect, we have estimated the Aboriginal share of expenditures on general programs.

Spending relating to Aboriginal people by all governments in 1992-93 is estimated to be in the order of $11.6 billion, with the provinces, territories and

TABLE 2.8
Estimated Total Expenditures by All Governments Related to Aboriginal People, 1992-93 ($ millions)

	Targeted Programs[1]	General Programs[2]	Total
Yukon	—	68	68
Northwest Territories	—	641	641
Newfoundland	2	61	63
Nova Scotia	2	40	42
Prince Edward Island	—	3	3
New Brunswick	—	28	28
Quebec	323	253	576
Ontario	260	845	1,105
Manitoba	25	472	497
Saskatchewan	52	393	445
Alberta	12	637	649
British Columbia	70	671	741

TABLE 2.8 (continued)
Estimated Total Expenditures by All Governments Related to Aboriginal People, 1992-93 ($ millions)

	Targeted Programs[1]	General Programs[2]	Total
Other provincial and local government expenditures[3]	—	736	736
Total provincial, territorial and local government expenditures	746	4,848	5,594
Federal expenditures on general programs[3]	4,852	1,182	6,034
Total expenditures of all governments[4]	**5,598**	**6,030**	**11,628**

Notes:

1. Targeted programs are those directed exclusively to Aboriginal people. For Ontario and Quebec, targeted programs also include other expenditures related to Aboriginal people, as estimated by the Ontario Native Affairs Secretariat and Quebec's secrétariat aux affaires autochtones.

2. Figures for general programs consist of the estimated Aboriginal share of all expenditures of governments other than those on targeted programs. For federal and provincial expenditures on elementary and high school education, post-secondary education and training, income transfers to persons, housing, health care, social services, and protection of persons and property, an Aboriginal share was estimated on the basis of the Aboriginal share of the client population of these programs and the relative rate at which Aboriginal people make use of the services. Relative rates of use by Aboriginal people were estimated using a variety of information and methods, such as the relative number of Aboriginal people in schools, child care facilities and correctional institutions. Estimates of expenditures by school boards financed by local taxes are included in the amounts for each province.

3. For federal expenditures on general programs, an Aboriginal share was calculated on the basis of the Aboriginal share of the population. A single amount was estimated for provincial and local governments together and listed as 'other provincial and local government expenditures'. For the territories, expenditures relating to Aboriginal people were estimated by applying the Aboriginal population share to total government expenditures.

4. Whereas Table 2.7 presents an historical perspective on federal expenditures on Aboriginal programs, Table 2.8 provides a snapshot of all expenditures of all governments relating to Aboriginal people for the most recent year for which all data were available (1992-93). Federal expenditures on targeted programs in Table 2.8 include, in addition to the expenditures identified in Table 2.7, a few small items as estimated in a research study prepared for RCAP by Goss Gilroy Inc. Included in Table 2.7 are the estimated Aboriginal shares of general transfers to territorial governments, but these are excluded from Table 2.8, as the expenditures of territorial governments are shown separately in this table.

The study by Goss Gilroy Inc. documents $10.1 billion in government expenditures relating to Aboriginal people. An additional $1.5 billion is included in Table 2.8 under two items, 'other provincial and local government expenditures' and 'federal expenditures on general programs', to take account of expenditures not considered in that study.

Source: Goss Gilroy Inc., "Federal, Territorial and Provincial Expenditures Relating to Aboriginal Peoples", research study prepared for RCAP (1995); and estimates by RCAP.

local governments adding $5.6 billion to federal expenditures of $6 billion. (For an explanation of how this estimate of federal expenditures relates to the data in Table 2.7, see the notes in Table 2.8.) This amounts to 4.1 per cent of the consolidated expenditures of all levels of government in Canada (excluding debt charges), which stood at $285.4 billion for that fiscal year.[17]

On a per capita basis, government expenditures relating to Aboriginal people were $15,714 in 1992-93.[18] This is 57 per cent higher than the spending of all governments per Canadian resident, which stood at $10,026 in the same year. In total, governments spent $4.2 billion more on programs and services for and used by Aboriginal people than they spent on programs for an equivalent number of Canadians in the general population.

These estimates demonstrate convincingly the existence of a significant difference in average government spending per person. We explore this difference further in Table 2.9, where government expenditures are presented by major function or policy area and expressed on a per capita basis in columns 4 and 6. Column 7 presents the ratio of per capita spending levels based on the amounts in columns 4 and 6. Ratios higher than one indicate government expenditures per Aboriginal person higher than per capita government expenditures for the general Canadian population.

As shown in Table 2.9, a high level of government expenditures on Aboriginal people is found across many policy areas. It is related to several factors: discrepancies in the cost of service delivery; some specific expenditures related to First Nations people and Inuit; and, most important, the high level of use of programs by Aboriginal people, resulting mainly from their economic marginalization and the social ills experienced in many communities. We examine each of these factors in turn.

Cost of services delivery

A disproportionate number of Aboriginal people live in small, remote, and northern communities. The cost of delivering government services varies substantially as a result of scale and distance from major centres. The cost of living in the north ranges from 25 per cent to 100 per cent higher than the Canadian average, a situation that is reflected in salaries and allowances for public servants working in the north. (See Volume 4, Chapter 6, particularly the discussion of support for the northern economy.) Municipal infrastructure, buildings and related services, and transportation, which make up a significant part of DIAND expenditures, are also more costly. Expenditures by the government of the Northwest Territories and local governments combined were about $19,400 per capita in 1992-93, almost double the national level. DIAND formulas for transfer payments to bands for education, social services and general administration take into consideration the size of the community, its distance from population centres, and latitude as cost factors. The amount DIAND pays per student in elementary or high school varies from a base amount of $4,500 to as much as $8,500 in the smallest northern communities.[19]

TABLE 2.9
Total Expenditures of All Governments on Aboriginal People and on All Canadians, by Function, 1992-93

	On Aboriginal People				On All Canadians		
	1 Federal ($ millions)	2 Provincial/ territorial/local ($ millions)	3 All governments ($ millions)	4 All governments, per Aboriginal person ($/person)	5 All governments ($ millions)	6 All governments, per Canadian ($/person)	7 Ratio of expenditure per Aboriginal person to expenditures per Canadian (col. 4 ÷ col. 6)
Elementary and secondary education	692	981	1,673	2,261	30,502	1,072	2.1
Post-secondary education and training	419	230	649	877	13,763	483	1.8
Income transfers	1,223	773	1,996	2,697	73,832	2,594	1.0
Housing	410	133	542	732	3,701	130	5.6
Health care	798	1,215	2,013	2,720	47,027	1,652	1.6
Social services	227	540	767	1,036	10,027	352	2.9
Protection of persons and property	342	648	991	1,339	25,505	896	1.5
Other government expenditures	1,924	1,074	2,999	4,052	81,026	2,847	1.4
Total	6,034	5,594	11,628	15,714	285,397	10,026	1.6

Notes: Column 7 gives the ratio of the amounts in columns 4 and 6. Columns 1 and 2 represent a regrouping of the data presented in Table 2.8. Column 5 is based on Statistics Canada, "Public Sector Finance", catalogue no. 68-212, Table 1.33.

Specific expenditures relating to First Nations people and Inuit

The federal government incurs a number of expenditures in fulfilling its obligations under the *Indian Act* and Aboriginal and treaty rights that have no counterpart in expenditures for all Canadians. These include expenditures associated with negotiating self-government, maintaining the Indian Register, and litigating with respect to Aboriginal rights. Expenditures associated with negotiating and settling land claims, for instance, totalled $173 million in 1992-93.

For status Indian people and Inuit, DIAND's post-secondary education assistance program (PSEAP) pays tuition fees and living allowances to students at post-secondary educational institutions, and Health Canada covers certain medical expenditures through its non-insured health benefits program (NIHB). In 1992-93, a total of $623 million was spent under these two programs, $201 million for PSEAP and $422 million for NIHB.

Although other federal programs for status Indian people living on-reserve and for Inuit communities generally adhere to provincial program rules and standards, there are differences, and they do not always favour Aboriginal clients. For instance, DIAND does not provide a shelter allowance to social assistance recipients living in band-owned housing, except those financed with CMHC assistance. In some instances DIAND will pay more for education services delivered by a province than it will to the Aboriginal community for the same services. For example, DIAND reimburses provincial school boards on the basis of their total costs averaged over all students. Schools in First Nations communities are funded on the basis of a formula providing only limited resources to address the special needs of Aboriginal children. (See Volume 3, Chapter 5.)

Some social services are in short supply in First Nations and Inuit communities. The availability of programs such as PSEAP and NIHB, therefore, does not necessarily mean better services overall. However, federal funding of medical services has resulted in the substantial development of health facilities for First Nations and Inuit communities across the country (see Volume 3, Chapter 3).

Use of services

The most important factors underlying differences in spending levels are relative levels of program use and differences in population structure. The relative level of program use by Aboriginal people is low in education, but high for most other program areas.

In education, level of use is indicated by enrolment of the school age population at learning institutions. Because Aboriginal youth on average leave school earlier than other Canadian youth, the rate of enrolment in elementary and secondary educational institutions is somewhat lower for Aboriginal people than for Canadians generally. However, the fact that a very large percentage of the Aboriginal population is of school age means that the number of Aboriginal students at these levels is disproportionately large. (Five- to 19-year-olds make up 33 per cent of the Aboriginal population but only 20 per cent of the general population.) The age structure of the Aboriginal population, therefore, is the main reason that per capita government expenditures on elementary and secondary education are approximately twice as much as for Canadians generally.

With respect to post-secondary education, we find that expenditures relating to Aboriginal people are also above the level for Canadians generally. Young Aboriginal adults constitute a large proportion of the Aboriginal population relative to the proportion of young adults in the general population, but they enrol at much lower rates and tend to leave university without completing a degree. At first glance, government spending on post-secondary education for Aboriginal students appears relatively low. However, also included in that category are funding of students through DIAND's PSEAP program and expenditures under the Pathways training program. Overall, therefore, spending per Aboriginal person on post-secondary education and training is approximately 80 per cent higher than per capita spending for all Canadians.

3. DEPENDENCE ON FINANCIAL ASSISTANCE AND REMEDIAL PROGRAMS

In contrast to relatively low participation rates in education, Aboriginal people make up a disproportionate share of the clients of the justice system and of federal, provincial and territorial social and income support programs. In this section we examine government expenditures on social programs and the justice system and identify the second major component of the cost of maintaining the status quo − the cost of extra government expenditures on remedial programs. We also estimate the share of the cost of forgone production that is shifted from Aboriginal people to governments (and thus all Canadian taxpayers) through financial assistance programs.

We focus on five program areas in two major groups: programs that provide financial assistance to persons in need and remedial programs. The former are intended to meet basic human needs and include social services, other forms of income transfers and housing subsidies. Remedial programs protect society, enforce the law and help individuals, families and communities cope with social, personal and health problems. Included in this category are health care programs, social services such as child welfare and alcohol and drug addiction treatment, and protection of persons and property (police and correctional services). As a group, Aboriginal people are frequent users of these services − the result of social disintegration in Aboriginal communities, poverty and racial discrimination, among other factors.

In each of these areas, governments jointly spend more per capita on services for Aboriginal people than they do for Canadians generally, as illustrated in Table

TABLE 2.10

Excess Expenditures of Governments on Financial Assistance and Remedial Programs, 1992-93

	Expenditures on Aboriginal people, per Aboriginal person ($)	All government expenditures, per Canadian ($)	Excess expenditures ($ millions)
Income support	2,404	1,968	323
Housing subsidies	732	130	445
Total: excess expenditures on financial assistance			**768**
Health care	2,282	1,652	466
Social services	1,036	352	506
Police and correctional services	1,106	492	454
Total: excess expenditures on remedial programs			**1,426**
Total excess expenditures			**2,194**

Notes: The per capita amounts for income support are derived from figures showing income transfers in Table 2.9 by excluding old age security and family allowance payments as these two benefits are not dependent on the economic situation of Aboriginal people. Health care spending per Aboriginal person was calculated by excluding non-insured health benefits, except for an excess component of the same relative size as for other health care expenditures. The per capita amounts for police and correctional services were derived by excluding expenditures on national defence from the category of protection of persons and property in Table 2.9. The amounts in the third column showing excess remedial expenditures were calculated by multiplying the difference between columns one and two by the Aboriginal population in 1992 (740,000).

Source: Estimates by RCAP, based on Table 2.9.

2.9. Table 2.10 shows that government expenditures on financial transfers and remedial programs for Aboriginal people exceeded expenditures for an equivalent number of Canadians by nearly $2.2 billion in 1992-93. Although high government expenditures indicate a high level of services, it should not be assumed that the needs of Aboriginal people are always fully or adequately met. During our hearings, Aboriginal people told us many times about the lack of certain services and difficulties they have experienced in making use of programs. We examined the need for government services of various kinds, the adequacy of services, and the effectiveness of past and present policies in previous volumes of this report.

Excess expenditures on financial assistance and remedial programs account for approximately half the difference between government expenditures on Aboriginal people and those on an equivalent number of Canadians in the general population, which is estimated at $4.2 billion (as discussed earlier in the chapter). Of the remaining $2 billion, $0.7 billion is federal expenditures relating to land claims, funding for post-secondary students and non-insured health benefits, and $0.9 billion is related to elementary and secondary education for Aboriginal people. These expenditures are relatively high because of the large Aboriginal population of young adults discussed earlier.[20]

An examination of statistics on the incidence of poverty, ill health and other indicators highlights the factors behind high dependence on financial assistance and remedial programs and the persistent nature of these factors. Perhaps most disturbing is the deterioration in economic conditions discussed in the first part of this chapter (see Table 2.5). One consequence of these conditions has been the increase in dependence on social assistance benefits to a point where, in 1992-93, 47 per cent of registered Indian persons living on reserves were receiving social assistance, compared to 40 per cent a decade earlier.[21] (These numbers include recipients and their dependents, as estimated by DIAND. They are higher than the numbers from the APS referred to in Volume 2, Chapter 5 on economic development and in Volume 3, Chapter 3 on health and healing. They are used here because they permit comparisons over time.) Dependence levels for other Aboriginal groups are also high, ranging from 20 to 25 per cent, or about three times the national average of 9.7 per cent.[22] Aboriginal people receive lower transfers than Canadian generally from several other income support programs, including employment insurance and the Canada and Quebec Pension Plans. The combined effect is a relatively low net transfer of income to Aboriginal people over and above what governments spend on financial assistance per Canadian in the general population.

Poverty also lies behind government expenditures on housing for Aboriginal people. The federal government, which provides the large majority of funding, assists Aboriginal households as a matter of social policy, based on financial need. Adverse economic trends affecting Aboriginal people over the past 10 years have meant that Aboriginal people were less able to look after their own housing needs by the end of the decade. Government programs have provided relief, but the housing stock remains inadequate, especially on First Nations territories (see Volume 3, Chapter 4).

Differences in per capita spending also relate to the incidence of ill health and social dysfunction among Aboriginal people. There have been some notable improvements in the health of Aboriginal people over the years. Medical advances and increased access to health services have resulted in lower infant mortality rates and a sharp decline in deaths from such diseases as tuberculosis, whooping cough and measles. Substantial progress in the prevention and treatment of respiratory and infectious disease accounts for the steady reduction in mortality rates since the 1950s.[23] Nevertheless, the high level of per capita spending on health care reflects the remaining gap between the health of Aboriginal people and that of Canadians generally, as documented in Volume 3, Chapter 3. First Nations people on-reserve make use

TABLE 2.11

Admissions to Provincial and Federal Custody, Showing Percentage Who Identified as Aboriginal, 1986-87 to 1993-94

	Sentenced Admissions to Provincial and Territorial Facilities	% Aboriginal	Warrant and Committal Admission to Federal Custody	% Aboriginal
1986-87	116,229	18	3,741	10
1987-88	117,325	22	3,988	11
1988-89	116,051	19	4,011	13
1989-1990	115,100	18	4,274	11
1990-91	114,834	19	4,296	12
1991-92	N/A	—	4,878	11
1992-93	N/A	—	5,583	13
1993-94	118,907	17	5,174	12

Notes:
N/A = not available.
— = not applicable.

Source: Statistics Canada, Canadian Centre for Justice Statistics, *Adult Correctional Services in Canada, 1993-1994*, pp. 67, 90; *Adult Correctional Services in Canada 1990-91*, pp. 35, 56.

of provincially insured services at more or less the same rate as other Aboriginal people and Canadians generally, and they receive federally funded services in communities as well. Because federal and provincial health services complement each other, this indicates a high rate of services use. The NIHB program also contributes to higher expenditures for Aboriginal people. Nevertheless, expenditures under the NIHB program also reflect the high incidence of ill health among Aboriginal people.

High rates of social services use reflect the social dysfunction that often accompanies poverty. Family breakdown, for example, and a lack of cultural sensitivity on the part of non-Aboriginal agencies have resulted in an inordinate proportion of Aboriginal children being placed in foster care. Although the percentage of First Nations children (on-reserve) in the care of foster parents or institutions declined from over six per cent in the mid- to late 1970s to just under four per cent in 1992-93, the percentage of all Canadian children in care decreased more rapidly, so the relative gap has widened (see Volume 3, Chapters 2 and 3). The incidence of children in foster care is also high for other Aboriginal groups.

Turning now to the justice system, we note that Aboriginal persons are incarcerated in provincial jails at 11 times the rate of other Canadians; in federal penitentiaries the rate is five times that of other Canadians. These rates, which have remained relatively constant over the last decade, point to social problems in Aboriginal communities and to problems in the way the justice and corrections systems deal with Aboriginal people.[24] As Table 2.11 shows, data on admissions to federal, provincial, and territorial correctional facilities do not reveal any strong trends over time. A high proportion of the cost of federal, provincial and territorial correctional institutions evidently is associated with Aboriginal people in custody, and has been for many years.

This brief survey of health care, social services and the justice system highlights the factors that give rise to large government expenditures on financial assistance and remedial programs for Aboriginal people. If the social and economic circumstances of Aboriginal people changed significantly for the better, and if remedial service systems were more culturally sensitive, the level of government expenditures for Aboriginal people would be more closely in line with expenditures for Canadians generally.

We conclude, however, that the conditions giving rise to large financial transfers to Aboriginal people and high remedial expenditures have not changed for the better and are not likely to do so in the absence of a fundamental reorientation of policies. On this basis, we estimate that excess government expenditures on financial assistance, which were nearly $0.8 billion in 1992-93 (see Table 2.10), will be the same in 1996, and that excess expenditures on remedial programs will increase from the $1.4 billion recorded in 1992-93 to $1.7 billion in 1996.[25]

Government financial assistance helps Aboriginal people in need obtain basic necessities such as food and shelter. If Aboriginal people had more and better jobs, they would be capable of meeting basic needs from their own incomes. Current government expenditures redistribute income between Canadians and Aboriginal people, shifting a part of the cost of forgone production from Aboriginal people to governments and thus to all Canadians.

Expenditures on remedial programs, however, pay for activities that could be eliminated if conditions changed for the better and services were more sensitive to Aboriginal needs and cultures. If Aboriginal people were healthier of body and spirit and their families less troubled, they would require less in the way of health care and social services, and there would be fewer cases of Aboriginal people in conflict with the law. As well, remedial services, especially the justice system, could be far more effective in dealing with Aboriginal people than they are now. Each of these improvements would mean that real productive resources could be freed for other uses. Many of the public sector employees now delivering remedial services could be redeployed to produce valuable goods and services. That these goods and services are not being produced now imposes a cost on Aboriginal people and all Canadians. Accordingly, excess expenditures on remedial programs, which we estimate at $1.7 billion in 1996, are a cost of the status quo. When we add this amount to the cost of forgone production, we find that the cost of the status quo in 1996 is $7.5 billion.[26]

4. Escalating Cost of the Status Quo

The analysis in this chapter leads us to conclude that the present circumstances of Aboriginal people impose large costs on them and on all Canadians. We have examined two categories of cost. The first and largest cost results from the economic marginalization of Aboriginal people. We have shown that under better conditions Aboriginal people could contribute an additional $5.8 billion to the Canadian economy. That they do not do so now is directly related to their low participation in the labour force, high unemployment, and lower productivity when they are employed. On further exploration we also found that a lack of full-time, year-round employment and low educational attainment relative to all Canadians are important aspects of the problem. These factors are not passing phenomena. On the contrary, as shown in Volume 2, Chapter 5, Aboriginal people have been on the fringes of the economy for several generations. In the first section of this chapter we showed that conditions deteriorated further over the 1980s, some modest improvements in educational attainment notwithstanding.

We have argued that it is realistic to expect that there can be a substantial increase in Aboriginal participation in wealth-creation activities. Our estimate of the economic potential of Aboriginal people is based on the known performance of the Canadian economy, taking into account its regional diversity and the aspirations of Aboriginal people. Indeed, in some parts of the country, where land claims have been settled or Aboriginal people have successfully launched businesses, we can already glimpse a better future with a stronger economic base for Aboriginal people.

The second cost of the economic marginalization of Aboriginal people consists of the extra expenditures by governments on remedial programs that address the adverse conditions facing many Aboriginal people. Many Aboriginal people and some entire communities are in poor health, struggling socially and economically. Expenditures on health care and social services, including child and family services, substance abuse programs, and the justice system, are higher for Aboriginal people than for Canadians generally. We estimate the combined cost of these expenditures, which we refer to as excess government expenditures on remedial programs, at $1.7 billion in 1996.

Like the economic circumstances of Aboriginal people, the social conditions that give rise to government expenditures on remedial programs are deeply rooted, and they have not improved significantly under the policies governments generally have chosen to apply.

The cost of the status quo is being borne by Aboriginal people and by all Canadians. The fact that Aboriginal people could be earning an estimated $5.8 billion more than they are means that governments are losing $2.1 billion in revenues they would otherwise collect through taxation.[27] The remaining $3.7 billion is a loss to Aboriginal people in income after taxes. They receive an estimated

TABLE 2.12
Present and Future Annual Cost of the Status Quo ($ billions)

	1996	2016
Cost to Aboriginal People		
Forgone earned income	5.8	8.6
Income taxes forgone	-2.1	-3.1
Financial assistance from governments	-0.8	-1.2
Net income loss of Aboriginal people	2.9	4.3
Cost to Governments		
Expenditures on remedial programs	1.7	2.4
Financial assistance to Aboriginal people	0.8	1.2
Government revenue forgone	2.1	3.1
Total cost to governments	4.6	6.7
Total cost of the status quo	7.5	11.0

Note: Under 'Cost to Aboriginal People', the total income forgone is estimated at $5.8 billion for 1996. Some of this cost is borne by Aboriginal people in the form of lost income. The rest is borne by governments, in the form of taxes forgone and various forms of assistance paid out. Costs to governments are removed from 'Cost to Aboriginal People' and included under 'Cost to Governments'.

$0.8 billion in income support payments and housing subsidies, so their disposable net income is $2.9 billion less than it could be.

When we took our estimate of $1.7 billion in excess government expenditures on remedial programs and added it to excess expenditures on financial assistance to Aboriginal people in the form of income support payments and housing subsidies, we concluded that government expenditures are $2.5 billion higher than they might be if Aboriginal people enjoyed the same quality of life as other Canadians. When we also considered the potential loss of revenues of $2.1 billion, we found that governments would experience a drain on their finances of $4.6 billion in 1996. This cost to governments, which occurs year after year and can never be recovered, is equivalent to the annual expenditures of the government of New Brunswick.

In sum, every year that the social and economic circumstances of Aboriginal people remain as they are, it costs the country $7.5 billion. That cost – the cost of the status quo – is the equivalent of nearly one per cent of Canada's GDP. It consists of a fiscal cost of $4.6 billion, borne by all Canadians, and a loss of net income to Aboriginal people of $2.9 billion.

If no effort is made to reduce the cost of the status quo, it is likely to increase. Unless economic opportunities and participation are enhanced and social conditions improve, the cost will increase in step with a growing Aboriginal adult population, or even more rapidly. This population is growing at almost twice the rate of the general Canadian adult population. Using demographic projections, we expect that the cost of the status quo could increase by 47 per cent over the next 20 years, from $7.5 billion to $11 billion by 2016 (see Table 2.12).[28]

The cost of the status quo is also likely to increase in relative terms. The Canadian population of working age is projected to increase by 23.5 per cent over the next 20 years, which is half the projected rate of increase in the cost of the status quo over the same period. This means an increase of close to 20 per cent in the burden of these costs per Canadian of working age. It also implies that the social cost of the status quo will increase to more than one per cent of GDP.[29]

It is possible to avoid this costly future, but not with current policies. To be sure, some improvements have been made, and we want to acknowledge these positive steps. Several major land claims have been settled in the north – a major step forward for the groups directly affected – and increasing resources are being devoted to negotiation and settlement of claims, a welcome move. Also worth mentioning are efforts to tackle specific health and social problems and the transfer of education and other public services to First Nations control. More generally, governments are also giving greater recognition to the particular needs of Aboriginal people, and there is growing awareness of Aboriginal concerns on the part of Canadians generally.

As we have shown, however, these measures, while constructive and offering some hope, do not go far enough. Only a more fundamental renewal of the relationship between Aboriginal people and other Canadians will lead to much improved conditions for Aboriginal people. The positive steps taken so far are likely to be overwhelmed by population growth, government expenditure restraint, and a lack of economic opportunity for Aboriginal people. Indeed, unrest in several parts of the country in the summer of 1995 was a reminder of the ever-growing sense of frustration with conditions in Aboriginal communities. Expectations have been raised; the younger generation is less willing to accept the enormous disparities that are the focus of this and other chapters of this report. Unless tangible progress is made soon, there is a serious risk of major conflict, with high human and economic cost, much higher than the cost of the status quo discussed here.

Notes

1. In 1996, Canada's Aboriginal population aged 15 years and over is calculated at 535,000. Of these, 153,000 (28.6 per cent) receive social assistance, based on the 1990 rate of dependence recorded in the Aboriginal peoples survey (APS). This is a con-

servative estimate, as dependence on social assistance has probably increased since 1990, as we show in this chapter. For a general discussion of the sources of data used by the Commission in this report, see Volume, Chapter 2, particularly the endnotes.

2. GDP is projected to be $821 billion in 1996, according to economic assumptions in the federal budget of February 1995. According to projections presented later in this chapter, the rapid growth of the Aboriginal population will cause the social cost of the status quo to increase to more than one per cent of GDP in the next 20 years.

3. This result is obtained by multiplying the participation rate (57 per cent for the Aboriginal population) by the percentage of the labour force that is employed (100 per cent less 24.6 per cent), and applying the same formula to the statistics for all Canadians. The difference between these employment rates is 18 per cent (61 per cent less 43 per cent), which when applied to the Aboriginal population aged 15 years and over (457,800) reveals a difference of 82,000 jobs.

4. For Canada, the labour force participation rate in 1990 was 76.4 per cent for males and 59.9 per cent for females; for Aboriginal people the rates were 65.4 per cent for males and 49.6 per cent for females. The unemployment rates are 10.1 per cent for Canadian males and 10.2 per cent for females. For Aboriginal people the rates are 27.2 per cent for males and 21.6 per cent for females. Statistics Canada, 1991 Census and Aboriginal Peoples Survey.

5. This result was obtained by applying the distribution of the Canadian population by level of education achieved to Aboriginal people and calculating what Aboriginal people would have earned at their actual rates of earning by level of education. The procedure consists of multiplying the corresponding elements in the second and third columns of Table 2.3, adding the resulting products, and scaling by the size of the Aboriginal population 15 years of age and over. This analysis is suggestive only and provides a snapshot, not a complete causal explanation. Although education can be a major lever for change, a major change in education cannot be realized in isolation and will likely result following other changes in Aboriginal society. As well, attitudes of many non-Aboriginal Canadians toward Aboriginal people are probably in part related to the gap in educational attainment between these two population groups. Thus, a narrower gap in education might facilitate the participation of Aboriginal people in the Canadian economy and give Aboriginal people with any amount of education access to better jobs and incomes. Improving educational attainment may be even more effective in improving overall conditions than our calculations indicate.

6. The percentage of Aboriginal groups living in urban areas is as follows: registered Indian people off-reserve, 80.8 per cent; non-registered Indian people, 69.3 per cent; Métis people, 64.9 per cent; and Inuit, 21.9 per cent. Of the Canadian population, 77.2 per cent live in urban areas (see Volume 2, Chapter 5).

7. This revised estimate of the earnings gap corresponds with a different estimate of the employment gap: 68,500 jobs in 1990, down from the 82,000 jobs mentioned earlier in the chapter.

8. In 1990, wages, salaries and supplementary labour income, together with income of unincorporated businesses, was $410,740 million. The GDP was $670,952 mil-

lion for the same year. Statistics Canada, "National Income and Expenditure Accounts, Annual Estimates 1981-1992", catalogue no. 13-201.

9. The gap in income from employment between Aboriginal people and an equivalent number of Canadians, $2.7 billion in 1990, is 61 per cent of the gap in total income. (The latter can be calculated as $100 \div 61 \times \$2.7$ billion = \$4.4 billion.) By the same method we find that actual earned income of Aboriginal people was $6.9 billion, while a value of $11.3 billion is found for potential earned income (that is, the income of an equivalent number of Canadians). In the absence of data it is assumed, as a first approximation, that the same relative gap exists for other income because economic activity tends to generate different types of income jointly. Most jobs in the economy involve capital investment by businesses that recover the cost of such investments and earn a profit as well as paying wages, salaries and benefits to their employees. However, the gap is probably larger than these estimates indicate. Income other than earnings from employment is derived largely from capital, and there are large disparities in wealth between Aboriginal people and Canadians in general.

10. The adjustment for population size is based on the growth in the Aboriginal population of working age (15 to 64 years) (see Volume 1, Chapter 2). The price level was adjusted using the Consumer Price Index for 1990 to 1994 (Statistics Canada, catalogue no. 62-001, vol. 74, no. 2), and the consensus forecast for 1995 and 1996 reported in the February 1995 federal budget.

11. The initial estimate of the employment gap derived from Table 2.1 – 82,000 for 1990 – was reduced to 68,500 when differences in economic opportunity reflected in Table 2.4 were considered. This latter estimate is updated to 80,000 for the year 1996 by applying the growth rate of the Aboriginal population of working age (15 to 64 years) over the period 1990 to 1996.

12. The experience of the James Bay Cree with the Hunter and Trapper Income Support Program is a good illustration of a dual lifestyle, one among many available. See Volume 2, Chapter 5 and Volume 4, Chapter 6. See also Ignatius La Rusic, "Subsidies for Subsistence: The Place of Income Security Programs in Supporting Hunting, Fishing and Trapping as a Way of Life in Subarctic Communities", research study prepared for RCAP (1993). For information about research studies prepared for RCAP, see *A Note About Sources* at the beginning of this volume.

13. We do not think that differences in lifestyle require further adjustments in our measures of economic potential and the earnings gap. In the small communities neighbouring many First Nations communities, people also live on the land and make trade-offs between employment and other pursuits that are not included in measured economic activity. As we show in this chapter, Aboriginal control of resources likely will lead to greater economic activity as more income from resource exploitation is retained in the region.

14. Mary Jane Norris, Don Kerr and François Nault, "Projections of the Population with Aboriginal Identity in Canada, 1991-2016", research study prepared by Statistics Canada for RCAP (1995) (the Aboriginal population aged 15 to 64 years is projected to increase from 507,000 in 1996 to 753,000 by 2016); Statistics

Canada, "Population Projection for Canada, Provinces and Territories, 1993-2016", catalogue no. 91-520; and Statistics Canada, "Revised Intercensal Population and Family Estimates, July 1, 1971-1991", catalogue no. 91-537.

15. Sources for total federal government expenditures: Statistics Canada, "Public Finance Historical Data 1965/66-1991/92", catalogue no. 68-512, and "Public Sector Finance 1994-95", catalogue no. 68-212.

16. For purposes of these calculations the following population growth rates over the period 1981-1991 were used: for the total Aboriginal population, including Métis and non-status Indian people: 48.5 per cent; for status Indian people and Inuit: 56.4 per cent; and for Inuit as well as status Indian people on-reserve and Crown land: 34.1 per cent. These rates are based on data from the APS and the Indian Register. The sharp increases in the growth rate for status Indian people reflects registrations under Bill C-31. The population of Canada increased by 12.9 per cent over the same decade.

17. Statistics Canada, "Public Sector Finance 1994-1995", catalogue no. 68-212.

18. Expenditures here are based on 740,00 persons who self-identified as Aboriginal, as measured by the Aboriginal peoples survey (APS), and after adjustment for under-reporting and updating to 1992. Federal and provincial programs directed to Aboriginal people generally take as clients those who self-identify. In calculations of the Aboriginal share of general programs for this chapter we used the identity population. When the number of status Indian people is taken from the Indian Register instead of the APS and adjusted for persons living abroad and other factors, the number of Aboriginal persons in 1992 is 787,000. Using this latter population estimate, and adjusting expenditures on general programs as appropriate, spending on Aboriginal people was estimated to be $14,900 per Aboriginal person in 1992-93, or 49 per cent higher than government per capita expenditures for Canadians in general.

19. The higher cost of delivering government services in small, remote and northern communities is reflected in expenditures for targeted programs but was not taken into account in calculating the Aboriginal share of general programs. As the amounts in Table 2.8 indicate, this cost factor may be significant for the federal government and Ontario and Quebec, but not for other provinces. The expenditures of territorial governments, as estimated and presented in Table 2.8, reflect the high cost of programs and services in the north.

20. Of the three factors affecting government expenditures, specific expenditures for First Nations and Inuit and differences in levels of service use play a significant role in differences in the level of government expenditures. The third factor, cost of service delivery, contributes to the difference in the level of expenditures in many areas of program delivery; it may also contribute to the unexplained residual of $0.4 billion.

21. DIAND, Basic Departmental Data – 1994, Tables 1 and 25.

22. Allan Moscovitch and Andrew Webster, "Social Assistance and Aboriginal People: A Discussion Paper", research study prepared for RCAP (1995).

23. The present brief discussion focuses on changes in health over time and is based on T. Kue Young, "Measuring the Health Status of Canada's Aboriginal Population: A Statistical Review and Methodological Commentary", research study prepared for RCAP (1994).

24. These matters are examined in RCAP, *Bridging the Cultural Divide: A Report on Aboriginal People and Criminal Justice in Canada* (Ottawa: Supply and Services, 1996). Chapter 2 of that report deals with Aboriginal over-representation in Canadian prisons and provides some data for Saskatchewan, Manitoba and the Northwest Territories.

25. To obtain a current estimate for the same period as the cost of forgone production, government expenditures on financial assistance and remedial programs for Aboriginal people were updated to the calendar year 1996 with information from the 1995-96 federal budget and estimates (see Table 2.7), including a projected three per cent increase in DIAND expenditures in 1996-97. It was assumed that provincial and territorial expenditures on Aboriginal people increased by four per cent between 1992-93 and 1996, reflecting a more rapid growth rate of the Aboriginal population within a constant overall level of expenditures. Excess expenditures were assumed to be constant as a share of expenditures for each of the five program areas.

26. The cost of excess expenditures and forgone production can be added together because both measure a loss of collective well-being in Canada. The cost of forgone output refers to under-utilization of the productive potential of Aboriginal people. The cost of excess government expenditures on remedial programs refers to a mis-allocation of other productive resources. Removing the former cost will result in higher employment and production in the Canadian economy. Eliminating the latter cost does not lead to more jobs and a higher GDP, but the people now delivering remedial services can be redeployed to produce goods and services not available at present. This would result in an increase in valuable output.

    Naturally, the economic potential of Aboriginal people and redeployment of a segment of public services will not be realized overnight, but such progress is realistic within a time frame measured in decades. In Chapter 4 of this volume, we suggest a schedule for implementing the recommendations of this report. Given the structural changes taking place continuously in the economy, as new products and technologies are introduced and the needs and preferences of the population change, these two shifts would not be extraordinarily large.

27. These potential revenues of federal, provincial and territorial and local governments are calculated by applying the share of government revenues in total income or GDP (41 per cent in 1993-94) to the income gain of Aboriginal people, with an adjustment for the tax exemption. The majority of Aboriginal people pay taxes in the same way as other Canadians. A tax exemption applies to "the personal property of an Indian or band situated on a reserve" (*Indian Act*, R.S.C. 1985, c. I-5, s. 87(1)(b)), and this is the basis for exemption of income earned by Indian people on-reserve and from sales taxes on goods and services acquired by Indian people on-reserve (this description captures only the general thrust of the tax rules, which

are intricate and, in the case of provincial sales taxes, vary by province). To calculate the government revenue share of additional income earned by Aboriginal people it was assumed that people on-reserve would pay no property or income taxes, with sales taxes at half the prevailing rates.

28. The cost of forgone output is assumed to be proportional to the size of the Aboriginal population of working age (15 to 64 years), which is projected to grow by 48.6 per cent between 1996 and 2016. This rate of growth is also applied to forgone government revenue. Excess government expenditures on financial assistance – social assistance and other income support payments, and housing subsidies – are projected to increase in step with the population aged 15 to 64. Excess expenditures on remedial programs are projected to increase by 45 per cent, with health care expenditures being proportional to the Aboriginal population aged 15 and over (an increase of 54.5 per cent between 1996 and 2016), and expenditures on social services and police and correctional services growing at the same rate as the Aboriginal population as a whole (34.8 per cent).

29. Based on these projections, the cost of the status quo will increase from 0.9 per cent of GDP in 1996 to 1.1 per cent by 2016. Our projections do not take into account future gains in productivity, which is, next to population growth, the most significant source of long-term growth in the economy. Productivity gains would increase GDP per Canadian in the work force and make the burden of social costs easier to bear. We note, however, that three-quarters of the social cost of the status quo consists of an economic gap between Aboriginal people and Canadians generally resulting from exclusion and marginalization. This gap will increase when productivity gains occur in the economy. Productivity gains, therefore, will not significantly change the relative cost of the status quo in relation to GDP.

3

THE COMMISSION'S STRATEGY
AS A GOOD INVESTMENT

THE COMMISSION'S PROPOSALS TO ESTABLISH a fundamentally different relationship between Canada and Aboriginal peoples are obviously not without cost; we are recommending that governments undertake major structural reform and a great many social and economic initiatives. We envisage a period, spanning a generation, in which the foundations of a renewed relationship are put in place and the day-to-day reality experienced by Aboriginal people is transformed. Governments will have to apply substantial resources to those tasks: fundamental change will be achieved only with great effort and commitment.

We believe that governments should commit significant additional resources to resolve historical claims, restructure the political relationship, and improve living conditions and economic opportunities for Aboriginal people. This expenditure is justified to correct the injustices of the past and present. As we have argued throughout this report, Aboriginal people are entitled to equal social, educational and health outcomes, to a fair share of the country's assets, and to a much greater share of opportunity than they have had so far. We also demonstrate in this chapter that the entire country stands to gain if our proposals are acted on. The additional government expenditures required to implement our recommendations are a good investment for all Canadians.

We approach the task of determining what additional resources governments should commit by taking several factors into consideration. First, our recommendations represent an interactive strategy for change and should be implemented in such a way that they reinforce each other. The breadth of our mandate has enabled us to consider the synergistic dimension of change, that is, the impact that change in one area has on a range of other areas. Thus we see a dynamic developing between structural reform and social and economic measures, each reinforcing the other. The principle that drives change and gives it direction is that Aboriginal people are empowered to create their own solutions by having both the authority and the tools to do so. We outlined this approach in the first chapter of this volume and will give more consideration to it here.

Second, we have been acutely conscious that governments are in the midst of the most fundamental reassessment of their activities and reduction of their expenditures since they first assumed a major role in the economic and social life of Canada. The resources are not available to do all that good public policy, or justice and morality, would dictate should be done.

Third, a further limitation constrains the pace of progress. We propose that change be implemented by Aboriginal people in the manner of their choosing. This means that the pace of change will be determined in part by their capacity to implement their chosen priorities, a capacity that is still developing.

Given these factors, we recommend strongly that, to give effect to our recommendations, governments increase their annual spending over the first five years of the strategy, so that by year five, expenditures are between $1.5 and $2 billion more than they are today. Governments will then need to sustain that level of additional expenditure for a number of years.

These resource requirements follow from the approach to implementation presented in Chapter 1. In the first few years following the government's receipt of this report, development of Aboriginal capacity to implement change through healing, improvement in economic and living conditions, and human resource and institutional development will require an immediate and major infusion of resources. By contrast, the initial focus with respect to structural reform will be on rebuilding Aboriginal nations and changing the land claims and treaty processes, which will require only limited funding in the early stages. But as more and more Aboriginal nations are reconstituted, increasing amounts will need to be allocated to implement self-government and the redistribution of lands and resources. Significant spending on social measures and structural reform will then need to be sustained for a number of years.

These investments represent an economic cost, in that productive resources will have to be devoted to the task. But in our view they will also result in substantial economic gains for all Canadians. They will lead to greater economic self-reliance for Aboriginal people and restore health and vitality to Aboriginal individuals and communities.

In Chapter 2 we demonstrated that the political, social and economic conditions facing Aboriginal people impose a cost of $7.5 billion per year on them and on all Canadians; this cost is likely to increase in future, reaching $11 billion per year 20 years from now. This cost of the status quo includes losses flowing from failure to develop and use the full economic potential of Aboriginal people and the cost of remedial action to deal with the effects of social disintegration. In Chapter 2 we showed that these costs can be reduced significantly. We believe that the recommendations in this report, taken together, will bring

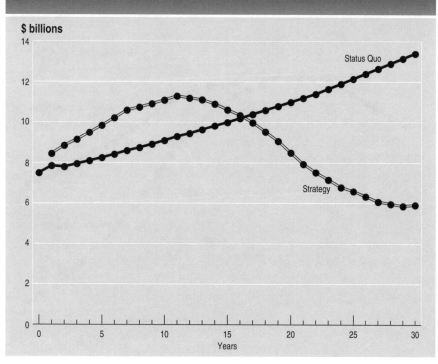

FIGURE 3.1

Projected Cost of the Status Quo and of the Commission's Strategy

about fundamental change in the circumstances of Aboriginal people and lead to the progressive reduction and eventual elimination of these costs. By eliminating the cost of the status quo, the strategy will yield economic benefits that far exceed the amounts governments will spend to implement it.

We estimate that these positive effects will begin to be realized in terms of the economy and government finances by about the tenth year following the adoption of our recommendations (though in terms of the impact on people's lives, the effects will be felt much sooner) and will become significant in the decade following that. Implementation will still involve significant costs 10 years hence, but as the gains from the strategy increase, the net cost will decline and in time become a net gain. The projected costs of the status quo and the strategy are displayed graphically in Figure 3.1. The net cost and net gain from the strategy are indicated by the distance between the two cost lines. As shown in Figure 3.1, the cross-over point, where net cost becomes net gain, is reached somewhere between year 15 and year 20 after the beginning of implementation. From this point on, Canadians and Aboriginal people will be better off than under the status quo.

Gains from the strategy will take the form of increased incomes for Aboriginal people and a fiscal dividend for governments. Governments will see

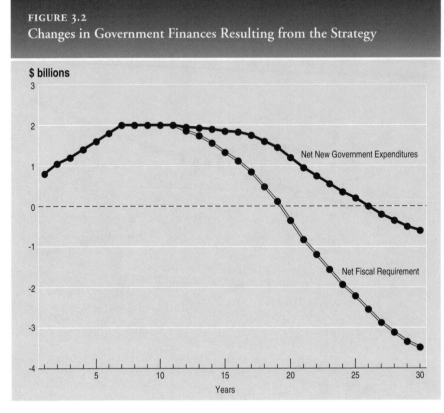

FIGURE 3.2
Changes in Government Finances Resulting from the Strategy

their revenues increase, as Aboriginal economic activity expands, and their expenditures on financial assistance and remedial programs decline as Aboriginal people's dependence on government diminishes. We propose that governments use a part of the fiscal dividend to increase the resources devoted to implementing the strategy and apply the remainder to general revenues.[1] This way of using the fiscal dividend makes it possible to complete the investments in healing, economic development and institutional reform, to implement Aboriginal self-government, and to make progress in reallocating lands and resources during the second 10-year period, without imposing an additional burden in excess of $2 billion in any year.

Indeed, governments will find their financial situation improve year after year as the fiscal dividend increases, until it reaches the same size as the additional expenditures needed for implementation. At that point governments would no longer have to raise taxes, borrow funds or reduce other spending to continue to work toward a renewed relationship with Aboriginal people. We expect that this point will be reached about 20 years after the beginning of implementation (Figure 3.2). From then on, governments jointly will have a smaller deficit (or larger surplus) than under the status quo.

TABLE 3.1

Net Long-Term Annual Gain from the Strategy Compared to the Status Quo ($ billions)

Aboriginal People

Increase in earned income	*8.6*	
Government revenues from increased Aboriginal income	(3.1)	
Reduction in financial assistance from governments	(1.2)	
Change in net income of Aboriginal people		4.3

Governments

Reduction in expenditures on remedial programs	*2.4*	
Expenditures to maintain the strategy	*(1.2)*	
Reduction in financial assistance to Aboriginal people	1.2	
Net change in government expenditures	2.4	
Increase in government revenues	3.1	
Net fiscal dividend to governments		5.5
Net gain for Aboriginal people and for all governments from the strategy compared to the status quo		*9.8*

Note: Real economic gains and costs are printed in *italics*. Other items relate to the distribution of these costs. Parentheses indicate negative entries. All values are based on the projected size of the Aboriginal population in 2016. This table is the same as Table 2.12, Chapter 2 in this volume, except that here 'Expenditures to maintain the strategy' has been added (see p. 74).

Looking beyond 20 years, the amount required to continue to implement the recommendations will decline when the major social and economic investments and the reallocation of lands and resources are completed. There are some permanent costs of maintaining the new governance arrangements and the higher standard of living of Aboriginal people, but these are considerably smaller than the present cost of economic dependency and social dysfunction. Thus, in the long run, government expenditures will be significantly lower than under the status quo (Figure 3.2).

The results that can be achieved by implementing the recommendations in this report are summarized in Table 3.1. Aboriginal people generate the larger share of the gain by producing greater economic output; but half this gain is transferred to governments through taxes and changes in financial assistance. Governments gain directly when demand for remedial programs declines, but they also bear the cost of maintaining the new reality. In all, more than half the net gain takes the form of a fiscal dividend for governments.

These time horizons and resource allocations – an investment of up to $2 billion per year for 20 years – should be seen against the background of four generations or more when the Canadian state marginalized Aboriginal people economically and politically and several more generations of welfare policies applied in a way that disregarded the social realities of Aboriginal communities and fostered deep dependency. Patience and consistency of effort will be needed as Aboriginal people heal themselves, take control of their futures and regain strength. Change cannot be expected to proceed in a uniform and steady manner or at a regimented pace.

Our recommendations are motivated first and foremost by a desire for social justice and for a restoration of historical rights, dignity and self-reliance to Aboriginal people. From this perspective the strategy will be a good investment for Canada. But the strategy is also a good economic investment. Greater productivity, higher incomes and improved government finances will result from it. At a time when the economy is not performing optimally and government finances are under severe strain, the realistic prospect of ending the economic dependency of many Aboriginal people and communities provides a powerful argument in favour of the strategy.

1. FINANCING FUNDAMENTAL CHANGE

In this and the next two sections we examine how the finances of governments will change as they implement the recommendations in this report. What is likely to happen if no major reforms are introduced is addressed in Chapter 2. There we showed that, in the absence of a fundamentally different approach and new policies, the social and economic conditions of Aboriginal people would remain more or less as they are at present and that government expenditures per Aboriginal person would remain at present levels. In support of this view, we provided extensive data showing that the circumstances of Aboriginal people and the level of government expenditures relating to Aboriginal people have shown little change over the past decade or two.

But the changing age structure of the Aboriginal population will bring about major shifts in the composition of government expenditures. Expenditures for education will remain close to their present level as a decline in the birthrate keeps the number of children and youth from increasing greatly; but expenditures on financial assistance will increase rapidly because large numbers of young people will be coming of age. Indeed, the age structure of the Aboriginal population will change in a way that would reduce government expenditures were it not for the high degree of economic dependence among Aboriginal people. The changing demographics add force to the economic argument for fundamental change, as reflected in the rapidly increasing cost of the status quo and the burden this imposes on all Canadians.[2]

A perspective on the future in which government expenditures remain more or less constant on a per capita basis is at odds with the present fiscal policies of most governments in Canada. It is worth noting that the starting point for the projections is 1996, so that projected expenditure levels reflect any cutbacks that occurred up to that point.

While governments will no doubt continue to practise expenditure restraint for some years, we would not expect reductions to the extent seen in recent years to continue after the public debt is stabilized. We believe that governments will continue to have a major role in the social and economic life of the country to maintain social peace, provide economic opportunity for all citizens, and support those in need. Should the future bring a major, sustained reduction in the scope of government responsibilities, there will likely be more hardship among Aboriginal people, and it would become very difficult to reach the goals we have set.

Governments should not ignore their obligations to Aboriginal people just because their role in society is being redefined. It would be a travesty of justice if concerted and effective action to correct the history of oppression and dispossession of Aboriginal people were set aside on grounds of financial restraint just at the point when this history is finally being recognized for what it is. A great debt is owing, a debt on which governments and Canadians cannot renege.

Our task is to show what resources are needed to establish a renewed relationship and end dependency on government by greatly improving social and economic conditions for Aboriginal people. We have not done this for individual recommendations but have projected resource requirements for 12 policy areas, using a global approach and with existing expenditures on similar activities as a guide.

The majority of the expenditures we propose are of a temporary nature, serving to bring about change. For example, land claims settlements will involve a redistribution of land, resources and money effected over a number of years and will be completed at some point. Future income streams will be transferred with the assets, but these would be reflected in the value of the assets or integrated into fiscal arrangements for Aboriginal governments.

Many of the Commission's recommendations concerning social and economic measures call on governments to change the content, delivery and control of existing services. The recommendations call for new Aboriginal institutions, restructuring of mainstream institutions and greater use of Aboriginal content, methods and knowledge. To achieve this, extra money will be needed for a period to effect change by involving Aboriginal people at all levels, by adding new functions or experimenting with new approaches that will later be merged with or substituted for present delivery mechanisms, and by developing new curricula and methods, as well as for bricks and mortar. As services reach more Aboriginal clients and are made more effective, and as the healing process proceeds, demand for services to deal with unmet needs will also increase funding requirements. But after the new structures are in place and fully operational, and the backlog of needs has been addressed, costs should revert to more or less the same level as before the introduction of changes.

Some costs of the strategy are of a permanent nature. For instance, investment in human resources for self-government and economic growth will mean greater enrolment rates among Aboriginal students. The central institutions of Aboriginal governments and the capacity to develop and implement policy where they assume jurisdiction are new functions that will require new resources on a permanent basis. But programs are already in place, and on the whole they can be delivered as efficiently by Aboriginal organizations as by existing agencies, or perhaps even more so. (Services to Indian people living on reserves and Inuit are already being delivered for the most part by Aboriginal organizations; any effects this may have on costs are reflected in the present level of expenditures and are not a cost of the strategy.)

Two stages of implementation are set out in detail in Table 3.2. The first column, showing government expenditure allocations for 2001, five years after the beginning of the strategy, represents the early implementation phase, when spending is focused on social and economic measures. The structural reform measures, although an indispensable part of the strategy and essential to its success, do not as yet involve large government outlays.

But 20 years after the strategy is launched this has changed completely, as shown in the second column of Table 3.2. The allocations for that year reflect the operations of Aboriginal nation governments and financial transfers associated with land claims and treaty settlements. Significant outlays will be required. While some of the social and economic investments will have been completed, other measures will still require major funding. (The expenditure allocations for social and economic measures for 2016 are scaled up to reflect changes in the size of Aboriginal client groups.)

Also shown in the second column of Table 3.2 is the fiscal dividend generated by the strategy in 2016. Significant annual savings will accrue in a number of program areas by that time, and these will be larger than the expenditures on the strategy's social and economic measures.[3] As government revenues also increase as a result of progress on the economic front, government finances overall will have returned to more or less the same state as under the status quo, that is, as shown in Table 3.2, an improvement of $375 million.[4]

This favourable result will be reached when half the cost of the status quo has been eliminated through improvements in the social and economic circumstances of Aboriginal people. While recognizing that the effects of the strategy will take time to emerge and that progress will not be steady or uniform, we believe it is possible that half the potential gains from the strategy can be real-

TABLE 3.2
Changes in Government Finances under the Strategy ($ millions)

Additional allocation in the year	2001	2016
Structural measures		
1. Tribunal and treaty commissions	50	50
2. Nation rebuilding	50	0
3. Nation governments	50	425
4. Land claims settlements	0	1000
Total for structural measures	**150**	**1475**
Social and economic measures		
Healing		
5. Education, youth and culture	300	150
6. Health care	100	(450)
7. Social services	100	(425)
8. Justice	25	(325)
Economic opportunity and living conditions		
9. Economic development	350	225
10. Income transfers	0	(250)
11. Housing and infrastructure	400	350
12. Human resource development	150	425
Total for social and economic measures	**1,425**	**(300)**
Government revenue gains	—	**(1,550)**
Overall total	**1,575**	**(375)**

Notes:
1. In this table, expenditures (numbers without parentheses) represent increases in spending by all governments required to implement the strategy. Reductions are shown by the numbers in parentheses in the column for 2016. These relate to amounts saved as a result of the strategy that, in its absence, would have been incurred under a continuation of the status quo and to additional revenues collected by governments.
2. Figures are rounded to the nearest $25 million.

ized 20 years from now. (We comment on the pace of progress later in the chapter). In the next two sections we discuss in detail the expenditure allocations and savings presented in Table 3.2.

2. ESTABLISHING A NEW RELATIONSHIP: STRUCTURAL MEASURES

As proposed in Chapter 1 of this volume, policies and processes to effect change in the political relationship between Aboriginal people and other Canadians and in the distribution of lands and resources would be put in place through a new royal proclamation and companion legislation. Initially the focus of action will be on rebuilding Aboriginal nations through processes that are to a large extent internal to such nations. Aboriginal groups will enter into these processes when they are ready and proceed at their own pace. The process may be time-consuming for many nations. Once reconstituted, Aboriginal nations will begin to exercise increased jurisdiction on their territories. Following negotiation of a Canada-wide framework agreement, recognized Aboriginal nations entering into treaty negotiations would use the framework agreement to arrive at more definitive arrangements respecting self-government jurisdiction, fiscal arrangements, and territory.

Compared to existing processes concerning treaties, governance and lands, we are proposing major changes in scope and orientation, with significant effects on financial requirements. Nation building and achieving recognition will require more resources than are allocated to existing community-based self-government and tripartite processes. The operations of new bodies such as the treaty commissions and the Aboriginal lands and treaties tribunal will also cost more than the institutions that are now part of the process. But the cost of these process innovations is modest compared to the resources needed to effect a reallocation of lands and resources and a resolution of treaty issues with all Aboriginal nations.

At present, federal, provincial and territorial governments spend some $200 to $250 million per year on negotiation, implementation and litigation related to treaties, lands and self-government, not including the value of claims settlements.[5] The settlement process will change but the activity will continue. There will still be a need for research and preparation of claims, evaluation and negotiation, but after new policies and processes are introduced, we would anticipate less litigation. Given the current large backlog of specific claims, and with more than 45 comprehensive claims filed in British Columbia alone, we expect that no financial resources currently committed to these activities can be freed up.

We propose that governments, while continuing to fund these various activities, commit an additional amount of up to $150 million per year during the initial five years of the strategy for structural reform measures. New funds are required, temporarily, for consultations about the royal proclamation and companion legislation and for negotiation of the framework agreement. These processes will involve the national Aboriginal organizations, which will require funding to support their participation, amounting to perhaps $15 million per year for consultations with their constituents, researching, preparing for and conducting negotiations, commissioning technical studies, and so on; this need will cease once an agreement is in place. These funds are included in the $150 million, as expenditures on other items (detailed below) will not be required during the early years of consultations. (Adoption of new policies and processes by federal, provincial and territorial governments will also involve costs such as for consultation within the government and with the public, drafting of legislation, and so on. We consider these part of governments' usual cost of doing business.)

The Aboriginal Lands and Treaties Tribunal will involve new outlays that are likely to be similar in scale to those of the Federal Court of Canada. These costs can be met in part by reallocating funding now devoted to other institutions, in particular the Indian Claims Commission. The net demand on the federal government may be $25 million per year. Our proposals also include treaty commissions. To these we assign an allocation of the same magnitude, bringing annual funding for the tribunal and treaty commissions to $50 million by year five of the strategy (Table 3.2, line 1).

Rebuilding Aboriginal nations will begin in earnest after the royal proclamation is promulgated. Nation building involves several stages: animation and preliminary self-definition, an initial referendum to launch the self-government process, development of a citizenship code, enumeration and resolution of citizenship cases, and developing a constitution.

Expenditures of $2.5 million per year for each nation, for two to four years on average, should be sufficient, although in certain cases a larger amount may be necessary. Accordingly, we would expect costs to range from $5 million to $10 million per nation over the time needed to complete the process. If 20 to 30 nations embark on the process in the three years following the royal proclamation and some of them complete it by the fifth year, as we think possible, expenditures should not exceed $50 million a year at that time (Table 3.2, line 2).

Once reconstituted, Aboriginal nations will seek formal recognition and establish nation governments. Nations will determine their own forms of governance, but all will need some type of legislature, an executive, and a capacity to develop and implement legislation and policy in each area of jurisdiction. The expenditures needed to establish and operate these institutions are the costs of Aboriginal self-government. We do not regard the cost of delivering existing programs and services by Aboriginal organizations as a cost of self-government.

DIAND spends close to $250 million per year in band government allocations, that is, expenditures for financial administration and general management functions relating to devolved programs.[6] With the creation of nation-level government, these functions will continue, and so will the need for funding. Some economies of scale will be realized. Band-level governments will likely continue with municipal-type responsibilities, but policy responsibility and specialized technical expertise can be concentrated at the nation level.

New funds will be needed to operate the governments and legislatures of Aboriginal nations. The institutions we proposed in Volume 2 for lands and resources and economic development will need a capacity to manage resources and regulate their exploitation, a sophisticated activity demanding skilled staff in numerous areas of expertise.

In our view, additional spending of $250 million equivalent to current band government allocations (approximately $735 annually per capita) will provide a strong funding basis for self-government by First Nations.[7] The combined amount of $1470 per capita, while higher than the per capita amounts spent by federal and provincial governments, is well below the per capita spending of the two territorial governments.[8] These are relevant comparisons, as Aboriginal nations will ultimately assume wide-ranging jurisdiction. The small size of communities and the distances between them will make for higher operational costs than those of federal and provincial governments, but the territory of Aboriginal nations generally will not be so large, or transportation and communications so costly, as to warrant spending at the levels found north of the 60th parallel.[9]

Other Aboriginal groups, in particular Métis groups, will also seek recognition as nations, assume jurisdiction, and take over program delivery from provincial and territorial governments. We estimate that this may involve $175 million in additional funding.[10] Thus, in the long run, an additional $425 million will be needed when the current Aboriginal population is regrouped into some 60 self-governing nations. As noted earlier, it may take 15 to 20 years to rebuild and recognize these nations and to reach the stage where many have assumed jurisdiction. If 10 nations are in operation by 2001, $50 million will be required in that year to meet their incremental cost of self-government (Table 3.2, line 3). Thus, five years after the beginning of the strategy, structural reform measures will require expenditures of $150 million – $50 million each for new institutions, nation rebuilding, and nation governments.

Following recognition, an Aboriginal nation may also begin to negotiate a treaty on self-government, territory and other treaty matters. Even when guided by a framework agreement, such negotiations are likely to be extensive and time-consuming. There will be a need to research traditional territory, and issues like land selection, third-party interests, and municipal tax bases will be more complex south of sixty than they are in the North. This activity will require additional funding, since the scope of the redistribution of lands and resources that we envisage well exceeds the specific and comprehensive claims being addressed by the government under its current claims policy.

As land claims settlements are reached, Aboriginal nations will acquire a land base and an economic base. If cash transfers under new treaties are similar in size to per capita cash payments awarded under modern comprehensive claims – about $35,000 – more than $26 billion will be required to accommodate nations without modern treaties. But these agreements also included the direct transfer of substantial amounts of Crown land, something that may not be possible to the same extent in the more developed and densely populated parts of the country. However, lands and resources may not be as significant a factor for economic development in areas close to urban centres, where the range of economic opportunities provides other options. Whatever the precise outcomes of negotiations, payment of the settlements will be spread out over a long period and will increase as more settlements are reached. Our strategy includes $1 billion per year in new funding for land claims, a level that should be reached before or early in the second decade of the strategy, and then maintained for as long as needed (Table 3.2, line 4).

Thus, after 20 years, governments would be spending close to $1.5 billion on structural reform in the following categories: $425 for Aboriginal self-government operations, $50 million for the Aboriginal Lands and Treaties Tribunal and treaty commissions, and $1 billion on land claims and treaties, mainly for the financial transfer component of settlements.[11]

3. SOCIAL AND ECONOMIC MEASURES: GATHERING STRENGTH

In Chapter 1 of this volume we set out four major dimensions along which social, economic and cultural initiatives should proceed: healing; improving economic opportunity and living conditions; human resources development; and development of Aboriginal institutions and adaptation of mainstream institutions. The following discussion of the resources required for implementation and the resulting gains is organized according to this framework. However, the fourth dimension, institutional reform, is so much a part of the first three dimensions that its funding allocation is included in those for the other three dimensions and is not shown separately in Table 3.2.

3.1 Healing

To foster a climate conducive to healing, we propose a number of strategies for education and culture, health care, social services and justice.

With respect to education and culture, our approach focuses on children, youth and cultural institutions. For year five, we allocate $300 million in new funding to education, youth and cultural strategies (Table 3.2, line 5). The first of these strategies is the development of Aboriginal curricula and teaching materials, where the diversity of cultures and languages necessitates a major investment over a decade. We allocate $50 million per year to this task. (The diversity of Aboriginal cultures, languages and history means that culturally appropriate educational materials will need to be developed for each. Our allocation is based on an expected number of Aboriginal nations and an annual allocation of up to $1 million per nation. Examples of new approaches in education are given in Volume 3, Chapter 5.)

Second, establishing Aboriginal schools and school boards for Métis and urban Aboriginal populations, and bringing high school education into Aboriginal communities, will require planning, investment in new institutions and instructional programs, construction of schools, and installation of long-distance facilities where these are more cost-effective. No doubt this reform can be financed in part within existing budgets for capital investment, program development and operations. We allocate an additional $100 million a year in this area. This amount represents an increase of about 10 per cent over current expenditures by provinces and school boards on education of Aboriginal children and youth.

Third, $100 million annually is allocated to the proposed youth strategy, reflecting an amount of $1,000 per year for each Aboriginal youth between the ages of 16 and 20. This level of funding allows for development of recreation and sports programs with a high degree of volunteer involvement for the large majority of Aboriginal youth, along with return-to-school programs, counselling and other targeted interventions.

The fourth item in this group concerns cultural institutions, to which we allocate $50 million. This injection of funds would more than double recent government spending on northern and Aboriginal broadcasting, support for Aboriginal languages, and cultural and educational centres. It would make possible the establishment of an Aboriginal languages foundation and an Aboriginal arts council, provide core funding for Aboriginal media, and support production of Aboriginal programs.

The first three components are investments that require a higher level of funding for only a limited period. Once the education system is restructured, Aboriginal content is developed, and Aboriginal people are involved in every aspect of it, cost per student should return to the levels now spent by governments. As well, when youth are motivated by opportunity and a positive environment, spending on the youth strategy can be reduced to $25 million a year. However, we estimate that cultural institutions will still require incremental funding 20 years from now and have allocated $50 million per year for that purpose. The $150 million noted in Table 3.2 also includes $75 million for the added cost of educating Aboriginal youth for a longer period when their rate of high school attendance and completion reaches the Canadian rate. This allocation is calculated as four per cent of government expenditures on elementary and secondary education. Based on 1991 data it is estimated that the duration of schooling is approximately four per cent shorter for Aboriginal people than for other Canadians.

In the medium term, extra resources will be needed in health care to enhance services selectively, based on community needs, and to integrate health and social services while they are brought increasingly under Aboriginal control. The task of restructuring is greatest in urban and rural off-reserve communities, where most of the additional funding should be directed to establish Aboriginal healing centres. An allocation of $100 million a year in year five is intended to ensure that this change takes place (Table 3.2, line 6).[12]

We take the same view of social services. Many of our recommendations with respect to the family, health and healing, education and economic development are aimed at protecting and enhancing the development of young children. Culturally appropriate services, maternal and child health, early childhood education, and high quality child care are proposed to complement the role of the family in nurturing young children. The federal government has recently implemented several early childhood initiatives for Aboriginal people. On First Nations territories, resources are being provided for a transfer of child and family services to Aboriginal control, while the focus is shifting to education and prevention. For year five, we allocate $100 million to social services to fund a wide range of early childhood initiatives to complement the federal measures; these focus mainly on urban and rural off-reserve Aboriginal communities (Table 3.2, line 7).[13]

As vitality and self-reliance are restored in Aboriginal communities, a re-allocation of government expenditures will ensue. The analysis in Chapter 2 indicated that significant reductions are possible in government expenditures on health care and social services, as well as in some other program areas. We project that by 2016 half the possible maximum savings will be realized (Table 3.2, lines 6 and 7).[14]

The changes in needs that make these expenditure reductions possible should be felt in a wide range of programs – child welfare, suicide prevention, alcohol and drug counselling, family violence, and other mental and physical health care. These services are not generally in abundant supply at present. We urge that, as social conditions improve, governments ensure that services are supplied at a more adequate level in relation to need and reduce expenditures only when there is solid evidence that needs are fully met. We are confident that the strategy will bring about a fundamental transformation in the next 20 years that will make the projected savings possible. The savings may appear in the form of a levelling off of funding for many Aboriginal institutions. Over the longer term, given a constant level of demand for services, program funding would be expected to increase with the size of the client population. A decline in demand would make it possible for governments to increase funding at a slower rate. Thus governments can reduce per capita spending and realize the savings we project without reducing their expenditures, abolishing programs, or shutting down delivery institutions.

With respect to justice, a modest amount of $25 million is allocated in the medium term for new initiatives (Table 3.2, line 8). We expect savings to emerge early in this area, as a result of a reduction in the extraordinarily high rate of incarceration of Aboriginal people as justice systems learn to deal with Aboriginal people more fairly and effectively, and these savings can be used to intensify measures for reform. When Aboriginal communities heal themselves and begin to offer more economic opportunities, further savings are bound to occur. It is not difficult to see the sources of possible savings when 72 per cent of prisoners in provincial prisons are Aboriginal, as is the case in Saskatchewan.[15] Entire facilities could be closed. The estimated reduction in government expenditures on police and correctional services, like the reduction in health care and social services expenditures, reflects a reduction of one-half of excess government expenditures that would otherwise occur by 2016 with the escalation of costs under the status quo.

There are other dimensions to healing, not least of which is the role of non-Aboriginal Canadians in gaining greater knowledge and understanding of the history and aspirations of Aboriginal people and acknowledging the errors of the past. We are calling for restitution, in particular of a land and resource base. The allocation under structural measures for this major item should be regarded as including all forms of restitution, including compensation to individuals and collectivities as recommended in Volume 1.

3.2 Improving Economic Opportunity and Living Conditions

The second thrust of action to revitalize Aboriginal societies is a direct attack on economic disparities and intolerable living conditions. With regard to economic development we propose an increase in government expenditures of $350 million by 2001, allocated to three components (Table 3.2, line 9). First, spending on small business advisory services, equity capital and small business loans has been reduced sharply in recent years, with a total federal effort of $105 million in 1995-96, compared to $177 million four years earlier.[16] Restoring funding to past levels and responding to increased demand resulting from population growth will require an increase in funding of $100 million in the medium term, followed by further increases in the future. This level of funding will accommodate initiatives such as a national Aboriginal development bank and expansion of funding for Aboriginal capital corporations, as well as the financial requirements of regional and sectoral development institutions, which were severely affected by cuts in the early 1990s. These institutions are the precursors of the economic development institutions of self-governing Aboriginal nations. Continuing to build these institutions serves the dual purpose of building capacity for self-government and pursuing business development.

The second component in the economic development envelope is a 10-year special training and employment initiative. We estimate that additional funds at the rate of half the Pathways program will be needed to implement this initiative on the scale required to have a significant impact. Thus, $100 million should be allocated to this initiative.[17]

Reform of social assistance is the third component. More active use of social assistance for economic and social development in Aboriginal communities does not necessarily require additional funding. Training and re-employment can be actively encouraged within existing budgets, in a way similar to reform of unemployment insurance over the past several years. Other funds coming into the community, in particular those for housing and infrastructure, could be used creatively in combination with social assistance benefits. However, we estimate that some additional funds will be required for support of hunting and trapping and the mixed economy. We allocate $150 million, which is equivalent to approximately 10 per cent of social assistance expenditures at this time. (An increase of 10 per cent normally could not be expected to have a significant effect on the nature and impact of government programs like social assistance. However, these funds should be applied selectively to support those whose main economic pursuits are of a traditional nature, so that they have a larger relative impact. As reform of social assistance and support for traditional activities are intended to stimulate economic activity and self-reliance, the related allocations are classified under economic development, not income transfers. Reform of social assistance is discussed in Volume 2, Chapter 5.)

Of these three components of additional funding for economic development – which together would amount to $350 million per year by 2001 – the first, an allocation for business development, can be phased out when economic development gains momentum and investments begin to be financed by private capital and reinvestment of revenues from natural resources and profits. The second component, the special training and employment initiative, is intended to accelerate skills upgrading over a 10-year period. Twenty years into the strategy, governments will still be funding training and business development, but we assume that current budgets, adjusted for population size, will be adequate to the task. Of the three components, only support for the traditional and mixed economies is likely to be long-term. Accordingly, 20 years from now, new funding for economic development is projected to be $225 million for support of traditional activities. (This estimate is equivalent to the allocation of $150 million for 2001, adjusted for changes in the adult Aboriginal population.)

As an allocation for social assistance has been included in new expenditures for economic development, no further new funding is required for income transfers. But as Aboriginal people achieve more success in the economy, there will be less need for income transfers. We project that, by 2016, expenditures in this area can be reduced by $250 million – one-half the excess expenditures that would occur if the status quo were maintained (Table 3.2, line 10).

We propose that funding be committed immediately to improve housing and infrastructure for Aboriginal people. Adequate water and sanitation systems should be installed and operated, so that within the next five years acute threats to health are eliminated. Within ten years, Aboriginal people should live in adequate and suitable housing, as a result of a major catch-up effort undertaken jointly by governments and Aboriginal people.

According to estimates presented in Volume 3, Chapter 4, these undertakings will require $228 million in 1997, growing to $774 million by 2006, most of it in the form of subsidies for loans. In 2001, as the halfway mark approaches, $400 million in new spending will be needed (Table 3.2, line 11).[18] These estimates include an allocation of $15 million in new funds for program delivery and development of Aboriginal institutions.

Beyond the 10-year horizon of Volume 3, Chapter 4, it becomes important to consider changes in ability to pay. We would expect Aboriginal people to spend a significant portion of gains in earned income on housing. Under the policies we propose in Volume 3, Chapter 4, government assistance for housing on- and off-reserve would be geared to financial need and would therefore decline as incomes rose. Based on a reduction of one-half in economic dependency, a saving of one-half of projected excess government expenditures on housing will reduce financial requirements by $350 million by the year 2016. As the cost of the housing proposals under the strategy at this time is $700 million, a net amount of $350 million is allocated.

3.3 Human Resources Development

The third major dimension of social and economic change is human resources development. In many parts of our report we have emphasized the need to prepare Aboriginal people for positions in Aboriginal governments and public services and for participation in the general economy. We have proposed many initiatives, including an education for self-government funding initiative and a scholarship fund for Métis and non-status Indian people, and called for expansion of assistance to First Nations and Inuit students to cover additional students and changes in costs.

In the early years, resources should be devoted to encouraging greater post-secondary attendance and establishing new Aboriginal institutions of post-secondary training, including an Aboriginal Peoples' International University. An allocation of $100 million by year five will enable governments to undertake the many initiatives we are proposing. This level of spending will need to be increased gradually to accommodate rising enrolments in post-secondary education once awareness programs have had their effect and new institutions are past the start-up stage.

We are also proposing that a scholarship fund be established for Métis and non-status Indian students. Assuming the average level of assistance per student is equivalent to that of the DIAND program, but with access based on merit, this initiative would require $50 million per year in new funding at the time it is introduced.[19] Thus, $150 million is required for human resources development by 2001 (Table 3.2, line 12).

In the longer run, the cost of the human resources development proposals flows from an increase in the number of Aboriginal students in post-secondary education, so that they achieve the same levels of enrolment and completion as other Canadians. At present, Aboriginal enrolment is at about 60 per cent of the rate for other Canadians, so that an increase of two-thirds is required, and expenditures on post-secondary education for Aboriginal people will have to increase by the same ratio. Using estimates of government expenditures developed for Chapter 2, we estimate that by 2016 this will create an annual requirement for $225 million in new funding for post-secondary institutions. Outlays for student funding will also increase with enrolment. Financial assistance for status Indian people and Inuit under the DIAND program and for Métis and non-status Indian people through the new scholarship fund will require approximately $200 million more annually when parity in enrolment is achieved. The $225 million figure is based on an estimate of $230 million spent by provinces and territories for post-secondary education in 1992-93 (Chapter 2, Table 2.9), projected to 2016. Note that this allocation reflects only expenditures of provinces and territories, not the total cost of post-secondary education which is covered partly through tuition fees, other charges to students, and other income of post-secondary institutions.

In the longer term, when Aboriginal people participate in and complete post-secondary education at the same rate as all Canadians, funding for Aboriginal human resources development will be $425 million higher than it would be if the present situation continues. This is the allocation for 2016, as 20 years should be sufficient to achieve parity in participation and performance in post-secondary education. It is assumed that the cost of funding Aboriginal students will increase by two-thirds as a result of higher enrolment. On the basis of the 1996 population, this creates a requirement for $200 million in incremental funding. It is assumed that the same amount is needed 20 years from now, despite growth in the population of student age, as the need for entry-level programs will be much reduced when more students have completed high school.

3.4 Institutional Development

The fourth major dimension of social and economic change is institutional reform. The establishment of Aboriginal institutions throughout the public sector will create room for Aboriginal initiative and approaches that are essential to the healing and revitalization of Aboriginal societies. Institution building is an integral part of reforms in education and culture, health and social services, economic development, and housing. In each of these areas we have allocated funds to the task of building new organizational and physical structures.[20] When change is complete and the new institutions are operating effectively, costs of service delivery should revert to normal levels.

4. Beyond the 20-Year Horizon

In the long term, well beyond the 20-year time horizon shown in Table 3.2, there will still be a requirement for financial resources to maintain the new institutional arrangements and the much improved circumstances of Aboriginal people. Five items are identified in Table 3.3, two of which relate to structural reform. A small amount is needed for the Aboriginal Lands and Treaties Tribunal and the treaty commissions, whose scale of operations will be much reduced after the major land and treaty issues have been dealt with. As well, the operations of Aboriginal governments will require funding.

As for social and economic measures, Aboriginal cultural institutions will need continuing support through public funds, not unlike Canadian cultural institutions. As well, higher high school retention and completion rates will need to be accommodated through greater expenditures on schools. A larger item is the funding of post-secondary educational institutions, as well as allowances and scholarships for students, to accommodate higher enrolment, an investment essential for maintaining economic self-reliance and effective self-government.

There will also be a continuing need for financial support from governments for individuals and communities. Although economic self-reliance is a realistic prospect for many Aboriginal communities, economic opportunity is not evenly distributed. We took this into account in estimating economic potential in the previous chapter. This suggests that governments may be called upon to provide income support and housing subsidies, over and above what they make generally available, in some parts of the country where economic opportunity is limited. To a large extent this may take the form of financial assistance for traditional activities, which is considered a permanent cost of the strategy.[21]

Taken together, about $1.2 billion will be needed in these five areas, which are essential to continuous implementation of the strategy. This long-term annual cost of the strategy is only a portion of the cost at year 20, because two of the largest allocations will eventually be phased out. Expenditures related to land claims and treaty settlements will still be high at year 20, but at some point this financial transfer will come to an end. The same can be said about housing subsidies: after 20 years, large outlays are still required to meet loan obligations assumed during the 10-year catch-up program and to meet the needs of a growing population. But eventually these loans will be paid off, and governments will be called upon to assist only rarely when Aboriginal people achieve their full economic potential. (When the reallocation of lands and resources is completed, the federal government could also eliminate existing expenditures on land claims,

TABLE 3.3
Changes in Government Finances under the Strategy: Long-Term Gains ($ millions)

	2016	Long Term
Structural measures		
Tribunal and treaty commissions	50	25
Nation rebuilding	0	0
Nation governments	425	425
Land claim settlements	1000	0
Total for structural measures	1475	450
Social and economic measures		
Healing		
Education, youth and culture	150	150
Health care	(450)	(900)
Social services	(425)	(850)
Justice	(325)	(650)
Economic opportunity and living conditions		
Economic development	225	225
Income transfers	(250)	(500)
Housing and infrastructure	350	(700)
Human resource development	425	425
Total for social and economic measures	(300)	(2800)
Government revenue gains	(1550)	(3100)
Net fiscal gain from the strategy	(375)	(5450)

Notes:
1. All amounts for the longer term are scaled to the size of the Aboriginal population in the year 2016.
2. In this table, expenditures (numbers without parentheses) represent increases in spending by all governments required to implement the strategy. Reductions are shown by the numbers in parentheses. These relate to amounts saved as a result of the strategy that, in its absence, would have been incurred under a continuation of the status quo and to additional revenues collected by governments.
3. Figures rounded to the nearest $25 million.

which are in excess of $300 million. This is not considered part of the gains from the strategy, as presumably governments would cease spending money on claims under current policies as well.)

On the other side of the ledger are government revenue gains, which increase over time to a level twice that in the year 2016. How this occurs was described earlier in the chapter: economic progress generates more government revenue and reduces dependence on financial assistance, while healing of individuals and communities and greater effectiveness of service delivery systems reduce expenditures on remedial programs. The entries in parentheses in the second column of Table 3.3 are based on calculations presented in Chapter 2 of this volume.[22]

As shown in the second column of Table 3.3, the net fiscal gain from the strategy increases dramatically compared to the situation at year 20. Most important is the full realization of the fiscal dividend from the strategy, as reflected in a number of entries in the table. However, phasing out two major costs – financial transfers related to land claims and treaty settlements, and government expenditures to achieve and maintain adequate housing – also contributes significantly to the net fiscal gain from the strategy, which eventually reaches $5.45 billion. In other words, in the long run, governments would be better off by $5.45 billion annually as a direct result of the strategy.

In summary, we expect the strategy to result in greater economic opportunities and in greater health and social well-being for Aboriginal individuals and communities. This should result in a larger contribution of Aboriginal people to the Canadian economy and in the freeing up of productive resources now devoted to dealing with the effects of social disintegration in Aboriginal families and communities. These are the fundamental gains that give rise to the changes in government finances just reviewed. Economic self-reliance also means greater wealth for Aboriginal people. We calculate that an increase of $4.3 billion in the net private incomes of Aboriginal people can be realized. Together with the changes in government finances detailed in the second column of Table 3.3, this gives the results presented at the beginning of this chapter and summarized in Table 3.1.

5. The Distribution of Costs and Gains among Governments

The federal government and the governments of the provinces and territories should each assume a share of the additional government expenditures required to implement the strategy, according to their established jurisdiction and our proposals for sharing the cost of social programs between orders of government and for fiscal arrangements involving Aboriginal governments. Each government also stands to collect a share of the considerable fiscal dividend we expect the strategy to generate – in other words, to gain from its own efforts to improve the social and economic conditions of Aboriginal people. Collaborative efforts among governments are likely to yield greater benefits within a shorter period.

The cost of developing and implementing Aboriginal self-government, both on and off Aboriginal territories, falls to the federal government; funding for nation rebuilding and the operations of nation governments would be provided by the federal government. This is broadly similar to the approach taken by the federal government and the government of British Columbia in treaty negotiations taking place in that province. Under a memorandum of understanding between Canada and British Columbia respecting cost sharing, the federal government is to pay for establishing and operating core institutions required for governance, while the cost of negotiating self-government, including contributions to First Nations for their participation, is to be shared between the two governments.[23]

With respect to lands and resources, we expect the costs of negotiation will be shared equitably between the two orders of government. The provinces should contribute provincial Crown land to the settlements, and the federal government will be responsible for providing most of the cash transfers. In areas where adequate provincial Crown land is not available, funds will be required for cash payments in lieu of land and to finance third-party buy-outs. The extent to which the federal government compensates provinces for loss of future income from lands transferred to Aboriginal control can have a major bearing on the distribution of costs between the two orders of government. All this will be negotiated between them, but it should be clear that provincial governments, which have been the principal beneficiaries of the absence of treaties or the misinterpretation or abuse of treaty provisions where this has occurred, will have to bear a substantial portion of the cost of settling lands and resources issues.[24]

With regard to social and economic measures, the federal government will also carry the larger share of the cost, but the provincial share will be more significant than for structural reform and may be between one-quarter and one-third. As proposed in Volume 4, Chapter 7, the federal government should fund changes in social programs on Aboriginal territories, where 42 per cent of the Aboriginal population lives at present.[25] Although this group is the most socially and economically disadvantaged among Aboriginal people, we have concluded that there is also an urgent need for reform in urban and non-reserve communities, where the provinces have a major role. They have an obligation to make programs more culturally sensitive and effective and therefore should provide funds for institutional reform of their public services. Affirmative action programs to bring about greater equality between Aboriginal people and other Canadians would be cost-shared between federal and provincial governments.

The distribution of costs between governments will be different for each major dimension of change. With respect to healing, the provinces will carry a large share of the cost of the strategy, as the proposals encompass the off-reserve population, including Métis and non-status Indian people. Economic development, including training, has been funded to a large extent by the federal government, and this should continue. (The transfer of responsibility for labour market programs and training to the provinces that is currently before Parliament will lead to a larger provincial share of the allocation for economic development.) With respect to housing assistance, the federal share has been approximately 75 per cent off-reserve, where half the incremental funding will be directed. The cost of the human resources strategy will fall fairly evenly on both orders of government, with the provinces funding institutions and the federal government supporting students.

To sum up our observations about sharing the costs of the strategy, provincial governments are called upon to implement a major share of the social and economic measures, which require most of the additional funding in the initial years. The federal government will assume a larger share later on, when the agenda shifts to definitive arrangements for structural reform, more and more Aboriginal nations move to self-government, and their territories expand and become home to more Aboriginal people. As the federal government is also the central player in fiscal arrangements with governments of Aboriginal nations, it will assume a predominant role.

In the previous chapter we showed that the federal government and the governments of the provinces and territories all have extensive expenditure commitments relating to Aboriginal people. Both orders of government provide financial assistance and remedial programs. Accordingly, both orders will share in savings flowing from the strategy. If conditions on First Nations territories and in Inuit communities improve, the federal government will see the demand for remedial programs and services decline. Off-reserve, the provinces and territories now carry the cost of remedial programs and will therefore gain when the need for these programs is reduced; but the federal government will also benefit where it now shares the cost of provincial programs for Indian people living off-reserve and through income transfer programs like employment insurance and housing subsidies.[26] Thus, every government stands to gain from efforts to improve social and economic conditions for Aboriginal people.

Increases in tax revenues flowing from economic growth will accrue to all governments, according to their share of various tax revenue sources. Both existing orders of government can expect to collect a share of additional personal and corporate income tax as well as sales tax revenues from greater activity off-reserve. Increases in economic activity on-reserve would be exempt from taxation to a large extent under the present system but would be subject to taxation by Aboriginal governments.

Indeed, we are proposing that governments of Aboriginal nations should have extensive taxation and spending powers. When Aboriginal governments assume jurisdiction, they may take over sources of revenue and spending responsibilities from federal, provincial and territorial governments. Naturally, they would then receive a share of the fiscal dividend commensurate with their tax and spending powers. However, under the financial arrangements we propose, much of this dividend will be passed on to other governments.

The revenues that will be available to the majority of Aboriginal governments in the medium term are likely to be inadequate to fund their normal operations, owing to the great needs of the Aboriginal population and the low level of market-oriented economic activity generally prevailing at present. If the federal government supplements the finances of Aboriginal governments in the manner that we recommend – to equalize fiscal capacity and to meet fiscal need – then the federal government will be the main beneficiary of improvements in the fiscal fortunes of Aboriginal governments.

First, through transfers aimed at correcting for weak fiscal capacity, the federal government will top up revenues of Aboriginal governments to a level that reflects average revenues of governments in the country. As economic conditions improve, Aboriginal governments will collect more revenue, and federal transfers will be reduced. This is entirely analogous to the effect on federal equalization payments when a province receiving the payments experiences an increase in its own revenues as a result of economic growth.

Second, we propose that the federal government also make transfers to Aboriginal governments to assist them in meeting needs such as high expenditures for social assistance related to a lack of employment opportunities, and for housing subsidies, health care and social services. These transfers will be reduced if social and economic conditions improve. Thus, as the fiscal dividend is passed through from Aboriginal governments to the federal government under the proposed new fiscal arrangements, the distribution of gains from the strategy between the after-tax incomes of Aboriginal people and the revenues of governments will see most of the gains flowing to non-Aboriginal governments, as they bear most of the costs today.

Aboriginal governments may choose to collect revenues in different ways and at different rates than other governments have done to date. The current on-reserve tax exemption leaves room for First Nations governments to raise new revenues. In the first instance this is an internal matter for First Nations, which will have the authority to determine taxation levels. With fiscal arrangements based on tax effort by the Aboriginal nation, fiscal transfers from the federal government will be determined to a degree by how and how much these nations tax. These matters will no doubt receive a great deal of attention in future and are the subject of analysis in the section on financing self-government in Volume 2, Chapter 3.

6. Realizing the Gains: The Pace of Progress

In this chapter we have estimated the dimensions of potential change and indicated a time frame for its realization. To close half the economic gap between

Aboriginal people and Canadians generally and improve social conditions to a similar degree in two decades is a great challenge indeed. In this final section we attempt to provide some perspective on this challenge.

In the previous chapter we analyzed economic disparities between Aboriginal people and other Canadians, showing that the economic gap between Aboriginal people and Canadians is equivalent to about two-thirds of the economic output of Aboriginal people. Thus, closing half the gap requires that output by Aboriginal people be increased by one-third. Over 20 years, this means increasing the economic output of Aboriginal people by 1.5 per cent per year on average, in addition to growth of 2 per cent per year associated with the projected increase in the Aboriginal population of working age.

In Chapter 2 we also showed that half the economic gap is attributable to a lack of full-time jobs for Aboriginal people and estimated that 80,000 additional jobs are needed to eliminate the disparity in employment if the population remains at 1996 levels. It would thus be possible to eliminate half the economic gap by creating 80,000 full-time jobs, or 4,000 jobs per year. In the context of a healthy Canadian economy, which creates jobs at a rate of 200,000 or more per year, this seems to be a modest challenge.[27] A different perspective emerges, however, when total requirements resulting from population growth are considered. In those circumstances an additional 225,000 jobs have to be created for Aboriginal people over the period to 2016. The potential employment level is projected to increase in step with growth in the Aboriginal population aged 15 to 64, that is, by 48.6 per cent. Thus, a total of 305,000 more jobs will be needed by 2016.

This rate of growth exceeds the rate of growth of employment in the Canadian economy as a whole by a significant margin, reflecting a closing of the gap as well as the high rate of growth of the Aboriginal adult population. Nonetheless, Aboriginal people make up only a small fraction of the Canadian population, and the adaptability of the Canadian economy and its past record of employment creation suggest that much progress is possible in 20 years. Over this period the majority of the baby boom generation will be retiring. This may permit greater upward mobility in jobs for qualified individuals and increase the importance of contributions by working Canadians to pension plans and social programs.

Job creation is not the only way to make progress. A complementary and equally productive strategy would be to find not only more but better jobs for Aboriginal people. In the previous chapter we pointed to the importance of closing the gap in educational attainment to achieve employment levels and earnings more comparable to those of other Canadians. Specifically, we showed that the gap in educational attainment accounts for 41 per cent of the difference in total earnings. Progress achieved in recent years in keeping Aboriginal students in school longer, together with the prospect of good jobs in the Aboriginal public sector and in Aboriginal and mainstream businesses, new education strategies, new Aboriginal institutions and student funding – all integral parts of the strategy – are bound to create a positive education climate and induce many more Aboriginal youth to continue their studies past high school. Possibly the next generation of Aboriginal people will achieve parity in high school completion and close most of the gap in post-secondary diplomas and degrees. Given that this generation is rather large, this will drastically change the educational qualifications of the Aboriginal labour force, and in due course this will translate into more and better jobs.

Many new jobs for highly qualified Aboriginal people will be found in an emerging Aboriginal public sector, in schools, health centres, governments. Most of these jobs already exist in mainstream and Aboriginal institutions, and more and more Aboriginal people will move into these positions, first in junior roles, and increasingly at more senior levels. The public sector, including government departments and education and health institutions, accounts for about one-quarter of the work force in Canada and a larger portion of the highly trained labour force. There will be new jobs, too, in economic development and land management institutions and to meet the needs of a rapidly growing population.

Education is also vital for success in the general labour market, and we can expect progress on this front, coupled with more effective placement activities and new approaches to affirmative action to help boost Aboriginal employment. Employment equity can be a powerful instrument. For instance, Aboriginal participation in the work force under the federal *Employment Equity Act* increased from 0.66 per cent in 1987 to 1.04 per cent in 1993.[28] Over a period of six years, close to 2,100 new jobs were created for Aboriginal people by the businesses subject to the federal employment equity policy, which account for 4.5 per cent of employment in Canada. If this pace of job creation for Aboriginal people were to be realized in the entire economy, more than 150,000 jobs would be created between 1996 and 2016. This would not be enough to close the employment gap, and a greater effort is therefore needed.

In many Aboriginal communities, access to mainstream jobs is limited, and the Aboriginal business sector will have to generate the necessary employment. Jobs, profits and tax revenues will be generated by greater Aboriginal control over lands and resources. The interim measures proposed in Volume 2, Chapter 4 will stimulate business development and job creation, and land claims settlements will add to this impact. Aboriginal people have demonstrated that when they obtain access to resources, they can mount successful business operations.[29]

Harvesting and processing of resources on traditional Aboriginal lands is an economic opportunity that will be opened up for Aboriginal people in many parts of the country as the land reform measures we propose are implemented and agreements are reached. Many communities and nations now have some of the technical and business skills needed to exploit these opportunities and can move forward quickly through joint ventures. Success stories can also be found in the United States, and these, too, suggest that significant gains can be made by communities that assume control over resources on their traditional territories or get cash settlements.[30]

In Canada, comprehensive land claims agreements are used as a tool of economic development. Evidence is still limited, but there is reason to be cautiously optimistic about the longer-term benefits of these agreements. A recent study comparing census data for 1981, 1986 and 1991 found that "over time, the Inuvialuit maintained a rapid increase in development while the James Bay communities maintained a modest increase".[31] As for specific claims, a recent evaluation prepared for DIAND found that there had been no noticeable improvement in economic conditions in the communities affected, but that some of the settlement money had been used to improve community infrastructure. Such investments are important to well-being and improve pre-conditions for economic development.[32]

Greater progress can be made as the full scope of regional economic opportunities is exploited and Aboriginal governments gain in legitimacy and competence and establish the right frameworks for their business ventures. It is also important to resume the building of economic development expertise and capacity that was interrupted by cutbacks.

This review is far from definitive about the likely pace of economic and social progress in the years ahead. But it suggests that significant progress can be made over a 20-year period. As we believe that our strategy will set in motion a broad process of profound change, we estimate that through new employment and Aboriginal people moving to more skilled and better paying jobs, half the economic gap can be eliminated by that time. This will entail changes in government revenues and expenditures on income support and housing subsidies.

With respect to remedial programs, we also take the view that significant progress is possible over a 20-year period. Certainly it is possible to establish the new Aboriginal institutions we propose and to make the investments in Aboriginal content and approaches within two decades, and within that period much can be accomplished in making mainstream institutions more culturally sensitive as well. Community and individual healing will be greatly stimulated by the commitment of governments and Canadians to a renewed relationship and to concrete steps toward its realization. More investment in early childhood development, reform of education, new youth programs, and greater economic opportunities should establish a far more positive environment for the next generation of Aboriginal people coming of age.

Perhaps it will take longer. If it takes 25 years instead of 20 to reach the halfway mark, Aboriginal people and Canadians may have to demonstrate more patience and more determination. Perhaps the investments in social and economic measures need to be sustained over a longer period, pushing up the total cost of implementing the recommendations in this report. Our strategy will still produce great and lasting improvement over the status quo and change of the dimensions sketched out in this chapter. The bottom line of our strategy for renewal is a large gain for Aboriginal people and for Canadians.

Notes

1. What governments do with the part of the fiscal dividend that is not reinvested in the strategy lies outside the terms of our mandate. Our purpose is to show that governments will gain more revenues and will be able to reduce expenditures by implementing our recommendations. To simplify matters, we assume that these gains will go directly to the bottom line, that is to say, increase the budget surplus or reduce the budget deficit.

2. To project government expenditures it is assumed that in each program area expenditures will remain constant in relation to the size of the client group. Using the expenditure categories identified in Chapter 2, Table 2.9, and the age groups most closely associated with each of these categories, the following rates of increase are projected for 1996-2016: for elementary and secondary education, 1.4 per cent, which is the growth rate of the 5 to 19 age group; post-secondary education and training, 22.3 per cent, the growth rate of the 15 to 34 age group; for income support and housing subsidies, 48.6 per cent, which is the rate of growth of the population aged 15 to 64; for health care, 54.5 per cent, the growth rate of the population aged 15 and over; and for social services, police and correctional services and other expenditures, 34.8 per cent, the growth rate of the Aboriginal population as a whole. This gives an overall growth rate of 34.8 per cent, equal to the rate of growth of the Aboriginal population. Expenditures on financial assistance and remedial programs taken together are projected to increase more rapidly than total expenditures relating to Aboriginal people, as also reflected in the projected rate of increase of 47 per cent for excess expenditures over 1996 to 2016, as discussed in Chapter 2 of this volume.

3. Savings are projected in five program areas where government spending is high as a result of the current circumstances of Aboriginal people. One of the five areas is housing subsidies. While experiencing some reduction in housing subsidies after 20 years of change, because Aboriginal people will then be on the way to economic self-reliance, governments will also still be spending extra funds to ensure that Aboriginal people have adequate housing. The combined result is a net extra expenditure of $350 million, as per the second column of Table 3.2.

4. It will be noted that governments spend more and collect more revenue at this point. The increase in revenue is not the result of extra taxation, but rather of economic gains made by Aboriginal people. The net cost of the strategy is reduced as the strategy becomes increasingly self-financing as a result of these economic

gains. The net cost (net gain) is measured by the change in the surplus/deficit of governments.

5. Process expenditures for 1995-96 included the following: for DIAND, operating expenditures of the Claims and Indian Government Branch, $37.2 million; transfers related to land claims research, negotiation and implementation, $42.9 million; loans, investments and advances relating to claims, $76 million; share of the Claims and Indian Government Branch in DIAND overhead, Indian Claims Commission, analysis of claims by the department of justice, $30 million (estimated); and community-based self-government negotiations, $17.8 million, for a total of $203.9 million. To this should be added the costs incurred by provincial and territorial governments relating to claims and self-government negotiations and the cost of litigation involving the federal government (at present more than 400 cases, many for breach of trust and fiduciary duty). These latter items are not negligible, but estimates of related expenditures are not available.

6. For fiscal year 1995-96, band government allocations by DIAND were as follows: $165.8 million for band support funding (including chief and council, basic administrative overhead, and additional amounts for administration of various programs); tribal council funding of $24.1 million (advisory services to bands) plus $21.6 million (administration); advisory services for unaffiliated bands, $1.5 million; and band employee benefits of $40 million. The total was $253 million, or $735 per reserve resident.

7. The government has been pursuing community-based self-government without increasing DIAND's budget. To finance self-government for the Yukon communities that have signed final agreements, DIAND is reallocating expenditures internally. The self-government policy announced on 11 August 1995 also takes the DIAND budgets as given. Nevertheless, it is simply not realistic to imagine that effective self-government can be achieved without incremental funding. It would be wrong to introduce self-government and at the same time reduce funding for essential government services. In the long run, self-government is likely to lead to savings in federal expenditures, as we show later in this chapter. These savings will take time to be realized, however.

8. The average annual operating cost of government per Canadian is $700 for all levels of government combined. The annual cost of operating the territorial governments is about $2,000 per resident for the Yukon and $3,800 for the Northwest Territories. These amounts represent expenditures for general government services, mainly the operating costs of the legislature, the executive and central agencies. The data and definitions can be found in Statistics Canada, "Public Sector Finance 1994-1995, Financial Management System", catalogue no. 68-212.

9. Incremental funding of $250 million averages out to $5 million per First Nation, assuming that about 50 First Nations will be established. On average, each First Nation will have from 5,000 to 7,000 citizens living on Aboriginal lands, a larger number on the nation's traditional territory, and several thousand citizens living elsewhere in Canada. The nation government will exercise some functions for all its citizens and some only for those living on Aboriginal lands.

10. This estimate reflects the relative size of the Métis and Inuit populations compared to the population of First Nations living on their own territories. Note that this estimate includes funding for Inuit, which may be an overstatement as the creation of Nunavut falls under existing policy. As the number of nations is not known, costs are extrapolated on the basis of the size of the population. While program delivery has already been devolved to First Nations and Inuit, this is not the case for Métis people. The related cost, which is regarded as being of a temporary nature, is addressed later in the chapter.

11. The allocations for operations of Aboriginal self-government and for land claims and treaties for year 20 are not adjusted for changes in the size of the Aboriginal population over the next 20 years. The cost of self-government is the cost of operating the central institutions of Aboriginal governments and is not related very closely to population size. The financial transfer associated with claims may depend on the size of the population affected. Additional costs related to future population increases may be met by extending the transfers over many years.

12. The transfer of First Nations health services to community control gives some indication of the cost of restructuring. Health Canada provides funding for management, financial adminstration, training, and so on, in a way broadly analogous to band support funding provided by DIAND. In 1995-96, $61.6 million will have been transferred to 142 First Nations; 24 per cent of this amount is for management and administration. Some costs (training) are transitional. Continuing costs of administration will be offset in the long run by savings in administration in governments and institutions currently doing this work and by greater effectiveness. The federal Building Healthy Communities strategy, with $243 million in funding over five years, is an example of service enhancement in response to needs. This strategy focuses on crisis intervention with respect to mental health, home care nursing and solvent abuse in First Nations and Inuit communities. The proposed funding allocation for health care would make possible restructuring and service enhancement of similar scope in non-reserve and urban settings. The orientation of program enhancements would not be limited to those of the Building Healthy Communities strategy but should be responsive to local needs. Restructuring would be focused on integrated service delivery through healing centres as recommended in Volume 3, Chapter 3.

13. The amount is allocated to the social services item in Table 3.2 but also covers initiatives that could be classified under health care and education. In First Nations and Inuit communities, child and family services are being transferred to Aboriginal control, with additional funding for preventive interventions. According to the 1995-96 federal estimates, DIAND spending on social services support could increase from $253 million in 1993-94 to $380 million in 1995-96, but it will probably take longer to achieve complete devolution of program management. As noted in Volume 3, the federal government has introduced several initiatives in recent years with respect to early childhood: Aboriginal Headstart, with $84 million for four years, focusing on non-reserve communities in the west and north; the First Nations and Inuit Child Care Initiative, with funding of $72 million for three years

and $36 million per year thereafter; and the Child Development Initiative (Brighter Futures in First Nations Communities), a child and community mental health program with funding of $177 million for five years. These examples indicate that within existing federal expenditures significant amounts are allocated to this important area and suggest that an allocation of $100 million per year for up to 20 years should make possible a transfer of control and selective enhancements in response to needs, especially in non-reserve and urban settings.

14. As shown in Chapter 2, governments incur excess expenditures on remedial programs as a result of the adverse circumstances of Aboriginal people. These excess expenditures are projected to reach $2.4 billion by 2016 unless action is taken (see Chapter 2, Table 2.12). If half these excess expenditures are eliminated by 2016, a gain of $1.2 billion will be realized, with a $450 million saving in health care and a $425 million saving in social services. Savings of $325 million will occur by 2016 in the third remedial program area, police and correctional services. Using the same approach, savings through reduction of excess government expenditures on financial assistance to Aboriginal people are projected to be $250 million for income support programs, also by 2016.

15. See RCAP, *Bridging the Cultural Divide: A Report on Aboriginal People and Criminal Justice in Canada* (Ottawa: Supply and Services, 1996), Chapter 2.

16. Chapter 2, Table 2.7. DIAND funding is also for community development and basic human resource development in First Nations communities. The increase in funding that we propose should be allocated to business development and regional capacity building, rather than to these community-based activities.

17. An average expenditure of $10,000 per trainee would make it possible to assist 10,000 persons per year under the initiative. Costs would include tuition fees, income allowances during classroom training, wage subsidies to encourage hiring, as well as planning and delivery by Aboriginal institutions. The assumed cost per trainee is similar to that of the current Aboriginal training program, Pathways, which has an annual budget of $200 million, but it may be higher (and the number of trainees lower) if training of longer duration is emphasized.

18. As discussed earlier in the chapter, it is assumed that in the absence of new policies, government expenditures in each program area will increase in step with the size of the client population. Expenditures on existing housing programs are projected to increase by 48.6 per cent over the period 1996-2016 (see note 2). This increase reduces the net expenditures required to implement the housing recommendations, as calculated in Volume 3, Chapter 4, to $400 million in 2001 and $700 million in 2016.

19. The budget for the DIAND program is $261 million in 1995-96. The number of Métis and non-status persons in the 15 to 34 age group, which includes most students in post-secondary institutions, is 46 per cent of the number of status Indians and Inuit in the same age group.

20. Consider the following funding allocations in year five, indicating levels of spending to be maintained for a number of years, possibly to year 20, which may also

be exceeded by drawing on the fiscal dividend as needed: $100 million for elementary and secondary schools, in part to establish new schools and school boards; $50 million for culture and languages; $100 million for health care; $100 million for social services; $100 million for economic development institutions; and $15 million for housing on First Nations territories.

21. In Chapter 2, the initial estimate of the gap between potential and actual production by Aboriginal people was reduced by one-quarter to account for regional variations in economic opportunity. As a first approximation, we could assume that savings in social assistance expenditures realized by governments when Aboriginal people participate fully in the economy will also be lower by the same fraction. In 2016, this would amount to $300 million, which is not greatly different from the $225 million allocated to support of traditional activities.

22. The amount of $700 million for housing and infrastructure reflects the complete elimination of excess expenditures and the absence of any cost associated with the strategy. The change from net cost in 2016 is particularly large because it reflects two changes that will occur when Aboriginal people achieve economic self-reliance: not only can the projected expenditures under existing policies be reduced sharply, but the expenditures under the strategy to improve and properly maintain the housing stock will also cease.

23. "Memorandum of Understanding (MOU) Between Canada and British Columbia Respecting the Sharing of Pre-treaty Costs, Settlement Costs, Implementation Costs and the Costs of Self-Government", Vancouver, 21 June, 1993.

24. The MOU between Canada and British Columbia provides for a rather complex approach to sharing the cost of settling treaty negotiations, in which each government's share of the cash cost depends on the mix of land and cash, the categories of lands transferred, and other factors in the settlement agreement. The sharing of costs, therefore, depends on the outcome of the treaty negotiations. According to the formula in the MOU, the federal share of the cash cost of settlement ranges from 75 to 90 per cent. Under the MOU, the federal government will partly reimburse the provincial government for ceding productive forest lands of high value and for loss of revenues from resources. The amounts involved are not part of the cash cost of settlements, but they are financial transfers between governments and shift a greater part of the financial cost of the settlement to the federal government.

25. First Nations people living on-reserve and Inuit made up 42 per cent of the Aboriginal population in 1996, according to projections based on the Aboriginal peoples survey. As a rough estimate, assuming that costs per Aboriginal person are the same on- and off-reserve, that 42 per cent of the Aboriginal population lives on Aboriginal territories, and that the federal government pays 50 per cent of costs for those not living on Aboriginal territories, the federal share of expenditures would be 71 per cent.

26. Cost sharing was terminated under the Social and Health Transfer of the *Budget Implementation Act*, S.C. 1995, c. 17 (Parts IV and V). As the federal government will no longer share the cost of provincial programs, it will not experience a direct

financial gain when demand for these programs is reduced. Employment insurance is a contributory program with rates set in a way that balances contributions and benefit payments over several years. A reduction in benefit payments would thus be passed on to contributors through lower rates. It is not certain that employment insurance benefits payments to Aboriginal people will decline when they participate more fully in the economy. Many Aboriginal people do not have employment of a type that qualifies them for benefits.

27. From 1984 to 1994, employment in the Canadian economy increased from 11,402,000 to 13,292,000, or by 189,000 per year on average. This period includes the 1990-92 recession and the weak economic recovery that followed it.

28. Human Resources Development, *Annual Report, Employment Equity Act, 1994* (Ottawa: Supply and Services, 1994).

29. The Meadow Lake Tribal Council's activities in the forestry sector are a good example. In 1988, the council purchased a sawmill owned by the province that had been struggling to survive for 20 years and established a tree harvesting and reforestation company. Success soon followed for the two joint ventures, which now boast 243 employees and account for an estimated 730 indirect jobs in northwestern Saskatchewan. Key to their success was a 20-year Forest Management Licence Agreement that made planning possible, has protected hunting and trapping rights and the interests of residents, and provided for reforestation and a preference to northern residents in harvesting, hauling and reforestation. The profitable companies have generated $10.7 million in corporate taxes and personal income taxes paid by their employees between 1992 and 1994. See Price Waterhouse, *Evaluation of Various Financial Results*, MLTC Logging and Reforestation Inc., NorSask Forest Products Inc., November 1994.

30. In six Indian reservations that gained control over resources or undertook business ventures with funds received in settlement of claims, the proportion of adults with incomes above the poverty line increased from an average of 21 per cent to 31 per cent over the period 1977-1989. Stephen Cornell and Joseph P. Kalt, "Reloading the Dice: Improving the Chances for Economic Development on American Indian Reservations", in *What Can Tribes Do? Strategies and Institutions in American Indian Economic Development* (Los Angeles: American Indian Studies Center, University of California, 1992). The authors also report that average unemployment in these six communities was 28 per cent of the labour force at the end of the study period, indicating that a substantial economic gap remained. In *Tribal Assets: The Rebirth of Native America* (New York: Henry Holt and Company, 1990), Robert White tells the stories of five U.S. tribes that have gained significant control over resources and have successfully exploited business and employment opportunities.

31. James Saku, "The Socio-Economic Impact of the Inuvialuit Final Agreement", PH.D. thesis, Department of Geography, University of Saskatchewan, 1995. The author measured social and demographic development as well as economic variables and found that changes in social and cultural indicators had been more pro-

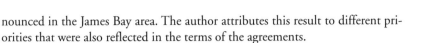

nounced in the James Bay area. The author attributes this result to different priorities that were also reflected in the terms of the agreements.

31. DIAND, *Report on the Evaluation of the Specific Claims Negotiation and Settlement Process,* Draft 1, 1994. If moneys received in settlement of land claims are applied to any of the elements of infrastructure or in any other way to improve the social and economic conditions of Aboriginal people, they add to the momentum of change either directly or indirectly by enabling Aboriginal governments to pursue other priorities.

4

Public Education: Building Awareness and Understanding

Public education is essential in confronting the problems posed by ignorance and misconceptions regarding our place in Canadian history and the nature of our rights. All Canadians should have the knowledge required to understand our situation, as well as the knowledge that what we have sought all along is mutual respect and coexistence.

Robert Debassige
Tribal Chairman and Executive Director
United Chiefs and Councils of Manitoulin
Toronto, Ontario
18 November 1993*

The Métis voice has been silent for far too long. Our non-representation or misrepresentation in mainstream media must be countered by effective and ongoing communication of our realities, both to our own people and to non-Aboriginal people of this country....[I]f the rate of growth of Native development and awareness is not increased dramatically, then the probability of [our] people assuming their rightful place in society in the future is very low.

Gerald Thom
President, Metis Nation of Alberta
Ottawa, Ontario
4 November 1993

There is a whole lot of misinterpretation as well as misconceptions about Native people. People who may live right next to an Indian

---

* Transcripts of the Commission's hearings are cited with the speaker's name and affiliation, if any, and the location and date of the hearing. See *A Note About Sources* at the beginning of this volume for information about transcripts and other Commission publications.

reserve will not have the slightest idea of what Native people are all about and that is very sad. It is only through education that both cultures can overcome this barrier.

Sheena Jackson
Lethbridge, Alberta
24 May 1993

FROM THE COMMISSION'S FIRST DAYS, we have been reminded repeatedly of the limited understanding of Aboriginal issues among non-Aboriginal Canadians and of the obstacles this presents to achieving reconciliation and a new relationship. As one intervener described it, there is a "vacuum of consciousness" among non-Aboriginal people. We would go further to suggest a pervasive lack of knowledge and perhaps even of interest.

Most Canadians still give low priority to the issues of importance to Aboriginal peoples. Aboriginal people in Canada continue to suffer the damaging effects of bias and racism at the hands of other Canadians. The news media generally devote little effort to providing information on Aboriginal issues. Very few institutions try to bridge the differences between Aboriginal and non-Aboriginal people or between different Aboriginal peoples.

Without accurate knowledge it is all too easy for negative stereotypes and simple ignorance to strangle communication. As François Trudel, a Laval university anthropologist, told us,

The first principle [of cultural accommodation] is knowledge of the other...I believe that it is the most fundamental principle in any human relationship, whether between individuals or between groups, and that so long as there is a lack of knowledge of the other, any prospect for establishing or re-establishing the ethnic and social relationship between Aboriginal and non-Aboriginal may be illusory, if not utopian. [translation]

François Trudel
Head, Department of Anthropology, Laval University
Wendake, Quebec, 17 November 1992

Yet knowledge alone is insufficient to change fundamental attitudes. Despite an overlay of concern, it does not take much provocation to uncover prejudiced attitudes and deep-seated hostility among Aboriginal and non-Aboriginal people alike. Sound information is an important element in overcoming this hostility. But also needed are opportunities for meaningful interaction as well as strong public role-modelling by leaders of both sectors – and not only the political leadership. Finally, ways need to be found to make discriminatory and racist behaviour unacceptable in private as well as public circles. The building of an open and inclusive society is a complex process that extends well beyond what is commonly understood as public education.

Brian Dickson, the former chief justice of Canada appointed to advise the prime minister on the Commission's mandate, emphasized the importance of public education. He saw the Commission itself as a vehicle for increasing public awareness of Aboriginal issues. Acting on his advice, we conducted extensive public hearings and round table consultations and published commentaries, discussion papers, special reports, and research studies. Special initiatives have included information videos, a telephone hot-line in Aboriginal languages as well as in English and French, and the CD-ROM version of our final and special reports, public hearings transcripts, and some of our research studies.

In this chapter, our purpose is to address the practical question of how to approach public education and the changing of public attitudes in a period of tight budgets and limited attention spans. If a major and sustained effort in public education is required, as we believe it is, where and how should it begin?

By public education we mean activities that can help increase public awareness of Aboriginal issues and contribute to reconciliation and understanding. They include news coverage and media activity of all sorts; conferences and seminars; awareness activities in schools, workplaces and communities and in local and national organizations; the use of symbols and cultural activities; and special initiatives such as exchanges between families, communities and associations and twinning between Aboriginal and non-Aboriginal communities or organizations.

Ultimately the kinds of activities we are advocating will influence social change, affecting people's behaviour and attitudes. They need to be undertaken as a long-term endeavour, for it will take time to change biased perceptions that have developed over generations. Innovative techniques will be required to break through the veil of indifference among non-Aboriginal Canadians and create opportunities for direct contacts between people.

Aboriginal and non-Aboriginal people alike have a common interest in creating a new relationship based on mutual respect and reconciliation. The benefits to Aboriginal people and their communities are obvious, whether measured in terms of autonomy, healing, cultural recognition or economic development. For non-Aboriginal people, the benefit lies in the opportunity for Canadians to move beyond policies that are the failed relics of colonialism. This will change Canada's reputation abroad and people's self-respect at home, as Nora Dewar Allingham commented in an essay on racism submitted at our public hearings by the Canadian Teachers' Federation:

> If I work to maintain the power of the dominant White group, I can continue to participate in the privilege that power confers. If I work to empower others, I am unlikely to be a direct recipient of any privilege that they may gain. I will, however, be a member of a society for which I feel less shame and anger and in which I may be able to participate more equally and more richly. I fear a social order which diminishes groups and individuals – I am equally diminished.[1]

Public education should be interactive and promote dialogue, balance, and a sense of sharing. Many of the successful examples of public education involve local consultation, face-to-face contact and collaboration between Aboriginal and non-Aboriginal people on a basis of equality. Direct personal contact works to dispel stereotypes and lower barriers to co-operation.

A number of corporations and governments have been successful in developing a focus on Aboriginal issues, through approaches such as affirmative action, cross-cultural training, and the appointment of Aboriginal people to boards of directors, senior executive positions, and government agencies and commissions.

Our public hearings stimulated a number of non-Aboriginal organizations to establish internal task forces and mechanisms to ensure they are sensitive to Aboriginal issues. These pioneering initiatives have not yet become common, but they are valuable precedents for the future.

RECOMMENDATION

The Commission recommends that

Principles for Public Education

5.4.1

Public education on Aboriginal issues be based on the following principles:

(a) Building public awareness and understanding should become an integral and continuing part of every endeavour and every initiative in which Aboriginal people, their organizations and governments are involved and in which non-Aboriginal governments and stakeholders have a part.

(b) Public education should involve both the sharing of information and a process of interaction, leading in time to a shared sense of advocacy and of public support.

(c) Non-Aboriginal organizations and corporations should establish internal mechanisms to make themselves aware of the distinctive needs of Aboriginal people whom they serve or employ and to ensure that they respond to those needs.

1. MAKING PUBLIC EDUCATION A REALITY

1.1 Creating Dialogue

We turn now to specific suggestions and ideas that can contribute to raising public awareness. One of the priorities brought to our attention is the need for personal contact and interaction between Aboriginal and non-Aboriginal people, both individually and in groups. A number of interveners spoke of the need for bridging, for opportunities for dialogue. One was an ad hoc group of 22 Aboriginal and non-Aboriginal young people, formed with the support of Quebec's youth advisory committee (Comité permanent de la jeunesse). The other, the Forum paritaire (Quebec Equality Forum), brought together Aboriginal leaders with leaders of non-Aboriginal unions and other groups to seek common ground on the future of Aboriginal people in Quebec.

Another group, the Aboriginal Rights Coalition (ARC, initially known as Project North), acts as a collective voice on Aboriginal issues for Canada's churches and has attempted to perform a bridging role. Its membership includes some Aboriginal representatives. ARC has been effective in many of its efforts in public education, notably during the time of the northern pipeline inquiry, when the question of developing a pipeline on the Mackenzie River was opened to direct input from the communities concerned. Project North helped to make northern development an issue across the country by bringing Aboriginal speakers from the North to town meetings and public forums in southern Canada.

Some organizations have already shown a capacity to bridge the gap between Aboriginal and non-Aboriginal people – notably a few municipal governments serving a significant Aboriginal population; some churches; some trade unions; a number of educational institutions at every level; friendship centres; and, on occasion, federal, provincial and territorial governments. Together, these institutions have the potential to touch the lives of most Canadians. They present a fertile field for action, and there are many precedents on which to build.

1.2 Cross-Cultural Communication

The goal of cross-cultural training is to sensitize persons whose work brings them into contact with people of another culture to the others' characteristics and needs. Some employers have begun to provide such training in the workplace. B.C. Hydro provides cross-cultural training workshops for its employees across the province. Hydro-Québec has a similar program for employees whose work involves Aboriginal people or communities. In Ontario, the provincial government supported an initiative of the Ontario Public Service Employees Union that has taken more than 300 of its leaders and senior staff through cross-cultural training schools held on Aboriginal territory.[2]

Many opportunities exist for cross-cultural communication. There is a tremendous need for accessible materials that can be used in schools, in adult education and by community organizations. The abridged version of this report and the CD-ROM version (which is accompanied by a guide for educators) are intended to help fill that need, as are certain key chapters from this report itself, such as the chapters on the Aboriginal dimension of Canadian history in Volume 1 and the treaty relationship in Volume 2.

Cross-cultural education can take place through the print and broadcast media and through community conferences, workshops and task forces. Quebec has shown a particular aptitude for bringing diverse groups together through the use of *tables de concertation*, a form of round table or task force involving community leaders meeting regularly for a period of several weeks or months.

Aboriginal communities can open their doors to visitors from surrounding areas as well as to eco-tourists from abroad and create jobs in the process. Friendship centres and communities can help bring the Aboriginal past to life by producing information profiles on local Aboriginal history. The potential exists almost everywhere for exchange visits, participation in ceremonies and festivals, work placements, and various forms of twinning to encourage communication between cultures.

Australia has taken several initiatives in recent years aimed at creating a new relationship with its Aboriginal population. These include the very successful use of a network of hundreds of community-based reconciliation study circles, which are linked with other activities such as public meetings with Aboriginal speakers and projects to identify Aboriginal sacred sites. The Australian government produced 4,000 local history kits to assist the efforts of parents' committees and Aboriginal organizations to promote learning about local indigenous history.

In 1990 Australia established a national Council on Aboriginal Reconciliation with a distinguished Aboriginal and non-Aboriginal membership. Its mandate includes educating non-Aboriginal Australians about Aboriginal history and cultures and developing proposals for a treaty or some other form of national reconciliation. It has produced an impressive series of booklets outlining major issues and calling for public response. Similar initiatives would be of benefit in Canada. We have recommended the creation of a major project to develop a general history of Aboriginal peoples (see Volume 1, Chapter 7) as well as agreements to identify and set aside sites that are sacred and of historical significance to Aboriginal peoples for Aboriginal management and, where appropriate, development of public information.

2. STAKEHOLDER GROUPS

Two main groups of stakeholders can be distinguished for purposes of public education: those with a broad mandate and a constituency that includes both Aboriginal and non-Aboriginal people and those with particular interests that may be affected by changes in Aboriginal communities and by the exercise of Aboriginal rights. Religious institutions, municipalities, and the education sector belong to the first group. Those with particular interests include service providers, people with environmental concerns, resource users such as hunters and outfitters, and a range of business organizations and companies. The labour movement has a foot in each camp.

2.1 Religious Institutions

Of all the non-governmental institutions in Canadian society, religious institutions have perhaps the greatest potential to foster awareness and understanding between Aboriginal and non-Aboriginal people. This potential exists even though the Christian churches' historical role was often that of supporting the dominant society and contributing to the marginalization of Aboriginal people.

Religious institutions can make a unique contribution today and in the future for several reasons. They are physically present in most communities across the country; through their organizational structures they can participate in public discussions at every level of Canadian society, from the neighbourhood to the national scene. Churches have had a long, albeit problematic, historical association with Aboriginal people. Some also have a track record in promoting public awareness of Aboriginal concerns. This is evident in activities such as the Aboriginal Rights Coalition and in internal restructuring to encourage greater Aboriginal involvement in church affairs, such as the All Native Circle of the United Church of Canada.

These institutions can provide a channel for distributing accurate information about Aboriginal culture and society along with the facilities to encourage public discussion of issues as they emerge. They have the capacity to facilitate interaction between Aboriginal and non-Aboriginal people not only at worship, but through the wide range of related service clubs and other organizations serving all ages that are found in most congregations.

Canada's religious bodies bring an ethical framework to issues of community and interpersonal relations, both nationally and locally. They are perceived as carrying moral authority and the capacity to exert leadership in their communities. This is a valuable resource, for the work of reconciliation has just begun, and they have a vital role in this process.

They can also engage in advocacy at the local level, particularly in cases where Aboriginal and non-Aboriginal people are becoming polarized around conflicts relating to lands or resources. Local bodies often have the stature to step in and help moderate such conflicts. Better still, they can try to anticipate situations of this kind and to help develop strategies to avoid polarization.

2.2 Municipalities

In Volume 4, Chapter 7 we offered several recommendations that address the relationship of Aboriginal people to municipal governments and mainstream institutions in urban centres. These included the creation of designated positions for Aboriginal representatives on local agencies, boards and commissions and the creation of Aboriginal affairs committees to advise city councils and school boards.

Like the religious institutions, municipal governments have enormous potential to promote public education and to contribute to constructive interaction between Aboriginal and non Aboriginal people. There is some form of local government in every corner of Canada. Mayors and local councillors hold positions of respect and can use their influence to fight racism and to bring communities closer together. Local governments have the capacity to organize forums, festivals, and cultural events that give Aboriginal people and issues a higher profile. Town halls, public libraries and community centres have the physical facilities to host displays on Aboriginal history and culture and events aimed at promoting understanding. Initiatives like Calgary's annual Native Awareness Week provide models that could be emulated in every city across Canada.

Municipalities should be leaders in ensuring that police and other employees receive regular cross-cultural training. They should be addressing practices that have tended to restrict the access of Aboriginal people to municipal employment in many communities. If a municipality supports community economic development or provides grants for groups involved in the arts and social services, it should give Aboriginal groups the same consideration as other citizens.

In its submission to the Commission, the Federation of Canadian Municipalities (FCM) cited a number of promising innovations through which local governments are building links with Aboriginal populations and creating awareness in the process. The FCM called for a joint strategy to strengthen ties between Aboriginal and non-Aboriginal communities. Their recommendations reflect a spirit that we wholeheartedly support:

> Municipal leaders must combine efforts with Aboriginal leaders, both nationally and locally, to identify barriers of mistrust, misperception, racism and systemic discrimination....Municipalities must be proactive and supportive [in achieving successful relations with Aboriginal people]...Improved Aboriginal political participation and managerial representation at the municipal level must be pursued.
>
> Federation of Canadian Municipalities
> Montreal, Quebec
> 1 December 1993

2.3 Educational Institutions

Since formal education is examined at length in Volume 3, our concern here is how the education system can contribute to building awareness and understanding of Aboriginal issues outside regular classroom instruction. Like municipalities, school boards have an obligation to Aboriginal constituents that is often not fulfilled. They too have the physical facilities and the resources to organize programs and events that reach out to inform the non-Aboriginal population and promote interaction.

Community colleges (CEGEPs in Quebec) and universities are similarly endowed. They can organize continuing education programs on a collaborative basis with Aboriginal communities and organizations. They have the skills to work with students and outside bodies to develop a knowledge of local Aboriginal history and to make it known throughout the community. They have the capacity to prepare discussion guides and information kits on Aboriginal issues and to assist people to organize study groups in the community. They can bring Aboriginal and non-Aboriginal people with common interests together through conferences and workshops, particularly when there are contentious issues – such as British Columbia's treaty process – that need to be better understood. We also hope that these institutions will be catalysts for discussion of our report and recommendations.

Post-secondary institutions can give their students direct experience of Aboriginal communities by organizing work placements. The recent emergence of Aboriginal student centres and resource centres at several universities is an important development, both for the support they provide to Aboriginal students and for their contribution to understanding of Aboriginal issues among non-Aboriginal students.

2.4 Labour Unions

Although unions have a significant number of Aboriginal members, they have only recently begun to acknowledge Aboriginal people as a constituency and to address their concerns. Unions have traditionally supported the cause of Aboriginal rights but have not devoted much time to exploring how the exercise of those rights may affect their current members. Some Aboriginal people have risen to senior positions within the labour movement, including Ethel LaValley, who was elected to the newly created position of Aboriginal vice-president of the Canadian Labour Congress (CLC) in 1994.

Clearly there are still many problems in the relationship between Aboriginal people and unions. Rules designed to protect the job security of unionized workers can serve as obstacles to Aboriginal people seeking to be hired or trained. The union may be blamed if an employer decides not to take on Aboriginal workers. When jobs are scarce, as is the case in most northern areas, these problems are inevitably more acute. This can be particularly difficult as Aboriginal communities seek to increase the number of Aboriginal people working in fields such as education, child welfare and other social outreach activities where cultural awareness and understanding have a high importance.

At our hearings, the CLC put forward a comprehensive program to develop awareness of Aboriginal issues at all levels of the labour movement, using resources such as union newspapers, videos, and training programs. It said that unions should reach out to Aboriginal students and communities in an effort to counter the negative perceptions of unions among Aboriginal people. It proposed that employers agree to collaborative employment equity programs in the workplace and allow Aboriginal awareness and anti-racism training to be provided during working hours.

We welcome the approach taken by the CLC, as well as other signs that the labour movement is taking constructive steps to reach out to Aboriginal people. Unions have a history of commitment to social justice and have established programs to train and educate their members. These assets can and should be used to help raise awareness and understanding of Aboriginal issues. At the same time there is a need to develop more creative and flexible solutions to practical problems in relations between Aboriginal people and unions, especially at the local level.

2.5 Professional Organizations

Our hearings indicated that many professional bodies are beginning to look at the concerns of their Aboriginal membership or the need for greater awareness and understanding of Aboriginal issues. Two examples illustrate the progress being made. Beginning in 1990, the Canadian Medical Association (CMA) established a two-year working group on Aboriginal health; brought an Aboriginal physician onto its staff through an executive interchange with Health Canada; held a conference to examine Aboriginal health issues; and developed a series of proposals dealing with government policy and the CMA's own activities. It also supported the development of the Native Physicians' Association, which operates independently but has become a strong influence on Aboriginal health issues within the CMA.

The organization of Quebec lawyers, the Barreau du Québec, has also taken steps that promise a continuing focus on Aboriginal issues. It created a standing committee on Aboriginal law in 1993 and established a program of information and training on Aboriginal issues for Quebec jurists in 1994. At our hearings the organization undertook to designate members who could assist in providing information to the public and to Aboriginal communities with respect to Aboriginal rights. It expressed particular interest in learning from Aboriginal people about non-judicial means of dispute settlement.

Professional bodies are generally seen as credible by their members, and they have mechanisms to provide education and training. These bodies can have a substantial influence if they decide to make Aboriginal issues a priority.

2.6 Other Stakeholders

Many other stakeholders are potentially affected by changes in Aboriginal communities and by the development of Aboriginal rights. Their diversity is reflected, for example, in the broad range of third-party interests represented on the treaty advisory committee established as part of the British Columbia treaty process.

These other stakeholders sometimes raise obstacles to the exercise of Aboriginal rights, but many are also in a position to help the non-Aboriginal population gain a greater understanding of Aboriginal issues. A number of national associations have established task forces or special committees, for example, to focus their members' attention on Aboriginal issues.

As the economic strength of Aboriginal people increases, corporations and financial institutions have begun to focus on Aboriginal issues by establishing Aboriginal business units and moving Aboriginal people into senior executive positions. The Bank of Montreal, the Royal Bank, the Toronto Dominion Bank and certain provincial utilities are examples. Syncrude, a large producer of synthetic oil in Alberta, has linked awareness activities and cross-cultural training with recruitment of Aboriginal workers and programs to support the development of Aboriginal communities and businesses.[3] For business, the value of these initiatives can be measured not just in goodwill but in opening doors for profitable collaboration in Aboriginal economic development.

RECOMMENDATION

The Commission recommends that

Cross-Cultural **5.4.2**
Understanding Bodies that represent or serve both Aboriginal and non-Aboriginal people
   (a) be proactive and innovative in promoting understanding of Aboriginal issues; and
   (b) review their own activities to ensure that they contribute to cross-cultural understanding and enhance relations with Aboriginal people.

3. ABORIGINAL ORGANIZATIONS

Aboriginal people and their organizations have a critical role to play. National Chief Ovide Mercredi of the Assembly of First Nations made this point to an Australian conference in 1993. He warned that Indigenous peoples need to act and went on to offer this counsel:

> [Y]our strongest ally in the end will be public opinion. Not the government's but public opinion. You have to organize to shape it. You have to organize so that they become your friends, your supporters....You have to focus on the conduct of their governments and you make their governments the issue, not the people whose support you need.[4]

Aboriginal people living in Canada have many agendas. For some the priority is self-government and control of their own territory; for others, notably in urban areas, it is how to maintain a distinct culture in a context of continuing interdependence. Whatever the issues, it is critical that Aboriginal people reach out for support to advance their cause. The need for networks and linkages to non-Aboriginal organizations must be recognized even if the cause being advanced is greater autonomy.

Aboriginal organizations can be the key to creating opportunities for interpersonal contact. Visits to reserves to meet with elders, educators and leaders should be encouraged; Aboriginal speakers could be made available for public forums where they can explain issues and respond to questions; pow wows and other events should encourage access by people from surrounding non-Aboriginal communities. The content of these encounters does not have to be political; understanding can develop through visits of youth groups or sports teams or through exchanges between school classes.

Aboriginal organizations can also be agents of change, prodding and lobbying society's institutions to examine how they can respond better to the needs and aspirations of Aboriginal communities. These initiatives can provide graphic illustration of the problems facing Aboriginal people, as, for example, the Assembly of Manitoba Chiefs did in its mass filing of employment equity complaints in 1991 involving discrimination against Aboriginal workers.

We heard statements at our hearings, mainly in Quebec, about the reluctance of Aboriginal leaders and governments to accept invitations to speak or to establish advisory links with neighbouring municipalities. People in Quebec also asked that Aboriginal leaders in that province be prepared to communicate in French as well as in English, as a sign of mutual respect. These concerns should be addressed.

Aboriginal youth should be singled out for attention, in particular those growing up in urban areas away from direct contact with their home territories. In Volume 4, Chapter 7, we commended friendship centres for their work in providing a social and cultural focus for urban Aboriginal people as well as a point of contact with the non-Aboriginal population. We proposed the creation of urban cultural education programs that would extend services to Aboriginal people and allow for more outreach to non-Aboriginal residents.

RECOMMENDATIONS

The Commission recommends that

Role for Aboriginal   **5.4.3**
Organizations   Aboriginal people and organizations participate in the process of public education through direct involvement, by creating opportunities for interpersonal contact and by acting as agents of change in Canadian society.

5.4.4
Aboriginal organizations and governments include their own members and citizens in efforts to build greater public understanding of Aboriginal issues and the changes now affecting Aboriginal communities.

4. The Media

Most of the information Canadians acquire about Aboriginal people and societies comes from the news and entertainment media. (See Volume 3, Chapter 6, for a more detailed discussion.) When the media address Aboriginal issues, the impressions they convey are often distorted. As the Assembly of First Nations put it in its submission at our hearings:

> Many Canadians have little, if any interaction with First Nations peoples in their daily lives and are likely to develop images and perceptions from newspaper articles, television programs, and commercials. Too many of those still perpetuate stereotypes which foster racism and discriminatory practices....
>
> The tendency of the media is to emphasize conflict, differences, violence, death and destruction. The media pay less attention to harmony, consensus, peace, life and growth. The media's insistence on the immediacy of news accelerates public discussion and heightens tension. It...is at odds with the more leisurely pace of life in First Nations communities.
>
> Assembly of First Nations
> Ottawa, Ontario
> 5 November 1993

The Canadian Association of Journalists was equally critical:

> Canada's Aboriginal peoples are, in general, badly served by national and local media, whether Native or not. The country's large newspapers, TV and radio news shows often contain misinformation, sweeping generalizations and galling stereotypes about Natives and Native affairs. Their stories are usually presented by journalists with little background knowledge or understanding of Aboriginals and their communities.
>
> The large media outlets include shamefully few Aboriginals either on their staffs or among their freelance journalists. As well, very few so-called mainstream media consider Aboriginal affairs to be a subject worthy of regular attention....The result is that most

> Canadians have little real knowledge of the country's Native peoples, or of the issues which affect them.
>
> Charles Bury
> Chair, Canadian Association of Journalists
> Ottawa, Ontario, 15 November 1993

There are only a handful of Aboriginal people among the 2,600 journalists working at major newspapers across Canada. The situation is not much better in radio and television, apart from the vigorous, but poorly funded, Aboriginal broadcast media serving northern Canada. For the past decade there have been very few regular Aboriginal programs on the major television networks (a subject considered at greater length in Volume 3, Chapter 6). The popular CBC production, "North of 60", demonstrates the potential for quality treatment of Aboriginal themes.

The best way for news media to convey a more accurate understanding of Aboriginal issues is to include Aboriginal journalists on their staffs. This is more than a matter of waiting to be asked for a job:

> It is no longer acceptable for the mainstream media to use the excuse that Native people don't apply for jobs on their newspapers, radio stations or television stations. The mainstream media owe it to their communities to reflect their cities, towns and rural areas by making their newsrooms as diverse as their communities. They have to actively pursue Native journalists to fill those voids in their newsrooms and to enhance and reflect the coverage of Native issues.
>
> Lynda Powless
> Native Journalists Association
> London, Ontario, 11 May 1993

Aboriginal people are becoming a significant element in the audience of the major media, particularly in urban centres in western Canada. It is time for the media to recognize their presence by hiring Aboriginal journalists and broadcasters and by reporting on the achievements of Aboriginal communities, not just the problems. Some media outlets have begun to acknowledge this responsibility, for example, by providing background reports about complex issues such as treaty negotiations. This commitment should become the norm.

In Volume 3 we noted the contribution of Aboriginal media to public education in Aboriginal communities. Despite severe cutbacks in funding, Aboriginal communications societies continue to share in a national Aboriginal television service, Television Northern Canada (TVNC), as well as providing extensive community and regional radio programming. These services are not available in most southern cities, and there are no plans to provide an Aboriginal channel on cable TV. The absence of such services is unfortunate for urban Aboriginal people; it is also a serious loss for the non-Aboriginal population.

TVNC is already transmitted by satellite while continuing to serve the North; it could provide a foundation for regular Aboriginal programming that could reach the majority of Canadians in urban areas via cable. This would be an important instrument for popular education directed to the mainstream population and an important resource to support education about Aboriginal issues in the schools. A comparable service in French and Aboriginal languages should be available in Quebec.

Aboriginal performers such as Tom Jackson, Susan Aglukark and Robbie Robertson and groups like Kashtin have become increasingly prominent in popular entertainment. In recognition, the music industry has established a special Aboriginal category in the annual Juno awards. Lawrence Martin was the first winner of the award in 1994, followed by Susan Aglukark in 1995. The same year singer and songwriter Buffy Ste. Marie was named to the Canadian Music Hall of Fame for her contribution to greater international recognition of Canadian artists and music.

In drama, the flavour of life in Aboriginal communities has been conveyed with humour and understanding in productions such as "North of 60" and "The Rez", in Tomson Highway's plays, and in the work of writer/performers like Margo Kane. These breakthroughs build Aboriginal pride and erase stereotypical images among the mainstream population.

In 1993 the Canadian Native Arts Foundation launched the first annual Aboriginal Achievement Awards to honour Aboriginal people for cultural achievements and other contributions to the community. Many other opportunities exist to give visible recognition to the achievements of Aboriginal people; the creation of one or more Governor General's Awards for Aboriginal literature might be a good place to start.

A number of alternative media have begun to emerge that have significant potential to broaden public understanding of Aboriginal issues. These include the new speciality channels on cable television; data bases and interactive materials on CD-ROM; computer bulletin boards and the Internet; and a proliferation of new newspapers and magazines. Alternative media are hungry for material and are attracting loyal audiences, in part because of their capacity to respond to audience needs through their formats and the communication medium chosen.

Outside major cities it is difficult for journalists, researchers and policy analysts to obtain information on Aboriginal issues. New technology can be of particular use in this area. The cost of maintaining a computerized data bank on Aboriginal issues, with access via the Internet, would be low relative to the number of potential users and the amount of information available. An institution like the proposed Aboriginal Peoples International University would be an obvious candidate to provide this kind of resource. In Volume 3, Chapter 5, we recommend the creation of such an electronic clearinghouse.

RECOMMENDATIONS

The Commission recommends that

Aboriginal
Presence in the
Media

5.4.5

Canadian media reflect the growing presence of Aboriginal people in their audience or readership by hiring Aboriginal journalists and broadcasters and by giving greater priority to coverage of Aboriginal issues and communities.

5.4.6

Aboriginal radio and television programming be available to all Canadians via cable TV, building on the service of TV Northern Canada and the radio services of Aboriginal communications societies.

5. SYMBOLS AND SPECIAL OCCASIONS

We have already mentioned the successful evolution of Calgary's Native Awareness Week, a mid-summer celebration that now includes participation by elders, Aboriginal art and film exhibitions, drama and variety shows, a pow wow, and a conference on doing business with Aboriginal people. Originally a collaboration between the Calgary Friendship Centre and the city's Chamber of Commerce, the week is now organized by a board with equal representation from the Aboriginal and non-Aboriginal communities.

Marlena Dolan of the Calgary Aboriginal Awareness Society told us of the need for sharing and awareness that inspired the foundation of Calgary's celebration:

> An accumulation of misconceptions and stereotypical branding has manifested an ignorance of Native people and elements of their culture. Native Awareness Week has helped clarify some of these misconceptions by providing an opportunity for the community at large to get involved and, in some situations, break the silence that has perpetuated the obvious fear of the unknown culture.
>
> Marlena Dolan
> Calgary Aboriginal Awareness Society
> Calgary, Alberta, 26 May 1993

Similar success has been achieved by the three major Aboriginal organizations in Nova Scotia, which set out to establish a Treaty Day tradition in Nova

Scotia after the 1752 treaty between the Mi'kmaq Nation and the British Crown was declared valid in court a decade ago. The celebration, established by the Union of Nova Scotia Indians, the Mi'kmaq Grand Council and the Native Council of Nova Scotia, has grown into an event that now involves the provincial government, municipalities, businesses, and the non-Aboriginal community. In 1994 the Nova Scotia government sent a video explaining the significance of Treaty Day to schools across the province and formally declared October to be Mi'kmaq History Month across the province. Ceremonies that had been confined to Halifax are now spreading to include the whole province. A similar evolution could occur in Manitoba with the annual Métis commemoration of Louis Riel Day on November 16th. The 1994 celebration included a reception hosted by the Honourable Yvon Dumont, Canada's first Métis lieutenant governor.

Events such as these provide an occasion to focus attention on the history and achievements of Aboriginal people and on the relationship between Aboriginal and non-Aboriginal people in Canada. Care should be taken to ensure that these events are part of an evolving relationship and are not merely symbolic.

The Assembly of First Nations and some other Aboriginal organizations designate June 21st as a National Day of Solidarity for Aboriginal People across Canada.[5] The Quebec National Assembly has also designated a National Day of Aboriginal Peoples on the same date, which marks the summer solstice.[6] This concept of a national day should be extended to all Aboriginal peoples, on a date designated jointly by Parliament and the national Aboriginal organizations. This date could also mark the formal acceptance by Canada and by First Peoples of the new Royal Proclamation we recommended in Volume 2, Chapter 2.

The designation of a national First Peoples Day should not exclude continuing to celebrate Louis Riel Day and treaty days for their intrinsic value and as instruments of public education. Beginning in 1995, the United Nations designated 9 August as the International Day of Indigenous Peoples; it should also be honoured as part of Canada's commitment to the United Nations Decade of the World's Indigenous Peoples.

RECOMMENDATIONS

The Commission recommends that

Symbols and Occasions **5.4.7**

Parliament and the national Aboriginal organizations jointly designate a national First Peoples Day to coincide with the issuing of a new Royal Proclamation and to be celebrated annually across Canada.

5.4.8
Special events such as Aboriginal Awareness Weeks be organized under joint Aboriginal and non-Aboriginal direction in all municipalities with a substantial Aboriginal population.

5.4.9
The commemoration of important occurrences in Aboriginal history through events such as treaty days and Louis Riel Day be expanded as a means of building solidarity and a vehicle for public education.

Aboriginal people have a powerful understanding of the importance of symbols. Symbols demonstrate the uniqueness of a place, a group, or an idea. They are a vehicle for public awareness and popular education. This significance is not lost on other Canadians; the federal government highlights Canada's Aboriginal heritage in projecting this country's image abroad. A striking example is the monumental sculpture by the Haida artist, Bill Reid, the focal point of Canada's embassy in Washington, D.C.

At home in Canada, there could be more such symbols and monuments to demonstrate the importance of Aboriginal people in Canada's history and to bring more Aboriginal content into the daily lives of Canadians. Many opportunities exist. An excellent example is the strong Aboriginal influence in the Canadian Museum of Civilization in Hull, Quebec, by architect Douglas Cardinal.

Systematic efforts could be made to choose or restore Aboriginal names for communities and for geographic features such as lakes, rivers, and mountains. This approach has been implemented in a systematic way in the Northwest Territories and in Northern Quebec, where places like Iqaluit (formerly Frobisher Bay) and Kuujjuaq (formerly Fort Chimo) have become household names.

Dual naming has become an accepted practice in Australia, allowing both the Aboriginal and the non-Aboriginal name to be used for some geographic features and place names. This practice could be used in Canada to remind people living in cities of the Aboriginal origin of their communities. City street names often honour leaders and heroes; more of those honoured should be Aboriginal people.

Other opportunities that should be considered include the following:

- Aboriginal leaders and elders could be called upon to say prayers or to celebrate their ceremonies at the opening proceedings of Parliament and other elected bodies, citizenship courts, and important meetings and conventions. This is already a practice in some segments of the labour movement. The Commonwealth Games, held in Victoria in 1994, and the summit of the G-7 nations in Halifax in 1995 were opened with traditional ceremonies of welcome by the Aboriginal nations on whose territory the meetings were held.

- One or more Aboriginal languages could be used alongside English and French in important public documents such as the *Canadian Charter of Rights and Freedoms* and the oath of citizenship to make new citizens more aware of the role of Aboriginal people in Canadian society.

- Aboriginal meeting places and sacred sites could be designated in cities or towns and used for ceremonies, for community events, and perhaps as sites for meetings and study groups aimed at broadening awareness and understanding of Aboriginal issues.

- Important events and sites in Aboriginal history could be marked by plaques, sculptures and museums, in the same way we now commemorate important non-Aboriginal historical events.

- Ceremonies that recall Canada's colonial history, such as the changing of the guard on the lawns of Parliament, could be complemented by events marking Aboriginal history and culture.

- Highway signs could mark the boundaries of traditional Aboriginal territories, just as they are now used to mark municipal and county boundaries. Municipalities could fly the Aboriginal flag for their territory as well as their own municipal emblem.

- Libraries and museums could emphasize the history, culture and current presence of Aboriginal people through regular displays and exhibitions. Similar exhibits could be located in public spaces such as shopping centres, corporate offices and city halls.

RECOMMENDATION

The Commission recommends that

Use of Symbols, Place Names and Ceremonies

5.4.10

Canadian governments recognize Aboriginal people's contribution to Canada through much greater use of Aboriginal place names, languages, ceremonies and exhibits and by honouring Aboriginal meeting places and historic sites.

6. FEDERAL AND PROVINCIAL GOVERNMENTS

Governments have an obvious responsibility to foster greater understanding because of their role in national and provincial life, the extent of their involvement with Aboriginal communities, and the resources they command.

The federal government should commit itself to making public education an integral part of all federal programs that affect Aboriginal people. Departments and agencies should be directed to explain how their activities affect Aboriginal people. Some of this information should be in popular form. Some should address myths and misconceptions about Aboriginal people and set the record straight.

Recent initiatives in public education involving governments and First Peoples are valuable precedents to be emulated. One example is the formation of a Tripartite Public Education Committee bringing Aboriginal people together with provincial and federal government representatives as part of the treaty process in British Columbia. Members of the committee have co-operated in preparing material and in organizing public meetings in areas where a treaty claim is being submitted. The three parties are to be involved in establishing local consultation committees in these areas, representing a broad range of community interests.

In Manitoba, communications and consultation with First Nations were made a priority as part of the recent agreement between the Assembly of Manitoba Chiefs and the Department of Indian Affairs and Northern Development. One of the first steps was to second the Assembly's director of communications to work from the department's regional office to provide information to Manitoba First Nations. In Ontario, a series of tripartite open houses helped to defuse initial resistance from the non-Aboriginal community to the announcement of a land claim by the Algonquins of Golden Lake.

6.1 Federal Departments and Agencies

The federal government should ensure its departments, agencies and commissions live up to the standards it advocates for the private sector in hiring Aboriginal people and in responding to Aboriginal needs. This requires regular review of federal programs for their content and relevance to Aboriginal people and the formation of Aboriginal advisory bodies to offer independent advice.

Cross-cultural training must become a requirement for all employees who work with Aboriginal clients or communities or who develop policies that affect Aboriginal people. Public servants should be exposed to different aspects of Aboriginal life through work assignments with Aboriginal communities or organizations. Aboriginal people should be seconded to work in the federal public service, both to raise awareness and to acquire experience in administering programs that will eventually come under Aboriginal control.

We are concerned about the lack of federal commitment to inform immigrants and people becoming citizens about Aboriginal people and their rights. The printed material that Canada offers to newcomers pays almost no attention to Aboriginal people and treats them as relics of the past. People can qualify for Canadian citizenship even if they have no knowledge of Canada's Aboriginal heritage.

Federal agencies can be powerful vehicles for public education and for advocacy and should be encouraged to use this potential. New institutions set up by governments to respond to Aboriginal needs – including the Aboriginal Peoples Review Commission that we propose in Chapter 1 of this volume to monitor the implementation of our recommendations – should have a mandate and adequate resources to engage in public education.

The federal government spends many millions of dollars each year on advertising and other forms of direct communication with Canadians. Channels of communication such as monthly pension cheque mail-outs should be treated as an opportunity to raise awareness of Aboriginal issues. Government tourism advertising can also be used to emphasize the presence and contribution of Aboriginal peoples in Canadian society. Every opportunity for public education should be exploited, such as the Nova Scotia government's practice of including information about Aboriginal hunting and fishing rights, prepared by the province's Aboriginal organizations, with every hunting licence issued.

6.2 Parliament and the Legislatures

Members of Parliament and their counterparts in provincial legislatures help form public opinion. Legislative committees on Aboriginal affairs are particularly important vehicles for public education because they can monitor government activities and provide a forum for Aboriginal people and organizations. They can also be a vehicle for Aboriginal people to participate directly in legislative work that touches Aboriginal concerns.

One of the most effective such committees was the House of Commons special committee on Indian self-government of 1982-83, chaired by Keith Penner, M.P. Its impact was attributable in part to close co-operation with representatives of Aboriginal people, including the appointment of Roberta Jamieson of the Assembly of First Nations, Bill Wilson of the Native Council of Canada (now the Congress of Aboriginal Peoples), and Sandra Isaac of the Native Women's Association of Canada to sit with the committee as non-voting members. This precedent should be adopted as a model for the future. Legislative committees dealing with Aboriginal issues should plan to meet regularly with members of the Aboriginal Parliament once this is established. Joint committees or commissions of inquiry with membership from the House of Commons and the Aboriginal Parliament should be considered when issues of mutual concern arise.

6.3 Provincial Governments

Provincial governments have compelling reasons for wanting to raise public awareness and understanding of Aboriginal issues. Many of their responsibilities touch directly on the daily lives of Aboriginal people in a way that federal programs do not. They are also keenly aware of the value of building social harmony at the community level. Provincial governments can do a great deal to encourage local initiatives to build bridges of understanding and co-operation, and their commitment to public education on Aboriginal issues should be no less significant than that of the federal government. Many of the suggestions made with respect to the federal government can be adapted for use by the provinces.

Meetings of first ministers and Aboriginal leaders to discuss issues of common concern have enormous symbolic importance, particularly when they are seen by people across Canada through television coverage. First ministers conferences have also proved effective as instruments of public education, helping Canadians become familiar with Aboriginal issues and with concepts such as the inherent right of self-government.

In Chapter 1 of this volume we called for a conference of first ministers and leaders of the national Aboriginal organizations to initiate a process of fundamental reform leading to a new royal proclamation and companion legislation and the creation of a forum to develop a Canada-wide framework agreement.

RECOMMENDATIONS

The Commission recommends that

Public Education Integral to All Programs

5.4.11

Federal, provincial and territorial governments make public education an integral part of all programs that affect Aboriginal people and ensure that it is delivered in collaboration with Aboriginal organizations.

5.4.12

The federal government ensure that the history and present circumstances of Aboriginal peoples are communicated to immigrants and to persons becoming Canadian citizens.

7. RESOURCES

It is necessary to provide sufficient resources for First Nations to launch public education campaigns on all issues related to First Nations in schools and communities. This should be done on both the national and regional level. The products of the campaign must be made available as widely as possible, including to new immigrants and those wishing to emigrate to Canada.

Tobaonakwut kinew
Grand Chief, Treaty 3, Assembly of First Nations
Ottawa, Ontario, 5 November 1993

We have recommended as a basic principle that building public awareness and understanding of Aboriginal issues become an integral part of every endeavour and every initiative relating to Aboriginal people. If this principle is accepted, most of the necessary resources can come from existing programs and budgets.

Establishing internal task forces or executive positions to deal with Aboriginal issues in interest groups, corporations and non-governmental organizations is a matter of reordering existing budgets and priorities. As unions, municipalities and educational institutions make a commitment to address Aboriginal issues, they will increase public education activity without adding significantly to costs.

Some efforts to support public education and dialogue about Aboriginal people have also succeeded in attracting corporate support. Notable examples are the Canadian Native Arts Foundation, established by the Mohawk conductor, John Kim Bell, and the in-service training programs organized by the Canadian Council for Aboriginal Business. As the economic importance of Aboriginal communities grows, the opportunities for attracting sponsorship for public education activities can be expected to increase.

An alternative source of support that should be explored by Aboriginal organizations is the resources of their constituent members. At present the major Aboriginal organizations have almost no funds to support public information activities; yet the value of programs now being delivered under Aboriginal control, primarily by First Nations community governments, has risen to more than $3 billion per year. It is a difficult choice to divert funds from programs that are often overstretched. This may be an unavoidable alternative, however, if Aboriginal voices are to be heard in raising public awareness of Aboriginal concerns.

The area of public education where new resources will be required is the extension of Aboriginal radio and television broadcasting to all areas of Canada as we suggest in Volume 3, Chapter 6. This would be a powerful initiative with value to the non-Aboriginal community as well as the large numbers of Aboriginal people now living in urban areas.

8. IMMEDIATE STEPS

We conclude the chapter by turning to immediate issues. What can be done to ensure that the analysis and recommendations of this report are fully understood? What initial steps should be taken to start building the awareness needed for a new relationship between Aboriginal and non-Aboriginal people?

One of our priorities has been to help Canadians understand our findings and recommendations. To that end, we have produced an abridged version of our report, which will also be available in CD-ROM form. This electronic report is aimed at community groups, teachers, the media, researchers and students and includes a complete record of our hearings and special reports and much of our research. We hope it can be made available to students at every high school, college and university across Canada.

Our formal role as a Commission ends with the publication of this report. The task of turning its recommendations into reality rests with governments, with Aboriginal organizations, and with the stakeholders most directly involved. They will need to collaborate to build momentum for change and to overcome inertia and unfamiliarity.

This Commission conducted the most comprehensive review of issues affecting Aboriginal peoples ever undertaken in Canada and perhaps in the world. It will take time for interested parties, governments and the public to absorb our report and perhaps a generation to implement it.

We hope that our report will be studied by community groups, churches, schools, university and other stakeholder groups during the months after its release; that governments, corporations, and voluntary organizations will set up task forces to look at the report's implications for their mandates and activities; and that magazines and newspapers will publish excerpts from it and reviews from knowledgeable commentators.

We doubt whether a purely voluntary approach to following up on implementation of our recommendations will be adequate. Publication of the report will stimulate demands for information and explanations that neither governments nor Aboriginal organizations will be in a position to satisfy. Our experience also indicates that many non-Aboriginal organizations and associations will be more likely to devote time and resources to reviewing issues that affect their particular constituency if they are encouraged to do so.

A small task force working with interested parties, governments, Aboriginal organizations and the media could play a vital role in increasing awareness and understanding of the issues dealt with in this report. Its work would be most effective if carried out by a group of Aboriginal and non-Aboriginal sponsors, perhaps beginning with a core group of leaders working with the support of religious institutions, unions, corporations, and the national Aboriginal organizations. A task force sponsored only by government would not be appropriate for this task, although funding assistance from governments would be desirable.

In Chapter 1 we recommended establishment of a review commission – reporting to Parliament and funded by but independent of government – to monitor progress on many fronts, including the actions taken by governments and others to implement the recommendations in this report. We propose that the tabling of this commission's annual report be the occasion for special debates on Aboriginal issues in Parliament and the provincial and territorial legislatures.

Governments have the greatest opportunity to place Aboriginal issues in the national spotlight and to initiate change. They should begin by focusing on this Commission's report. We favour an early response from federal, provincial and territorial governments on the principles and overall approach of this report as well as on specific recommendations. This could be followed by a first ministers conference (FMC) with national Aboriginal organizations to begin a process of review and implementation. The FMC would be of enormous importance in terms of public education and as a symbol of the commitment of the parties to move to a new relationship. As we suggested in Chapter 1, the FMC could also be the instrument for establishing the administrative mechanisms of change.

Many of the recommendations for public education in this chapter are modest in cost, and most can be implemented relatively quickly. Some should be given priority. In the year after this report is published, for example,

- The House of Commons, the Senate, and provincial and territorial legislative assemblies could devote one or more days to debate on the report of the Royal Commission on Aboriginal Peoples, then follow up with more detailed consideration by their respective Aboriginal affairs committees.
- Federal and provincial governments and Aboriginal organizations could agree to designate a national First Peoples Day.
- Through their national and provincial associations, municipalities could be encouraged to organize an Aboriginal Awareness Week as a regular annual event in all major cities in Canada.
- The media could be encouraged to give special attention to the achievements of Aboriginal people, with the CRTC in particular promoting greater visibility for Aboriginal people and issues through radio, television, and cable networks.

RECOMMENDATIONS

The Commission recommends that

Immediate Steps **5.4.13**

The CD-ROM version of the Commission's final report, research studies and public hearings be distributed by the government of Canada free of charge to every Canadian high school, college and university library.

5.4.14

A task force be established by a coalition of interested organizations and funded in part by the federal government to promote understanding and wide public discussion of the findings and recommendations of the Royal Commission on Aboriginal Peoples for at least the first year following publication of this report.

NOTES

1. Nora Dewar Allingham, "Anti-Racist Education and the Curriculum – A Privileged Perspective", in Canadian Teachers' Federation (CTF), *Racism and Education: Different Perspectives and Experiences* (Ottawa: CTF, 1992), p. 1.

2. Hydro-Québec and the Ontario Public Service Employees Union (OPSEU) described these initiatives at our public hearings in Montreal and Toronto. See Hydro-Québec, transcripts of the hearings of the Royal Commission Aboriginal Peoples (hereafter RCAP transcripts) Montreal, Quebec, 27 May 1993; and OPSEU, RCAP transcripts, Toronto, Ontario, 18 November 1993.

3. The Syncrude approach was described at the Commission's round table on Aboriginal economic development and resources and in the report on that round table, *Sharing the Harvest: The Road to Self-Reliance* (Ottawa: RCAP, 1993), pp. 318-319.

4. Chief Ovide Mercredi, "Self-Determination", in Council for Aboriginal Reconciliation, "The Position of Indigenous People in National Constitutions: Speeches from the Conference" (Canberra, Australia: CAR, 1993), p. 66.

5. National Indian Brotherhood and Assembly of First Nations, National Day of Solidarity for Indian People, resolution 39 passed in Penticton, British Columbia, April 1982.

6. Quebec National Assembly, "Journée nationale des peuples autochtones", *Journal des débats*, 33/40 (17 June 1994), p. 2059.

5

CONSTITUTIONAL AMENDMENT: THE ULTIMATE CHALLENGE

THE CENTRAL DOCUMENT OF CANADA'S CONSTITUTION is the *Constitution Act, 1867* and its various amendments, the most significant being the *Constitution Act, 1982.* The constitution consists of far more than these acts, however. Constitution building began much earlier and reflects the evolution of relations among Aboriginal people and French and British settlers. (See Volume 2, Chapter 3 and our constitutional discussion paper, *Partners in Confederation.*[1])

Throughout our report, there are references to decisions of the Supreme Court of Canada that have helped shape and determine the meaning of Aboriginal and treaty rights under the constitution. Through such interpretations, the constitution takes on new meaning and direction. The constitution has also evolved through unwritten conventions and customs that are as much a part of the constitution as the written text. Perhaps the most familiar are the conventions concerning the operations of cabinet government and the role of the Crown in governance. There are also a number of statutes that breathe life into the concepts, values and structures embodied in the constitution. Obvious examples include the *Supreme Court Act*, the *Official Languages Act* and the *Canada Elections Act.* Clearly, then, the Canadian constitution is not static but rather a living, vibrant instrument that is constantly evolving.

How is constitutional change brought about? The most obvious method is formal amendment. Amendments may add provisions to the constitution, as with the *Canadian Charter of Rights and Freedoms*, added in 1982. They may change specific provisions such as the amendments made in 1965 to set a retirement age for senators. Formal amendment has not been the most common means of securing change, however. Decisions of the Supreme Court of Canada and before that the Judicial Committee of the Privy Council (until 1952) have had a profound influence on the constitution, its interpretation and its development. The results of federal-provincial jurisdictional disputes have had far-reaching and permanent effects on the division of powers between those two orders of government. Judicial interpretation and the advent of the Charter have clarified and developed Aboriginal and treaty rights.

Over time, parts of the constitution may fall into disuse, as the federal powers of disallowance and reservation have done. The same thing may ultimately happen to section 91(24) of the *Constitution Act, 1867* as federal powers in relation to "Indians, and Lands reserved for the Indians" are gradually replaced by Aboriginal self-government.

The constitution has also been altered through public policy development and implementation. Public policy can be developed in a number of ways, including legislation, spending decisions of government and treaty making. There is an array of processes for achieving policy goals, ranging from public consultation, parliamentary committees, royal commissions and referendums to federal-provincial meetings and general elections where a single theme may predominate.

When the constitution is changed through a formal amendment, people can see the change and assess its implications. The same is true of amendment by way of court decisions. Change through policy development is much more subtle, however, because the constitutional consequences may not be readily apparent for some time. A clear illustration of this is the evolution of the federal spending power over the last 50 years. We have referred a number of times in this report to the Canada Health and Social Transfer (CHST), which replaced the Canada Assistance Plan and Established Programs Financing with a single, unconditional transfer to provinces. This was the most recent and perhaps most significant development with respect to the spending power since the Second World War.

Often, a public policy decision is a result of intergovernmental agreements. In many instances, constitutional boundaries are stretched to new limits through the dynamic of intergovernmental relations. The range of matters covered by federal-provincial financial relations – tax collection agreements, equalization payments and the funding of social programs through the CHST – shows the importance of this process. Another example is the agreement on interprovincial trade signed by the federal and provincial governments in July 1994. This agreement was reached even though two years earlier most provincial governments were unwilling to consent to a constitutional amendment on this subject during the Charlottetown negotiations. Compared with a constitutional amendment, an intergovernmental agreement allows for greater flexibility in its provisions and reduces the role of courts in its interpretation.

Clearly, then, understanding the concept of negotiation is central to understanding and implementing many of the recommendations in this report. The Canada-wide framework agreement recommended in Volume 2, Chapter 3 is an excellent example of a multilateral negotiation process involving federal, provincial, territorial and Aboriginal representatives. That agreement, when concluded, will rank as a major constitutional document. In Volume 2, Chapter 2, in particular our discussions of treaty making, implementation and renewal processes, we make a critical distinction between 'negotiation' and 'process'. Whereas negotiation is seen all too often as a one-time event, process suggests a continuing dialogue. A close analogy in federal-provincial relations is Canada's system of fiscal federalism, which is the result of more than 50 years of discussion, negotiation, experimentation and consensus building. Indeed, it is still evolving, and no end to the dialogue is in sight. Through a comparable nation-to-nation process of treaty making, renewal and implementation, a renewed relationship will emerge between Aboriginal people and non-Aboriginal people in Canada. This too will be the product of continuing negotiations that result in agreements that themselves are capable of change and development over the years.

Rights contained in agreements resulting from the negotiation process with Aboriginal nations are protected under section 35 of the *Constitution Act, 1982*. While constitutional boundaries can be stretched to meet new circumstances or be given new meaning by mutual agreement, those charged with concluding and implementing agreements are usually conscious of the fact that they are negotiating in the shadow of the courts. Negotiating an agreement to further public policy is preferable to resorting to legal action. Indeed, when governments do go to court to resolve a jurisdictional dispute, it is usually because intergovernmental negotiations have failed.

Early in our mandate, Commissioners realized that significant and wide-ranging change with respect to Aboriginal self-government was possible within the existing constitutional framework.[2] In this report, therefore, our recommendations are presented in such a way as to ensure that they can be implemented without constitutional change. The one exception concerns entrenchment of the Alberta *Metis Settlements Act*, discussed later in this chapter.

Following the Quebec referendum of 30 October 1995, however, and the subsequent federal legislation giving a federal veto on constitutional amendments to Canada's regions, there is also a possibility that significant constitutional change will be considered in the coming years. In light of this new scenario, the Commission believes strongly that constitutional questions of vital importance to Aboriginal peoples must be given equal weight and consideration. We identify six essential elements:

1. explicit recognition that section 35 includes the inherent right of self-government as an Aboriginal right;
2. an agreed process for honouring and implementing treaty obligations;
3. a veto for Aboriginal peoples on amendments to sections of the constitution that directly affect their rights, that is, sections 25, 35 and 35.1 of the *Constitution Act, 1982* and 91(24) of the *Constitution Act, 1867*;

4. recognition that section 91(24) includes Métis people along with First Nations and Inuit;

5. constitutional protection for the Alberta *Metis Settlements Act*; and

6. alterations to section 91(24) to reflect the broad self-governing jurisdiction Aboriginal nations can exercise as an inherent right and to limit federal powers accordingly.

We would reiterate, however, that all but one of our recommendations can be implemented without a further constitutional round, and we would urge governments to proceed with implementation on that basis.

Based on the findings of extensive research conducted for the Commission and our own assessment of the constitution, Commissioners have reached a number of legal conclusions that clearly push the boundaries of the constitution to new limits. Critics of these conclusions may well disagree and offer alternative interpretations. Rather than risk conflict over what the constitution does or does not mean, some would prefer to resolve issues through formal constitutional amendment.

Some differences in constitutional interpretation are acknowledged in this report. One example is our conclusion about the applicability of the *Canadian Charter of Rights and Freedoms* to Aboriginal governments. In his study for the Commission, Kent McNeil concluded that it does not apply; other experts, including Peter Hogg and Mary Ellen Turpel, concluded that it does.[3] To compound the problem of interpretation, many Aboriginal people believe that, regardless of what the constitution says, the Charter should not apply to them because they never consented to it and it does not reflect their values.

The issue could be resolved through formal constitutional amendment or through litigation. The question raises the prospect of a legal challenge from adherents of one of the stated positions. How such a case might arise is perhaps of less significance than the eventual resolution, which is linked to an interpretation of section 35(1) of the *Constitution Act, 1982*. We conclude that the Aboriginal and treaty rights recognized and affirmed in that section include the right of self-government. It is impossible to predict whether the Supreme Court would reach the same conclusion, but it is a major premise upon which much of our report is based.

An alternative to judicial interpretation to decide this issue would be a constitutional amendment. In the past, most fundamental changes in the constitution have been the result of judicial decision or amendment. Aboriginal and treaty rights have been reinforced by both methods – by the addition of section 35 in 1982, and by the courts in decisions such as *Sioui* and *Sparrow*.[4]

The two processes are fundamentally different. In our discussion of treaties in Volume 2, Chapter 2, we questioned whether the courts are the appropriate forum in which to settle what are essentially political disputes and suggested that the courts have probably gone about as far as they can go. On the other hand, the level of political consensus required for constitutional amendment is not easy to achieve, as experience has demonstrated. In 1987, after four years of effort, a proposed constitutional amendment to recognize the inherent right of Aboriginal self-government failed to achieve the necessary provincial government consensus required during the negotiation phase. In June 1990, the Meech Lake Accord failed because it did not receive the support of two provincial legislatures, despite having been approved twice by the House of Commons and by eight other provincial legislatures. In 1992, the Charlottetown Accord was rejected in a Canada-wide referendum.

1. THE AMENDING FORMULA

As the fundamental law of the land, the constitution should be difficult to change. It is not unusual for constitutions to require an extraordinary majority of some kind, particularly in the case of federal systems. In other words, a high degree of consensus among the people and their governing institutions is an appropriate prerequisite for constitutional change.

The *Constitution Act, 1982* specifies complex formulas for amending the constitution, reflecting the fact that the constitution has its origins in an act drafted 130 years ago.[5] Thus the act reflects and combines the concerns and constitutional positions prominent in the 1970s and early '80s, when it emerged, as well as various constitutional conventions on amendment that had developed since Confederation.

Four provisions for changing the constitution are relevant to our discussion. The general amending formula (the process that would apply to most amendments) is contained in section 38(1) of the *Constitution Act, 1982.*[6] An amendment under section 38(1) requires an affirmative vote by both houses of Parliament and by two-thirds of the provincial legislatures representing 50 per cent of the population.[7] At present this means seven of the 10 provinces. Given the current distribution of the population among the provinces and the fact that the combined population of Ontario and Quebec is more than 60 per cent of the total population, an amendment would therefore require the consent of either the Ontario legislative assembly or the Quebec National Assembly. It should be noted that under section 38(1), Parliament is the only legislature with a veto on any amendment.[8]

Under section 41 of the *Constitution Act, 1982,* certain amendments require unanimity, which means that both houses of Parliament and the legislatures of the 10 provinces must concur.[9] The list of amendments subject to the unanimity rule is short and includes the following:

- the office of the Queen, the Governor General and the Lieutenant Governor of a province;

- the right of a province to a number of members in the House of Commons not less than the number of senators by which the province was entitled to be represented in 1982 (when the formula came into effect);
- subject to section 43 (discussed below), the use of the English or the French language;
- the composition of the Supreme Court of Canada; and
- an amendment to the amending formulas.

In the Commission's view, at least three of the items are potentially of interest to Aboriginal people, as discussed later in this chapter.

Section 42 identifies certain institutional amendments requiring approval under the general amending provisions set out in section 38(1):

- the principle of proportionate representation of the provinces in the House of Commons prescribed by the constitution of Canada;
- the powers of the Senate and the method of selecting senators;
- the number of members by which a province is entitled to be represented in the Senate and the residence qualifications of senators;
- the Supreme Court of Canada (except for amendments affecting the composition of the court);
- the extension of existing provinces into the territories; and
- the establishment of new provinces.

In effect, several provisions in sections 41 and 42 clarify the limits of Parliament's authority under section 44 to "make laws amending the constitution of Canada in relation to the executive government of Canada or the Senate and House of Commons".

The final way to amend the act is section 43, which provides for amendments that affect one or more but not all provinces. It was under this section that New Brunswick expanded the scope of its language guarantees under the *Canadian Charter of Rights and Freedoms* in 1993, and it is under this provision that Alberta is seeking constitutional protection for its law on the province's Metis settlements. It is also under section 43 that any alteration to boundaries between provinces would take place.

In addition to these specific requirements for approving constitutional amendments, several other provisions warrant consideration. The first is the 'opting out' provision in section 38(3). Most amendments can be secured upon agreement by both houses of Parliament and two-thirds of the legislative assemblies of provinces representing 50 per cent of the population. But what happens if one or two, but not more than three, provinces disagree with a particular amendment? Section 38 does not give any province a veto over an amendment but it does provide a protective shield. Section 38(2) identifies classes of amendments that derogate "from the legislative powers, the proprietary rights or any other rights or privileges of the legislature or government of a province".

Under section 38(3), an individual province can opt out of any amendment that falls within this category; in other words, it cannot veto an amendment, but it is not required to accept amendments to which it objects. This section applies to a wide range of constitutional provisions, including sections of the Charter, provincial legislative authority found in sections 92, 92A, 93, 94A and 95, proprietary rights with respect to natural resources in section 109, and intergovernmental immunity from taxation in section 125 of the *Constitution Act, 1867.* Thus, where an amendment diminishes provincial legislative authority or affects a province's natural resources or other rights, individual provinces have legal protection in situations where they are in disagreement with the amendment. However, under section 40, it is only when an amendment relates to education and other cultural matters that "Canada shall provide reasonable compensation to any province to which the amendment does not apply". Although the examples given apply to amendments to existing constitutional provisions, section 38(3) would also apply to any new provisions that fell within its scope.

Another provision of some importance is one regulating the time lines necessary to secure an amendment. Section 39 specifies that amendments proposed under section 38 that do not secure the required degree of support lapse after "three years from the adoption of the resolution initiating the amendment". It was on this rock that the Meech Lake amendment foundered. The same section establishes a minimum time limit as well, stating that no amendment can be proclaimed within a year of the adoption of a resolution unless all provincial legislative assemblies have dealt with the resolution. (The 1983 amendment on Aboriginal matters could not be proclaimed until 1984 because, even though it had met the necessary threshold under section 38(1), the Quebec National Assembly had not yet considered the matter.) In other words, consensus for an amendment must be developed and maintained within a fixed period of time. (There is no time limit for amendments initiated under section 41, the unanimity provision.)

It is instructive to compare the time limits set in the amending formula with the length of time it takes for a constitutional law case to move through the court system. Many of the most important Canadian constitutional law decisions have resulted from references by governments to the courts. A reference is a procedure by which a government asks a court for an interpretation of the constitution on a specific question. Only the federal government can refer questions directly to the Supreme Court. Most references are decided within a year of the request being filed. This does not include the lead time required to draft the question to be asked. References that originate at the provincial level take longer but they are also likely to be decided within the same time limits as the amending formula. Cases other than references take considerably longer and invariably would take much longer than the three-year maximum time limit contained in the amending formula.

As if the approval thresholds of the amending formula are not difficult enough, during Canada's recent experiences with constitutional amendment, governments have added some extra hurdles. Since 1982, when the amending formula was approved, our track record with respect to constitutional amendment has been marked more by failure, acrimony and complaints about the process than by success. These efforts in turn have spawned a variety of processes that are in effect supplementary procedures to the amending formula in the *Constitution Act, 1982*. These procedural innovations can be summarized in two words: public participation.

The doors to public participation were opened wide in 1980-81 during the parliamentary committee hearings on the draft text of the *Constitution Act, 1982*. With the addition of leaders of Aboriginal organizations and the two territorial governments, they were opened again, although in a different fashion, during the series of constitutional conferences "respecting constitutional matters that directly affect the Aboriginal peoples of Canada, including the identification and definition of the rights of those peoples to be included in the constitution of Canada", which took place between 1983 and 1987.[10] During the Meech Lake negotiations of 1987-1990 Canadians demanded a say on the proposed constitutional amendment, and public hearings were held by two parliamentary committees, one in the summer of 1987 and another in the spring of 1990, when the idea of a companion resolution to the Meech Lake resolution was given consideration. In addition, there were public hearings by legislative committees in Quebec, Manitoba, Ontario and New Brunswick. In 1992, all Canadians were involved in a new ratification process – the third country-wide referendum in Canadian history.

The recent focus on constitutional amendment has produced other policies as well. For example, in 1986, the 1983 proposed amendment to the language provisions of the *Manitoba Act* changed the Manitoba Legislative Assembly's rules on processing constitutional amendments, establishing a fixed number of days for debate in the legislature and setting a requirement for public hearings. It was because of these rules that Elijah Harper, the lone Aboriginal member of the Manitoba Legislative Assembly was able to delay a vote on the Meech Lake resolution until the time limit expired.[11] The Meech Lake experience caused both British Columbia and Alberta to enact legislation requiring a provincial referendum before the government can introduce a constitutional amendment in the legislative assembly. Quebec had two referendums on its constitutional status, one in 1980 and the second in 1995. Under federal referendum legislation, the government of Canada can conduct a constitutional referendum should it choose to do so. The difference between the federal law and those of British Columbia and Alberta is that the former is permissive while the latter are mandatory. These, then, are some of the additional challenges of constitutional amendment that have evolved over the past few years.

Before assessing the application of the amending formula to the specific concerns raised in this report, two other points should be mentioned. The first is that the Yukon and Northwest Territories have no formal role in the amending process. Both territories participated in negotiations on proposed amendments on

Aboriginal matters between 1983 and 1987 and in the negotiations leading to the Charlottetown Accord, but a vote by a territorial assembly has no direct effect on the outcome. The same applies to Aboriginal nations. The 1983 amendment to the *Constitution Act, 1982* commits, but does not require, federal and provincial governments to consult with Aboriginal peoples on amendments to sections of the *Constitution Act* in which they are mentioned, specifically section 91(24) of the *Constitution Act, 1867*, and sections 25, 35 and 35.1 of the *Constitution Act, 1982*. Thus, other than a probable say in drafting an amendment, Aboriginal people as individuals and Aboriginal nations as political entities have no formal role in ratification other than as voters in a federal or provincial referendum.

We believe, however, that a strong argument can be made that the participation of Aboriginal peoples and territorial governments in the Charlottetown negotiations established a constitutional convention requiring their participation in future constitutional conferences. Moreover, it should be understood that their participation covers all subjects on the agenda, not just those of immediate consequence to Aboriginal peoples. The reality is that the entire *Constitution Act, 1982* is of concern to them. The moral legitimacy of any future constitutional amendment would be brought into question if Aboriginal people did not have a say in its content.

2. CONSTITUTIONAL AMENDMENTS AND THE COMMISSION'S REPORT

How does this discussion of constitutional amendment apply to our recommendations? Again, we emphasize that the recommendations (save the one on the Alberta *Metis Settlements Act*) can be implemented without constitutional amendment. Nevertheless, in the event that proposals for constitutional change become the focus of government attention in the future, the matters addressed in this chapter should be on the table for consideration, with priority on the six essential elements identified at the beginning of the chapter. The Commission considered four categories of potential amendments: amendments for greater certainty, consequential amendments, institutional amendments, and others.

2.1 Amendments for Greater Certainty

Two groups of recommendations in this report rely on governments and courts accepting the Commission's interpretation of the *Constitution Act, 1982*. The first concerns our interpretation of section 35 and is found in our discussion of the inherent right of self-governance as it is entrenched in the constitution (see Volume 2, Chapter 3). We have concluded that section 35 recognizes and affirms the inherent right of self-government as an existing Aboriginal and treaty right, and that Aboriginal nations can assume jurisdiction without benefit of a new treaty arrangement in core areas, including education, health, social services, languages and culture. Furthermore, we have concluded that the *Canadian Charter of Rights and Freedoms* applies to Aboriginal nation governments under section 32(1) and that such governments have the benefit of section 33, the notwithstanding clause.

These conclusions may be challenged, and the Supreme Court may find our interpretation incorrect. Although we think this unlikely, without the certainty provided by a constitutional amendment, it remains a possibility. The way to resolve this uncertainty is with a constitutional amendment – a negotiated amendment with Aboriginal peoples at the table to assure that their position is protected. Advocates of constitutional amendment are unwilling to adopt a 'wait and see' attitude, contending that there is too much to lose if a court decision proves unfavourable. An adverse court decision would not rule out the possibility of constitutional amendment, but it would reduce proponents' leverage at the negotiating table. After the Supreme Court gives its interpretation, it would be up to those who disagree to persuade federal and provincial governments that an alternative interpretation is preferable. Moreover, Aboriginal nations have no formal role in the amending process at present and consequently would not participate as full partners.[12]

What would such an amendment look like? One possible starting point would be the text drafted during the 1992 Charlottetown negotiations, which recognized the inherent right of self-government in Canada and established a constitutional framework for negotiation. But while the referendum results suggest that it was favoured by Métis people and Inuit, many people in First Nations communities opposed that part of the amendment or the amendment on treaties. It cannot be assumed, therefore, that this text would be the starting point.

Governments might be willing to recognize the inherent right of self-government despite a restrictive interpretation of section 35 by the courts, but it is not certain they would.

We conclude that any forthcoming constitutional negotiations should include efforts to arrive at an agreed amendment to recognize explicitly Aboriginal peoples' inherent right of self-government, with Aboriginal nation governments forming one of three orders of government in Canada. Though existing treaty rights are recognized in section 35, treaty nations do not see section 35 on its own making a substantial difference with respect to Canadian governments' willingness to implement their treaty obligations. They want the question of treaty implementation on the agenda for constitutional reform.

The second amendment that could be made for greater certainty relates to section 91(24) and our conclusion that Métis people are included in the term "Indians" just as Inuit were included as a result of a Supreme Court decision in 1939 (see Volume 4, Chapter 5).[13] To date, the government of Canada has rejected the interpretation that section 91(24) includes Métis people. This issue may become the subject of a reference to the Supreme Court of Canada, initiated by the federal government acting on its own or at the request of the Métis National Council, which is anxious to have the issue resolved.[14] An amendment could be seen as the best means of providing the guarantees Métis people are seeking, an alternative that we propose in Volume 4, Chapter 5. (See our recommendation in Volume 4, Chapter 5 concerning the reference route if the government of Canada does not accept our interpretation of section 91(24) or is unwilling to pursue an amendment.)

During the negotiations leading to the Charlottetown Accord, the federal government agreed to amend section 91(24) to include Métis people.[15] The arguments for inclusion of Métis people varied. Some participants believed the amendment was no more than a clarification of the section, while others thought the amendment expanded the scope of the section. One issue associated with this amendment arises because jurisdiction implies the potential responsibility for expenditures. We use the term potential because the federal government does not accept financial responsibility for all Aboriginal people already within the scope of section 91(24). (See Volume 4, Chapter 7, particularly the discussion of financing social programs for Aboriginal people off Aboriginal territory.) Thus, the federal government does not consider that legislative jurisdiction necessarily implies expenditures. The implications of such an interpretation is another reason why this matter may go to court before any action is taken.

2.2 Consequential Amendments

A consequential amendment is one that becomes necessary as a result of another amendment or a different interpretation of the constitution. The one constitutional amendment the Commission is recommending as essential comes under this heading – an amendment to protect the Alberta *Metis Settlements Act*. If Métis people are included in section 91(24), then any legislation relating specifically to them passed by a provincial legislature is probably *ultra vires*. Also, since Alberta has set aside land for Métis settlements through provincial legislation, the only sure way of shielding the legislation from unilateral change by the legislature is through an amendment to the constitution. However, efforts by Alberta to have such an amendment approved by the procedures of section 43 have not been successful.

The Charlottetown Accord proposed two such amendments, one amending the *Constitution Act, 1867* and the other the *Alberta Act, 1905*.[16] In discussions on these amendments it became clear that the Alberta legislation required constitutional protection to prevent any future unilateral changes in it by the Alberta legislature and to prevent the provincial statute from being declared *ultra vires*. For these reasons, we recommended a constitutional amendment confirming the Alberta *Metis Settlements Act* (see Volume 4, Chapter 5).

2.3 Institutional Amendments

Institutional amendments relate to the structure and functioning of Parliament, the addition of new provinces and the amending formula.

In Volume 2, Chapter 3, we examined Aboriginal participation in the Senate and House of Commons and the idea of a third house of Parliament. Changes to the constitution in these areas require either the consent of Parliament and two-thirds of the provinces representing 50 per cent of the population (section 38) or unanimity (section 41). Most of these amendments are identified in either section 41 or section 42 of the amending formula. Amendments to the six matters listed in section 42 must meet the threshold requirements of section 38. The opting out provisions of section 38 do not apply to the amendments discussed under this heading.

The Senate

Canada is divided into four Senate divisions: Ontario, Quebec, the Maritimes and the West. Representation for Newfoundland and Labrador and the two territories is also provided for, the former as a result of Newfoundland's admission to Canada in 1949, and the latter through a constitutional amendment in 1975, made before the amending formula was adopted in 1982. During the Charlottetown negotiations, separate Aboriginal representation in the Senate was thought to be both necessary and desirable, but the details were left to post-referendum negotiations.[17] Any change in the overall composition of the Senate, such as the establishment of an Aboriginal division, would require a constitutional amendment under section 38(1).

The House of Commons

Section 42 details the procedures to be followed under section 38(1) in the event of amendments to "the principle of proportionate representation of the provinces in the House of Commons prescribed by the Constitution of Canada".[18] The Royal Commission on Electoral Reform addressed the question of separate representation for Aboriginal peoples in the House of Commons but did not propose a constitutional amendment.[19] If separate Aboriginal constituencies were established as part of the existing seats allocated to a province, no amendment would be necessary, because the principle of proportionate representation would not have been modified. However, establishing separate Aboriginal representation in the House of Commons where constituencies cross provincial boundaries or the principle of proportionate representation is altered will require a constitutional amendment.

An Aboriginal House of Parliament

Section 17 of the *Constitution Act, 1867* defines Parliament as follows:

> There shall be One Parliament of Canada, consisting of the Queen, an Upper House styled the Senate, and the House of Commons.[20]

In Volume 2, Chapter 3, we recommended that Parliament establish an Aboriginal parliament as the first step toward creating a House of First Peoples or a third house of Parliament with its own special role in the legislative process. This would be possible only through constitutional amendment. What is less clear is whether such an amendment requires the consent of Parliament and all the provinces (section 41) or Parliament and two-thirds of the provinces representing 50 per cent of the population (section 38). Unanimity might be required because such an amendment could be seen as affecting the office of the Queen. Given the significance of such a change in Canada's legislative institutions, unanimity would likely be desirable.

The Supreme Court

We believe that the Supreme Court of Canada should include at least one Aboriginal member. At any time, the federal government could appoint an Aboriginal person to fill a vacancy on the court. We believe that a requirement that one of the justices be Aboriginal should be the subject of an constitutional amendment. This would require provincial unanimity whether it involved designating one of the existing nine seats or expanding the size of the court.

Creating new provinces

Section 42(1)(f) provides for the establishment of new provinces through constitutional amendment. For example, converting the northern territories to provinces would require the consent of Parliament and two-thirds of the provinces representing 50 per cent of the population. The territories themselves would have no say in the matter other than submitting a request.

Creating new provinces has been controversial ever since accession to provincial status was included in the amending formula. The territorial governments and many Aboriginal people were extremely critical of the Meech Lake proposal to change the amending formula from two-thirds of the provinces with 50 per cent of the population to unanimity. The territories were not enamoured of the 1982 provisions, but they were even less enthusiastic about the proposed alteration. Indeed their criticism was one of a number that led eventually to the failure of the Meech Lake Accord.

Territorial leaders were full participants in the deliberations leading up to the 1992 Charlottetown Accord. They argued that admitting new provinces should be determined by Parliament alone, as it had been before 1982 under the provisions of the *Constitution Act, 1871*.[21] It was under these provisions that Parliament created the provinces of Alberta and Saskatchewan in 1905. Others at the table were concerned about new provinces being created by Parliament alone and the implications of this for the amending formula and representation in a reformed Senate organized around the principle of provincial equality. In the end a compromise was reached: the territories could be admitted as new provinces under an amended version of the provisions of the *Constitution Act, 1871*, but they would not participate in constitutional amendments under sections 38, 41 or 42, and their representation in the Senate would remain as it was before they became provinces.[22]

Some scholars have suggested that consideration be given to creating an Aboriginal province.[23] Should this idea be pursued, proponents would need to seek approval under section 42(1)(f). Presumably, the position of such a province within the overall constitutional framework – for example, representation in the Senate and House of Commons – would be addressed during negotiations leading to its establishment. It should be noted, however, that participation in constitutional amendments would be governed by the unanimity provisions of section 41.

Constitutional amendment

Apart from the federal government's commitment to consult Aboriginal peoples on amendments to sections of the constitution that mention them, Aboriginal peoples have no formal role in the amending procedure. Before Aboriginal people can have a say, the amending formula requiring unanimity under section 41 must be changed. The Charlottetown Accord provided for Aboriginal participation in amendments that refer specifically to them. Such amendments required "the substantial consent of the Aboriginal peoples referred to" in addition to the procedures already in place.[24] Given this rather vague wording and lack of clarity on the meaning of "substantial consent", it is evident that further attention would need to be given to devising a means not only to consult Aboriginal peoples, but also to obtain their consent to amendments that would affect their rights under sections 25, 35, 35.1 and 91(24).

These are areas of the constitution over which Aboriginal peoples should have a veto. As mentioned earlier, the Parliament of Canada, in February 1996, passed an *Act Respecting Constitutional Amendments* to 'lend' the federal veto to five regions as an interim step pending broader constitutional reform.[25] If that broader reform is not forthcoming or does not encompass an Aboriginal veto over sections 25, 35, 35.1 of the *Constitution Act, 1982* and section 91(24) of the *Constitution Act, 1867*, then this new act should be amended to lend the federal veto to Aboriginal peoples for those sections.[26]

2.4 Other Amendments

Several other possible constitutional amendments emerge from this report. They include amendments to clarify the current constitution, entrench certain constitutional principles and incorporate some of our recommendations.

Clarification

During our deliberations, questions were raised about the meaning of certain parts of section 35 of the *Constitution Act, 1982*. Apart from our conclusion about the inherent right of self-government, two other provisions may require clarification through amendment as opposed to court action. One relates to the term Métis in section 35(2) and what is intended by it. It is not clear whether it is limited to the western Métis Nation or has a broader meaning.

The second matter in need of clarification is section 35(3), which reads as follows: "For greater certainty, in subsection (1) 'Treaty rights' includes rights that now exist by way of land claims agreements or may be so acquired."[27] The basic understanding of this provision is that rights contained in modern land claims agreements are given constitutional protection under section 35(1) as soon as such agreements are concluded. Some might argue that this gives them the effect of constitutional amendments, but we do not think so. In our view, under section 35(3) the content of Aboriginal and treaty rights is simply expanded to include these recently acquired rights. If we are correct in this, there is no conflict between section 35(3) and the requirements of the amending formula.

Entrenchment of constitutional principles

The principle that comes to mind most readily is the fiduciary responsibility of governments to Aboriginal peoples, an issue that was also addressed during the Charlottetown round. Aboriginal leaders emphasized then that none of the changes in the division of powers set out in the final agreement in any way limited the federal fiduciary responsibility to Aboriginal peoples.[28] The more compelling question is whether it is even realistic to try to capture such a broad legal principle by means of a constitutional amendment.

Entrenchment of some measures we recommend

The two recommendations in this category are the proposed Royal Proclamation and the Aboriginal Lands and Treaties Tribunal. The Royal Proclamation is a highly symbolic act with no specific constitutional status other than as part of the constitution in the broader sense of the word. With constitutional recognition, however, it would also have constitutional protection. This principle of constitutional protection can also be applied to the tribunal. An amendment under section 38 would demonstrate provincial endorsement of the Aboriginal Lands and Treaties Tribunal and its role and would also resolve certain problems associated with its composition. Such an amendment could include provisions on the jurisdiction of the tribunal and the method for selecting members. This would solve any problems that might arise with respect to section 96 courts. (See Volume 2, Chapter 4 for a complete discussion of these issues.)

Equalization and regional disparities

An amendment to section 36 of the *Constitution Act, 1982*, concerning equalization and regional disparities, warrants consideration. Specifically, the section should be amended to reflect the Aboriginal order of government and state that the commitment of Parliament and the government of Canada to the principle of making equalization payments extends to Aboriginal governments (see Volume 2, Chapter 3).

Intergovernmental immunity from taxation

Another amendment that should be made to the *Constitution Act, 1867* concerns section 125 regarding intergovernmental immunity from taxation. (see Volume 2, Chapter 3). Since the principle is already established in the constitution, there is every reason to extend it to Aboriginal governments.

When the amending formula was drafted, it was thought prudent to examine its operation some time after it came into effect. Section 49 therefore required a review within 15 years of the date of the proclamation of the *Constitution Act, 1982*, which meant sometime before 17 April 1997. The only constitutional requirement was that the prime minister convene a first ministers conference to consider the operation of the amending formula.

On 21 June 1996, the government of Canada convened a first ministers conference. The government argues that this conference met the requirements of section 49. Efforts by Aboriginal organizations to be heard at the conference were unsuccessful. The conference did not result in recommendations for change in the amending process.

If history provides any guidance, federal and provincial governments will probably meet at some time to review the need for and possibly outline a number of constitutional amendments. When such a meeting might occur is a matter of conjecture. We are convinced, however, that Aboriginal people must be represented at any such conference. To do otherwise would be to repeat the mistakes of the past.

RECOMMENDATIONS

The Commission recommends that

Constitutional **5.5.1**
Conference Representatives of Aboriginal peoples be included in all planning and preparations for any future constitutional conference convened by the government of Canada.

5.5.2

A role for Aboriginal peoples and their governments in the amending process, including a veto for Aboriginal people on changes to sections 25, 35, 35.1 of the *Constitution Act, 1982* and section 91(24) of the *Constitution Act, 1867*, be one matter for consideration at any future conference.

5.5.3

Other matters of concern to Aboriginal peoples, including, in particular, explicit recognition of the inherent right of self-government, treaty making and implementation, the inclusion of Métis people in section 91(24), entrenchment of the Alberta *Metis Settlements Act*, and alterations to section 91(24) to reflect the broad self-governing jurisdiction of Aboriginal nations, form part of the constitutional agenda.

Taken together, the changes we propose to protect Aboriginal interests would constitute a comprehensive amendment to the constitution. Some of our proposals will be controversial. Nevertheless, if all governments and Aboriginal peoples accept the main premises of our report, the changes we propose are attainable.

Constitutional amendments do not happen overnight. They are usually the result of extensive negotiations. Even when negotiators reach agreement on an amendment, there is no guarantee that the amendment will be ratified. As recent experience has shown, constitutional amendment is anything but easy.

Even if discussions resume, a number of preliminary questions would arise: What is the likelihood of discussions succeeding? Would amendments related to Aboriginal peoples be part of a larger process of reform, comparable to the Charlottetown process, or would they be examined in a discrete process, as they were between 1983 and 1987? Did the 1992 referendum on the Charlottetown Accord establish a constitutional convention with respect to future constitutional amendments, at least for amendments of that magnitude? (In Quebec the referendum was conducted under the provincial law, whereas in the rest of the country the federal referendum law was used, including in British Columbia and Alberta, where a referendum is required for constitutional amendments. In those two provinces, at least, the decision is already made.) Who would initiate the negotiations? How much time should be devoted to the exercise? Would negotiation start with the Charlottetown text or would negotiators wipe the slate clean and start over again? How would public input, both Aboriginal and non-Aboriginal, be accommodated?

We have outlined the issues surrounding constitutional amendment because the subject kept recurring as we discussed our recommendations, although it surfaced very rarely during our hearings.[29] Constitutional amendment is certainly one way to achieve self-government. As we have stated repeatedly, however, and in light of what appears to be general acceptance that section 35 includes Aboriginal peoples' inherent right of self-government, we believe that the constitution already presents avenue for implementing the major structural changes recommended in this report. If this assessment is correct, the constitutional amendment route is no longer essential to secure the desired result. Meaningful change can be achieved within the existing constitutional framework, which has proved remarkably resilient and flexible.

Even so, the *Constitution Act, 1982* does not reflect the role and status that Aboriginal nations should have in the life of this country. There have been several attempts in the past two decades to rectify this omission – the amendments of 1982 and 1983, the constitutionally mandated first ministers conferences on Aboriginal matters, and the Charlottetown Accord. But the omission remains. We therefore believe strongly that the path to a renewed relationship between Aboriginal nations and Canada would be clearer and surer if the relationship of equality and respect we envisage were reflected in a constitution that was amended to include

1. explicit recognition that section 35 includes the inherent right of self-government as an Aboriginal right;
2. an agreed process for honouring and implementing treaty obligations;
3. a veto for Aboriginal peoples on amendments to sections of the constitution that directly affect their rights, that is, sections 25, 35, and 35.1 of the *Constitution Act, 1982* and 91(24) of the *Constitution Act, 1867*;
4. recognition that section 91(24) includes Métis people along with First Nations and Inuit;
5. constitutional protection for the Alberta *Metis Settlements Act*; and
6. alterations to section 91(24) to reflect the broad self-governing jurisdiction Aboriginal nations can exercise as an inherent right and to limit federal powers accordingly.

NOTES

1. Royal Commission on Aboriginal Peoples (RCAP), *Partners in Confederation: Aboriginal Peoples, Self-Government, and the Constitution* (Ottawa: Supply and Services, 1993).

2. See RCAP, *Partners in Confederation*.

3. For a more extensive commentary on these two perspectives, see Volume 2, Chapter 3 on governance, in particular the discussion of the *Canadian Charter of Rights and Freedoms*. See generally Kent McNeil, "Aboriginal Governments and the *Canadian Charter of Rights and Freedoms*: A Legal Perspective", research study prepared for RCAP (1994); and Peter W. Hogg and Mary Ellen Turpel, "Implementing Aboriginal Self-Government: Constitutional and Jurisdictional Issues", in *Aboriginal Self-*

Government: Legal and Constitutional Issues (Ottawa: RCAP, 1995). See also RCAP, *Bridging the Cultural Divide: A Report on Aboriginal People and Criminal Justice in Canada* (Ottawa: Supply and Services, 1996), pp. 257-267. For more information about research studies prepared for RCAP, see *A Note About Sources* at the beginning of this volume.

4. *R. v. Sioui*, [1990] 1 S.C.R. 1025; and *R. v. Sparrow*, [1990] 1 S.C.R. 1075.

5. Discussions on an amending formula began in 1927 (when the relevant statute was the *British North America Act*, now the *Constitution Act, 1867*) and continued inter- mittently until the proclamation of the *Constitution Act, 1982*. In 1964, consensus was reached on an amending procedure known as the Fulton-Favreau formula. In 1971, consensus was reached on a regionally based amending procedure known as the Victoria formula. The latter was the amending formula initially included in the patriation resolution introduced in Parliament in October 1980. As a consequence of federal-provincial negotiations in November 1981, the Victoria formula was dropped from the resolution and the amending formula now contained in the con- stitution was added. Discussions did not end at that point but have continued ever since. Proposed changes to the 1982 provisions can be found in both the Meech Lake and Charlottetown legal texts. The amending formula was also the subject of study by a special joint committee of the Senate and the House of Commons in 1991.

6. This would include most amendments to the *Canadian Charter of Rights and Freedoms*, the division of powers, interprovincial trade, intergovernmental tax immunity, equalization and regional disparities, the Senate and the Supreme Court other than its composition.

7. Note that under section 47 of the *Constitution Act, 1982*, the Senate has only a sus- pensive veto of 180 days on amendments. In 1987 the Senate delayed its approval of the Meech Lake resolution adopted by the House of Commons, and the House of Commons passed the resolution a second time, thereby giving federal approval.

8. Under *An Act respecting constitutional amendments*, S.C. 1996, c. 1, s. 1(1), "No Minister of the Crown shall propose a motion for a resolution to authorize an amendment to the Constitution of Canada, other than an amendment in respect of which the legislative assembly of a province may exercise a veto under section 41 or 43 of the *Constitution Act, 1982*, or may express its dissent under subsection 38(3) of that Act, unless the amendment has first been consented to by" provinces representing five regions: the Atlantic provinces, Quebec, Ontario, the prairie provinces and British Columbia.

9. Note that the Senate's role under section 41 is limited to a suspensive veto just as it is under section 38.

10. Section 37 of the *Constitution Act, 1982* required that a single conference be con- vened. The amendment that emerged from that conference continued the process until 1987.

11. See David C. Hawkes and Marina Devine, "Meech Lake and Elijah Harper: Native-State Relations in the 1990s", in *How Ottawa Spends: The Politics of*

Fragmentation, 1991-92, ed. Frances Abele (Ottawa: Carleton University Press, 1991).

12. One example of an amendment brought about as a direct result of Supreme Court decisions is section 92A, concerning natural resources. See J. Peter Meekison and Roy Romanow, "Western Advocacy and Section 92A of the Constitution", in J. Peter Meekison, Roy Romanow and William D. Moull, *Origins and Meaning of Section 92A: The 1982 Constitutional Amendment on Resources* (Montreal: Institute for Research on Public Policy, 1985). Consider also the complete lack of success Newfoundland has had in securing an amendment on offshore resources.

13. *Re term "Indians"*, [1939] 1 S.C.R. 104. See Bradford W. Morse and John Giokas, "Do the Métis Fall Within Section 91(24) of the *Constitution Act, 1867*?", in *Aboriginal Self-Government* (cited in note 3), p. 140.

14. This was raised as a possibility by Gerald Morin, president of the Métis National Council, in Toronto, 1 February 1994, at a meeting of ministers responsible for Aboriginal affairs, Aboriginal leaders, and the Royal Commission on Aboriginal Peoples.

15. Draft Legal Text, 9 October 1992 (based on the Charlottetown Accord of 28 August 1992), section 8: "91A. For greater certainty, class 24 of section 91 applies...in relation to all the Aboriginal peoples of Canada."

16. Consensus Report on the Constitution, Final Text, Charlottetown, 28 August 1992, section 55; and Draft Legal Text, sections 12 and 24.

17. See Consensus Report on the Constitution, section 9; and Draft Legal Text, section 2.

18. *Constitution Act, 1982*, section 42(1)(a).

19. Royal Commission on Electoral Reform and Party Financing, *Reforming Electoral Democracy* (Ottawa: Supply and Services, 1991).

20. *Constitution Act, 1867* (U.K.), 30 & 31 Vict., c. 3, s. 17.

21. *Constitution Act, 1871* (U.K.), 34 and 35 Vict., c. 28, reprinted in R.S.C. 1985, App. II, No. 11.

22. See Draft Legal Text (cited in note 15), sections 32 and 4. A new section 42.1 would have been added to the amending formula:

> 42.1 subsection 38(1) and sections 41 an 42 do not apply to allow a province that is established pursuant to section 2 of the *Constitution Act, 1871* after the coming into force of this section to authorize amendments to the Constitution of Canada and, for greater certainty, all other provisions of this Part apply in respect of such a province.

The composition of the Senate was controlled by section 21(2) which read as follows:

> 21(2) Notwithstanding subsection (1), where a new province is established from the Yukon Territory or the Northwest Territories, the

new province shall be entitled to the same representation in the Senate as the territory had.

Section 21(1) set provincial representation in the Senate at six for all provinces and provided for one senator per territory. Aboriginal representation was subject to future negotiations.

23. Thomas J. Courchene and Lisa M. Powell, *A First Nations Province* (Kingston: Institute of Intergovernmental Relations, Queen's University, 1992). See also David J. Elkins, "Aboriginal Citizenship and Federalism: Exploring Non-Territorial Models", research study prepared for RCAP (1994).

24. Draft Legal Text (cited in note 15), section 33. Section 45.1 would have been added to the current amending formula:

45.1* (1) An amendment to the Constitution of Canada, that directly refers to, or that amends a provision that directly refers to, one or more of the Aboriginal peoples of Canada or their governments, including

(a) section 2, as it relates to the Aboriginal peoples of Canada,** class 24 of section 91, and sections 91A, 95E and 127 of the *Constitution Act, 1867,* and

(b) section 25 and Part II of this Act and this section,

may be made by proclamation issued by the Governor General under the Great Seal of Canada only where the amendment has been authorized in accordance with this Part and has received the substantial consent of the Aboriginal peoples so referred to.

(2) Notwithstanding section 46, the procedures for amending the Constitution of Canada in relation to any matter referred to in subsection (1) may be initiated by any of the Aboriginal peoples of Canada directly referred to as provided in subsection (1).

* A mechanism for obtaining aboriginal consent would be worked out prior to the tabling of a Constitution resolution in Parliament.

** A reference to any provision relating to aboriginal representation in the Senate would be added here.

25. See note 8.

26. Note that in its report on Bill C-110, the Senate committee recommended that the bill be amended to provide an Aboriginal consent clause with respect to section 91(24) of the *Constitution Act, 1867* and sections 25, 35 and 35.1 of the *Constitution Act, 1982.*

27. Added by the *Constitution Amendment Proclamation, 1983.*

28. A new section 127 would have been added to the *Constitution Act, 1867* to give this protection. See Draft Legal Text (cited in note 15), section 18.

29. One notable exception was during a presentation by Ron George, president of the Native Council of Canada (now the Congress of Aboriginal Peoples) at our hearings in Moncton, New Brunswick, 15 June 1993. He noted that the constitutional conference required by section 49 would be "a major opportunity to set a clear progressive constitutional agenda".

Appendix 5A

Procedure for Amending the Constitution*

General procedure for amending Constitution of Canada

38. (1) An amendment to the Constitution of Canada may be made by proclamation issued by the Governor General under the Great Seal of Canada where so authorized by

(a) resolutions of the Senate and House of Commons; and

(b) resolutions of the legislative assemblies of at least two-thirds of the provinces that have, in the aggregate, according to the then latest general census, at least fifty per cent of the population of all the provinces.

Majority of members

(2) An amendment made under subsection (1) that derogates from the legislative powers, the proprietary rights or any other rights or privileges of the legislature or government of a province shall require a resolution supported by a majority of the members of the Senate, the House of Commons and the legislative assemblies required under subsection (1).

Expression of dissent

(3) An amendment referred to in subsection (2) shall not have effect in a province the legislative assembly of which has expressed its dissent thereto by resolution supported by a majority of its members prior to the issue of the proclamation to which the amendment relates unless that legislative assembly, subsequently, by resolution supported by a majority of its members, revokes its dissent and authorizes the amendment.

Revocation of dissent

(4) A resolution of dissent made for the purposes of subsection (3) may be revoked at any time before or after the issue of the proclamation to which it relates.

Restriction on proclamation

39. (1) A proclamation shall not be issued under subsection 38(1) before the expiration of one year from the adoption of the resolution initiating the amendment procedure thereunder, unless the legislative assembly of each province has previously adopted a resolution of assent or dissent.

Idem

(2) A proclamation shall not be issued under subsection 38 (1) after the expiration of three years from the adoption of the resolution initiating the amendment procedure thereunder.

---

* Part V, *Constitution Act, 1982*, "Procedure for Amending Constitution of Canada".

Compensation

40. Where an amendment is made under subsection 38(1) that transfers provincial legislative powers relating to education or other cultural matters from provincial legislatures to Parliament, Canada shall provide reasonable compensation to any province to which the amendment does not apply.

Amendment by unanimous consent

41. An amendment to the Constitution of Canada in relation to the following matters may be made by proclamation issued by the Governor General under the Great Seal of Canada only where authorized by resolutions of the Senate and the House of Commons and of the legislative assembly of each province:

(a) the office of the Queen, the Governor General and the Lieutenant Governor of a province;

(b) the right of a province to a number of members in the House of Commons not less than the number of Senators by which the province is entitled to be represented at the time this Part comes into force;

(c) subject to section 43, the use of the English or the French language;

(d) the composition of the Supreme Court of Canada; and

(e) an amendment to this Part.

Amendment by general procedure

42. (1) An amendment to the Constitution of Canada in relation to the following matters may be made only in accordance with subsection 38(1):

(a) the principle of proportionate representation of the provinces in the House of Commons prescribed by the Constitution of Canada;

(b) the powers of the Senate and the method of selecting Senators;

(c) the number of members by which a province is entitled to be represented in the Senate and the residence qualifications of Senators;

(d) subject to paragraph 41 (d), the Supreme Court of Canada;

(e) the extension of existing provinces into the territories; and

(f) notwithstanding any other law or practice, the establishment of new provinces.

Exception

(2) Subsections 38(2) to (4) do not apply in respect of amendments in relation to matters referred to in subsection (1).

Amendment by general procedure

43. An amendment to the Constitution of Canada in relation to any provision that applies to one or more, but not all, provinces, including

(a) any alteration to boundaries between provinces, and

(b) any amendment to any provision that relates to the use of the English or the French language within a province,

may be made by proclamation issued by the Governor General under the Great Seal of Canada only where so authorized by resolutions of the Senate and House of Commons and of the legislative assembly of each province to which the amendment applies.

Amendments by Parliament

44. Subject to sections 41 and 42, Parliament may exclusively make laws amending the Constitution of Canada in relation to the executive government of Canada or the Senate and House of Commons.

Amendments by provincial legislatures

45. Subject to section 41, the legislature of each province may exclusively make laws amending the constitution of the province.

Initiation of amendment procedure

46. (1) The procedures for amendment under sections 38, 41, 42 and 43 may be initiated either by the Senate or the House of Commons or by the legislative assembly of a province.

Revocation of authorization

(2) A resolution of assent made for the purposes of this Part may be revoked at any time before the issue of a proclamation authorized by it.

Amendments without Senate resolution

47. (1) An amendment to the Constitution of Canada made by proclamation under section 38, 41, 42 or 43 may be made without a resolution of the Senate authorizing the issue of the proclamation if, within one hundred and eighty days after the adoption by the House of Commons of a resolution authorizing its issue, the Senate has not adopted such a resolution and if, at any time after the expiration of that period, the House of Commons again adopts the resolution.

Computation of period

(2) Any period when Parliament is prorogued or dissolved shall not be counted in computing the one hundred and eighty day period referred to in subsection (1).

Advice to issue proclamation

48. The Queen's Privy Council for Canada shall advise the Governor General to issue a proclamation under this Part forthwith on the adoption of the resolutions required for an amendment made by proclamation under this Part.

Constitutional conference

49. A constitutional conference composed of the Prime Minister of Canada and the first ministers of the provinces shall be convened by the Prime Minister of Canada within fifteen years after this Part comes into force to review the provisions of this Part.

Appendix A

Summary of Recommendations
Volumes 1-5

VOLUME I
Looking Forward,
Looking Back

We have grouped the recommendations made in this volume by theme rather than in the order in which they appear in the text. The original numbering of recommendations has been retained (that is, with the first number representing the volume, the second the chapter number and the third the recommendation number) to facilitate placing them in their original context.

The Commission recommends that a renewed relationship between Aboriginal and non-Aboriginal people in Canada be established on the basis of justice and fairness.

The Commission recommends that

Commitment to Ethical Principles of Relations
1.16.1
To begin the process, the federal, provincial and territorial governments, on behalf of the people of Canada, and national Aboriginal organizations, on behalf of the Aboriginal peoples of Canada, commit themselves to building a renewed relationship based on the principles of mutual recognition, mutual respect, sharing and mutual responsibility; these principles to form the ethical basis of relations between Aboriginal and non-Aboriginal societies in the future and to be enshrined in a new Royal Proclamation and its companion legislation (see Volume 2, Chapter 2).

Terra Nullius and the Doctrine of Discovery
1.16.2
Federal, provincial and territorial governments further the process of renewal by
  (a) acknowledging that concepts such as *terra nullius* and the doctrine of discovery are factually, legally and morally wrong;
  (b) declaring that such concepts no longer form part of law making or policy development by Canadian governments;

(c) declaring that such concepts will not be the basis of arguments presented to the courts;

(d) committing themselves to renewal of the federation through consensual means to overcome the historical legacy of these concepts, which are impediments to Aboriginal people assuming their rightful place in the Canadian federation; and

(e) including a declaration to these ends in the new Royal Proclamation and its companion legislation.

That the appropriate place of Aboriginal peoples in Canadian history be recognized.

The Commission recommends that

Aboriginal History
Series Project

1.7.1

The Government of Canada

(a) commit to publication of a general history of Aboriginal peoples of Canada in a series of volumes reflecting the diversity of nations, to be completed within 20 years;

(b) allocate funding to the Social Sciences and Humanities Research Council to convene a board, with a majority of Aboriginal people, interests and expertise, to plan and guide the Aboriginal History Project; and

(c) pursue partnerships with provincial and territorial governments, educational authorities, Aboriginal nations and communities, oral historians and elders, Aboriginal and non-Aboriginal scholars and educational and research institutions, private donors and publishers to ensure broad support for and wide dissemination of the series.

1.7.2

In overseeing the project, the board give due attention to

• the right of Aboriginal people to represent themselves, their cultures and their histories in ways they consider authentic;

• the diversity of Aboriginal peoples, regions and communities;

• the authority of oral histories and oral historians;

• the significance of Aboriginal languages in communicating Aboriginal knowledge and perspectives; and

• the application of current and emerging multimedia technologies to represent the physical and social contexts and

the elements of speech, song and drama that are fundamental to transmission of Aboriginal history.

*That the nature and scope of the injury caused to Aboriginal people by
past policies in relation to residential schools be established and appropriate
remedies devised therefor.*

The Commission recommends that

Public Inquiry **1.10.1**
Under Part I of the *Public Inquiries Act,* the government of
Canada establish a public inquiry instructed to
(a) investigate and document the origins and effects of residential school policies and practices respecting all Aboriginal
peoples, with particular attention to the nature and extent
of effects on subsequent generations of individuals and
families, and on communities and Aboriginal societies;
(b) conduct public hearings across the country with sufficient
funding to enable the testimony of affected persons to be
heard;
(c) commission research and analysis of the breadth of the
effects of these policies and practices;
(d) investigate the record of residential schools with a view to
the identification of abuse and what action, if any, is considered appropriate; and
(e) recommend remedial action by governments and the
responsible churches deemed necessary by the inquiry to
relieve conditions created by the residential school experience, including as appropriate,
  • apologies by those responsible;
  • compensation of communities to design and administer
    programs that help the healing process and rebuild their
    community life; and
  • funding for treatment of affected individuals and their
    families.

Aboriginal **1.10.2**
Majority A majority of commissioners appointed to this public inquiry
be Aboriginal.

National **1.10.3**
Repository The government of Canada fund establishment of a national
repository of records and video collections related to residential

schools, co-ordinated with planning of the recommended Aboriginal Peoples' International University (see Volume 3, Chapter 5) and its electronic clearinghouse, to

- facilitate access to documentation and electronic exchange of research on residential schools;
- provide financial assistance for the collection of testimony and continuing research;
- work with educators in the design of Aboriginal curriculum that explains the history and effects of residential schools; and
- conduct public education programs on the history and effects of residential schools and remedies applied to relieve their negative effects.

That the nature and scope of the injury caused to Aboriginal people by past policies in relation to the relocation of Aboriginal communities be established and appropriate remedies devised therefor.

The Commission recommends that

Violation of **1.11.1**
Rights   Governments acknowledge that where the relocation of Aboriginal communities did not conform to the criteria set out in Recommendation 1.11.2, such relocations constituted a violation of their members' human rights.

Amend the **1.11.2**
Canadian Human   Parliament amend the *Canadian Human Rights Act* to authorize
Rights Act   the Canadian Human Rights Commission to inquire into, hold hearings on, and make recommendations on relocations of Aboriginal peoples to decide whether

(a) the federal government had proper authority to proceed with the relocations;

(b) relocatees gave their free and informed consent to the relocations;

(c) the relocations were well planned and carried out;

(d) promises made to those who were relocated were kept;

(e) relocation was humane and in keeping with Canada's international commitments and obligations; and

(f) government actions conformed to its fiduciary obligation to Aboriginal peoples.

15-Year
Mandate

1.11.3

The Canadian Human Rights Commission be authorized to conduct inquiries into relocations, including those that occurred before the Commission's creation in 1978, and that with respect to the latter relocations, its mandate expire 15 years after coming into force.

Violation
of the Act

1.11.4

Parliament amend the *Canadian Human Rights Act* to provide that it is a violation of the act if a relocation of an Aboriginal community does not conform to the six criteria listed in Recommendation 1.11.2, and that the provisions in Recommendation 1.11.11 apply in those circumstances where appropriate.

Alternative
Dispute
Mechanisms

1.11.5

The Canadian Human Rights Commission be authorized specifically to provide a range of alternative dispute resolution mechanisms, including mediation, facilitation, and consensual arbitration.

Powers

1.11.6

The Canadian Human Rights Commission be given subpoena powers with respect to documents, evidence and witnesses, and powers to compel testimony and appoint experts and counsel.

Remedies

1.11.7

The Canadian Human Rights Commission be given the authority to recommend a range of remedies to redress the negative effects of relocations, including

- provision for essential social infrastructure or services or special community initiatives;
- provision for relocatees to return to and re-establish in the home community;
- provision for visiting between separated families;
- funding of additional services, for example, to assist the readjustment of returnees, or all persons still adversely affected by the relocations;
- settlement of individual claims for compensation for, among other things, unpaid work done or services rendered during relocation and personal property lost or left behind; and
- costs, including future costs, incurred by relocatees or their representatives in attempting to resolve their complaints.

Public 1.11.8
Reports The Canadian Human Rights Commission be required to
describe activity on relocation claims in its annual report and
be authorized to make special reports as it sees fit and period-
ically review and report on action on its recommendations.

Governments 1.11.9
Co-operate Federal, provincial and territorial governments co-operate with
communities and the Canadian Human Rights Commission by
opening their files on relocation to facilitate research.

Funding for 1.11.10
Communities Aboriginal communities be given funding by the Canadian
Human Rights Commission, upon decision of a panel of advisers appointed by but independent of the Commission, as follows:
(a) seed funding, of up to $10,000, to conduct preliminary
research on their claims after *prima facie* assessment of the
merits of their applications; and
(b) adequate additional funding when, in the panel's judgement, the communities have claims sufficient to warrant
inquiry by the Commission.

Recourse 1.11.11
to Courts The Canadian Human Rights Commission be authorized to
apply to an appropriate tribunal to obtain any appropriate
measure against the government of Canada, or to demand in
favour of the Aboriginal community or communities in question any measure of redress it considers appropriate at the time,
where
(a) the parties will not agree to mediation or arbitration of the
dispute; or
(b) proposals of the Commission have not been carried out
within an allotted time to its satisfaction; and
(c) application to a tribunal or demand in favour of a community is with the consent of concerned communities.

International 1.11.12
Standards Canada participate fully in efforts to develop further international standards to protect Indigenous peoples against arbitrary relocation and ensure that Canadian law incorporates the
spirit and intent of international norms, standards and
covenants relating to relocation.

Repository of **1.11.13**
Records The national repository for records on residential schools proposed in Recommendation 1.10.3 and its related research activities also cover all matters relating to relocations.

That the nature and scope of the injury caused to Aboriginal people by past discriminatory policies in relation to Aboriginal veterans be established and appropriate remedies devised therefor.

The Commission recommends that

Acknowledge **1.12.1**
Contribution Acknowledge, on behalf of the people of Canada, the contribution of Aboriginal people within the Canadian Armed Forces during the wars of this century (the First World War, the Second World War and Korea) by
(a) giving a higher profile to Aboriginal veterans at national Remembrance Day services;
(b) funding the erection of war memorials in Aboriginal communities; and
(c) funding the continuing work of Aboriginal veterans' organizations.

Appoint **1.12.2**
Ombudsman Agree to Aboriginal veterans' requests for an ombudsman to work with the departments of veterans affairs and Indian affairs and northern development and national and provincial veterans' organizations to resolve long-standing disputes concerning
• Aboriginal veterans' access to and just receipt of veterans benefits; and
• the legality and fairness of the sales, leases and appropriations of Indian lands for purposes related to the war effort and for distribution to returning veterans of the two world wars.

Aboriginal **1.12.3**
Personnel Hire Aboriginal people with appropriate language skills and cultural understanding in the Department of Veterans Affairs to serve distinct Aboriginal client groups.

Foundation **1.12.4**
Establish and fund a non-profit foundation in honour of Aboriginal veterans to promote and facilitate education and research in Aboriginal history and implement stay-in-school initiatives for Aboriginal students.

VOLUME 2

RESTRUCTURING THE RELATIONSHIP

Conclusions and recommendations are grouped by theme and do not necessarily appear here in the same order as in the text. The original numbering of recommendations has been retained, however (with the first number representing the volume, the second the chapter, and the third the recommendation number), to facilitate placing them in their original context.

Chapter 2 Treaties

With respect to the historical treaties,
the Commission recommends that

Fulfilment of Historical Treaties

2.2.2

The parties implement the historical treaties from the perspective of both justice and reconciliation:
  (a) Justice requires the fulfilment of the agreed terms of the treaties, as recorded in the treaty text and supplemented by oral evidence.
  (b) Reconciliation requires the establishment of proper principles to govern the continuing treaty relationship and to complete treaties that are incomplete because of the absence of consensus.

Treaty Implementation and Renewal

2.2.3

The federal government establish a continuing bilateral process to implement and renew the Crown's relationship with and obligations to the treaty nations under the historical treaties, in accordance with the treaties' spirit and intent.

Principles of Implementation

2.2.4

The spirit and intent of the historical treaties be implemented in accordance with the following fundamental principles:
  (a) The specific content of the rights and obligations of the parties to the treaties is determined for all purposes in a just and liberal way, by reference to oral as well as written sources.
  (b) The Crown is in a trust-like and non-adversarial fiduciary relationship with the treaty nations.
  (c) The Crown's conflicting duties to the treaty nations and to Canadians generally is reconciled in the spirit of the treaty partnership.

(d) There is a presumption in respect of the historical treaties that

- treaty nations did not intend to consent to the blanket extinguishment of their Aboriginal rights and title by entering into the treaty relationship;
- treaty nations intended to share the territory and jurisdiction and management over it, as opposed to ceding the territory, even where the text of an historical treaty makes reference to a blanket extinguishment of land rights; and
- treaty nations did not intend to give up their inherent right of governance by entering into a treaty relationship, and the act of treaty making is regarded as an affirmation rather than a denial of that right.

With regard to new treaties and agreements,
the Commission recommends that

New Treaties and **2.2.6**
Agreements The federal government establish a process for making new treaties to replace the existing comprehensive claims policy, based on the following principles:

(a) The blanket extinguishment of Aboriginal land rights is not an option.

(b) Recognition of rights of governance is an integral component of new treaty relationships.

(c) The treaty-making process is available to all Aboriginal nations, including Indian, Inuit and Métis nations.

(d) Treaty nations that are parties to peace and friendship treaties that did not purport to address land and resource issues have access to the treaty-making process to complete their treaty relationships with the Crown.

In relation to all treaties,
the Commission recommends that

Matters for **2.2.11**
Negotiation The following matters be open for discussion in treaty implementation and renewal and treaty-making processes:

- governance, including justice systems, long term financial arrangements including fiscal transfers and other intergovernmental arrangements;
- lands and resources;

- economic rights, including treaty annuities and hunting, fishing and trapping rights;
- issues included in specific treaties (for example, education, health and taxation); and
- other issues relevant to treaty relationships identified by either treaty party.

Reconciliation of Laws and Policies 2.2.5

Once the spirit and intent of specific treaties have been recognized and incorporated into the agreed understanding of the treaty, all laws, policies and practices that have a bearing on the terms of the treaty be made to reflect this understanding.

With respect to establishing a new treaty process,
the Commission recommends that

Promulgating a Royal Proclamation 2.2.7

The federal government prepare a royal proclamation for the consideration of Her Majesty the Queen that would

(a) supplement the *Royal Proclamation of 1763*; and
(b) set out, for the consideration of all Aboriginal and treaty nations in Canada, the fundamental principles of
   (i)   the bilateral nation-to-nation relationship;
   (ii) the treaty implementation and renewal processes; and
   (iii) the treaty-making processes.

Enacting Companion Legislation 2.2.8

The federal government introduce companion treaty legislation in Parliament that

(a) provides for the implementation of existing treaty rights, including the treaty rights to hunt, fish and trap;
(b) affirms liberal rules of interpretation for historical treaties, having regard to
   (i)   the context of treaty negotiations;
   (ii) the spirit and intent of each treaty; and
   (iii) the special relationship between the treaty parties;
(c) makes oral and secondary evidence admissible in the courts when they are making determinations with respect to historical treaty rights;
(d) recognizes and affirms the land rights and jurisdiction of Aboriginal nations as essential components of treaty processes;
(e) declares the commitment of the Parliament and government of Canada to the implementation and renewal of

each treaty in accordance with the spirit and intent of the treaty and the relationship embodied in it;

(f) commits the government of Canada to treaty processes that clarify, implement and, where the parties agree, amend the terms of treaties to give effect to the spirit and intent of each treaty and the relationship embodied in it;

(g) commits the government of Canada to a process of treaty making with
  (i) Aboriginal nations that do not yet have a treaty with the Crown; and
  (ii) treaty nations whose treaty does not purport to address issues of lands and resources;

(h) commits the government of Canada to treaty processes based on and guided by the nation-to-nation structure of the new relationship, implying
  (i) all parties demonstrating a spirit of openness, a clear political will and a commitment to fair, balanced and equitable negotiations; and
  (ii) no party controlling the access to, the scope of, or the funding for the negotiating processes; and

(i) authorizes the establishment, in consultation with treaty nations, of the institutions this Commission recommends as necessary to fulfil the treaty processes.

Elements of Treaty Process

2.2.10

The royal proclamation and companion legislation in relation to treaties accomplish the following:

(a) declare that entry into treaty-making and treaty implementation and renewal processes by Aboriginal and treaty nations is voluntary;

(b) use clear, non-derogation language to ensure that the royal proclamation and legislation do not derogate from existing Aboriginal and treaty rights;

(c) provide for short- and medium-term initiatives to support treaty implementation and renewal and treaty making, since those processes will take time to complete; and

(d) provide adequate long-term resources so that treaty-making and treaty implementation and renewal processes can achieve their objectives.

Outcome of Treaty Processes

2.2.12

The royal proclamation and companion legislation in relation to treaties provide for one or more of the following outcomes:

(a) protocol agreements between treaty nations and the Crown that provide for the implementation and renewal of existing treaties, but do not themselves have the status of a treaty;

(b) supplementary treaties that coexist with existing treaties;

(c) replacement treaties;

(d) new treaties; and

(e) other instruments to implement treaties, including legislation and regulations of the treaty parties.

Crown Treaty Office **2.2.13**

The royal proclamation and companion legislation in relation to treaties:

(a) establish a Crown Treaty Office within a new Department of Aboriginal Relations; and

(b) direct that Office to be the lead Crown agency participating in nation-to-nation treaty processes.

With regard to provincial and territorial responsibilities,
the Commission recommends that

Provincial/ Territorial Participation **2.2.9**

The governments of the provinces and territories introduce legislation, parallel to the federal companion legislation, that

(a) enables them to meet their treaty obligations;

(b) enables them to participate in treaty implementation and renewal processes and treaty-making processes; and

(c) establishes the institutions required to participate in those treaty processes, to the extent of their jurisdiction.

2.2.14

Each province establish a Crown Treaty Office to enable it to participate in treaty processes.

Regarding the creation of treaty institutions,
the Commission recommends that

Treaty Commissions **2.2.15**

The governments of Canada, relevant provinces and territories, and Aboriginal and treaty nations establish treaty commissions as permanent, independent and neutral bodies to facilitate and oversee negotiations in treaty processes.

2.2.16

The following be the essential features of treaty commissions:

- Commissioners to be appointed in equal numbers from lists prepared by the parties, with an independent chair being selected by those appointees.
- Commissions to have permanent administrative and research staff, with full independence from government and from Aboriginal and treaty nations.
- Staff of the commissions to act as a secretariat for treaty processes.
- Services of the commissions to go beyond simple facilitation. Where the parties require specialized fact finding of a technical nature, commissions to have the power to hire the necessary experts.
- Commissions to monitor and guide the conduct of the parties in the treaty process to ensure that fair and proper standards of conduct and negotiation are maintained.
- Commissions to conduct inquiries and provide research, analysis and recommendations on issues in dispute in relation to historical and future treaties, as requested jointly by the parties.
- Commissions to supervise and facilitate cost sharing by the parties.
- Commissions to provide mediation services to the parties as jointly requested.
- Commissions to provide remedies for abuses of process.
- Commissions to provide binding or non-binding arbitration of particular matters and other dispute resolution services, at the request of the parties, consistent with the political nature of the treaty process.

Aboriginal Lands and Treaties Tribunal

2.2.17

The Aboriginal Lands and Treaties Tribunal recommended by this Commission (see Volume 2, Chapter 4) play a supporting role in treaty processes, particularly in relation to

(a) issues of process (for example, ensuring good-faith negotiations);

(b) the ordering of interim relief; and

(c) appeals from the treaty commissions regarding funding of treaty processes.

With regard to fostering public education and awareness,
the Commission recommends that

Public Education **2.2.1**
Federal, provincial and territorial governments provide programs of public education about the treaties to promote public
understanding of the following concepts:
(a) Treaties were made, and continue to be made, by
Aboriginal nations on a nation-to-nation basis, and those
nations continue to exist and deserve respect as nations.
(b) Historical treaties were meant by all parties to be sacred and
enduring and to be spiritual as well as legal undertakings.
(c) Treaties with Aboriginal nations are fundamental components of the constitution of Canada, analogous to the
terms of union whereby provinces joined Confederation.
(d) Fulfilment of the treaties, including the spirit and intent of
the historical treaties, is a test of Canada's honour and of
its place of respect in the family of nations.
(e) Treaties embody the principles of the relationship between
the Crown and the Aboriginal nations that made them or
that will make them in the future.

Chapter 3 Governance

With regard to the establishment of Aboriginal governance,
the Commission concludes that

1. The right of self-determination is vested in all the Aboriginal peoples of
Canada, including First Nations, Inuit and Métis peoples. The right finds its
foundation in emerging norms of international law and basic principles of
public morality. By virtue of this right, Aboriginal peoples are entitled to negotiate freely the terms of their relationship with Canada and to establish governmental structures that they consider appropriate for their needs.

2. When exercised by Aboriginal peoples within the context of the Canadian
federation, the right of self-determination does not ordinarily give rise to a
right of secession, except in the case of grave oppression or disintegration of the
Canadian state.

3. Aboriginal peoples are not racial groups; rather they are organic political and
cultural entities. Although contemporary Aboriginal groups stem historically
from the original peoples of North America, they often have mixed genetic her-

itages and include individuals of varied ancestry. As organic political entities, they have the capacity to evolve over time and change in their internal composition.

4. The right of self-determination is vested in Aboriginal nations rather than small local communities. By Aboriginal nation we mean a sizeable body of Aboriginal people with a shared sense of national identity that constitutes the predominant population in a certain territory or group of territories. Currently, there are between 60 and 80 historically based nations in Canada, compared with a thousand or so local Aboriginal communities.

5. The more specific attributes of an Aboriginal nation are that

- the nation has a collective sense of national identity that is evinced in a common history, language, culture, traditions, political consciousness, laws, governmental structures, spirituality, ancestry and homeland;
- it is of sufficient size and capacity to enable it to assume and exercise powers and responsibilities flowing from the right of self-determination in an effective manner; and
- it constitutes a majority of the permanent population of a certain territory or collection of territories and, in the future, will operate from a defined territorial base.

The Commission therefore recommends that

Recognition of 2.3.2
Self-
Determination All governments in Canada recognize that Aboriginal peoples are nations vested with the right of self-determination.

With regard to government recognition of Aboriginal nations, the Commission concludes that

6. Aboriginal peoples are entitled to identify their own national units for purposes of exercising the right of self-determination. For an Aboriginal nation to hold the right of self-determination, it does not have to be recognized as such by the federal government or by provincial governments. Nevertheless, as a practical matter, unless other Canadian governments are prepared to acknowledge the existence of Aboriginal nations and to negotiate with them, such nations may find it difficult to exercise their rights effectively. Therefore, in practice there is a need for the federal and provincial governments actively to acknowledge the existence of the various Aboriginal nations in Canada and to engage in serious negotiations designed to implement their rights of self-determination.

The Commission therefore recommends that

Identifying **2.3.3**
Nations   The federal government put in place a neutral and transparent process for identifying Aboriginal groups entitled to exercise the right of self-determination as nations, a process that uses the following specific attributes of nationhood:

> (a) The nation has a collective sense of national identity that is evinced in a common history, language, culture, traditions, political consciousness, laws, governmental structures, spirituality, ancestry and homeland.
>
> (b) The nation is of sufficient size and capacity to enable it to assume and exercise powers and responsibilities flowing from the right of self-determination in an effective manner.
>
> (c) The nation constitutes a majority of the permanent population of a certain territory or collection of territories and, in the future, operates from a defined territorial base.

With regard to the jurisdiction of Aboriginal governments,
the Commission concludes that

7. The right of self-determination is the fundamental starting point for Aboriginal initiatives in the area of governance. However, it is not the only possible basis for such initiatives. In addition, Aboriginal peoples possess the inherent right of self-government within Canada as a matter of Canadian constitutional law. This right is inherent in the sense that it finds its ultimate origins in the collective lives and traditions of Aboriginal peoples themselves rather than the Crown or Parliament. More specifically, it stems from the original status of Aboriginal peoples as independent and sovereign nations in the territories they occupied, as this status was recognized and given effect in the numerous treaties, alliances and other relations maintained with the incoming French and British Crowns. This extensive practice gave rise to a body of inter-societal customary law that was common to the parties and eventually became part of the law of Canada.

8. The inherent right of Aboriginal self-government is recognized and affirmed in section 35(1) of the *Constitution Act, 1982* as an Aboriginal and treaty-protected right. The inherent right is thus entrenched in the Canadian constitution, providing a basis for Aboriginal governments to function as one of three distinct orders of government in Canada.

9. The constitutional right of self-government does not supersede the right of self-determination or take precedence over it. Rather, it is available to Aboriginal

peoples who wish to take advantage of it, in addition to their right of self-determination, treaty rights and any other rights that they enjoy now or negotiate in the future. In other words, the constitutional right of self-government is one of a range of voluntary options available to Aboriginal peoples.

10. Generally speaking, the sphere of inherent Aboriginal jurisdiction under section 35(1) comprises all matters relating to the good government and welfare of Aboriginal peoples and their territories. This sphere of inherent jurisdiction is divided into two sectors: a core and a periphery.

11. The core of Aboriginal jurisdiction includes all matters that are of vital concern to the life and welfare of a particular Aboriginal people, its culture and identity; that do not have a major impact on adjacent jurisdictions; and that otherwise are not the object of transcendent federal or provincial concern. With respect to these matters, an Aboriginal group has the right to exercise authority and legislate at its own initiative, without the need to conclude federal and provincial agreements.

12. The periphery comprises the remainder of the sphere of inherent Aboriginal jurisdiction. It includes, among other things, subject-matters that have a major impact on adjacent jurisdictions or attract transcendent federal or provincial concern. Such matters require a substantial degree of co-ordination among Aboriginal, federal and provincial governments. In our view, an Aboriginal group cannot legislate at its own initiative in this area until agreements have been concluded with federal and provincial governments.

13. When an Aboriginal government passes legislation dealing with a subject-matter falling within the core, any inconsistent federal or provincial legislation is automatically displaced. An Aboriginal government can thus expand, contract or vary its exclusive range of operations in an organic manner, in keeping with its needs and circumstances. Where there is no inconsistent Aboriginal legislation occupying the field in a core area of jurisdiction, federal and provincial laws continue to apply in accordance with standard constitutional rules.

14. By way of exception, in certain cases a federal law may take precedence over an Aboriginal law where they conflict. However, for this to happen, the federal law has to meet the strict standard laid down by the Supreme Court of Canada in the *Sparrow* decision. Under this standard, the federal law has to serve a compelling and substantial need and be consistent with the Crown's basic fiduciary responsibilities to Aboriginal peoples.

15. In relation to matters in the periphery, a self-government treaty or agreement is needed to settle the jurisdictional overlap between an Aboriginal government and the federal and provincial governments. Among other things, a treaty will need to specify which areas of jurisdiction are exclusive and which are concurrent and, in the latter case, which legislation will prevail in case of conflict. Until such a treaty is concluded, Aboriginal jurisdiction in the periphery remains in abeyance, and federal and provincial laws continue to apply within their respective areas of legislative jurisdiction.

16. A treaty dealing with the inherent right of self-government gives rise to treaty rights under section 35(1) of the *Constitution Act, 1982* and thus becomes constitutionally entrenched. Even when a self-government agreement does not itself constitute a treaty, rights articulated in it may nevertheless become constitutionally entrenched.

The Commission therefore recommends that

Inherent Right of **2.3.4**
Self-Government   All governments in Canada recognize that the inherent right of Aboriginal self-government has the following characteristics:

(a) It is an existing Aboriginal and treaty right that is recognized and affirmed in section 35(1) of the *Constitution Act, 1982.*

(b) Its origins lie within Aboriginal peoples and nations as political and cultural entities.

(c) It arises from the sovereign and independent status of Aboriginal peoples and nations before and at the time of European contact and from the fact that Aboriginal peoples were in possession of their own territories, political systems and customary laws at that time.

(d) The inherent right of self-government has a substantial degree of immunity from federal and provincial legislative acts, except where, in the case of federal legislation, it can be justified under a strict constitutional standard.

2.3.5
All governments in Canada recognize that the sphere of the inherent right of Aboriginal self-government

(a) encompasses all matters relating to the good government and welfare of Aboriginal peoples and their territories; and

(b) is divided into two areas:

- core areas of jurisdiction, which include all matters that are of vital concern for the life and welfare of a particular Aboriginal people, its culture and identity, do not have a major impact on adjacent jurisdictions, and are not otherwise the object of transcendent federal or provincial concern; and
- peripheral areas of jurisdiction, which make up the remainder.

2.3.6

All governments in Canada recognize that

(a) in the core areas of jurisdiction, as a matter of principle, Aboriginal peoples have the capacity to implement their inherent right of self-government by self-starting initiatives without the need for agreements with the federal and provincial governments, although it would be highly advisable that they negotiate agreements with other governments in the interests of reciprocal recognition and avoiding litigation; and

(b) in peripheral areas of jurisdiction, agreements should be negotiated with other governments to implement and particularize the inherent right as appropriate to the context and subject matter being negotiated.

With regard to the right of self-government, which is vested in Aboriginal nations, the Commission concludes that

18. The constitutional right of self-government is vested in the people that make up Aboriginal nations, not in local communities as such. Only nations can exercise the range of governmental powers available in the core areas of Aboriginal jurisdiction, and nations alone have the power to conclude self-government treaties regarding matters falling within the periphery. Nevertheless, local communities of Aboriginal people have access to inherent governmental powers if they join together in their national units and agree to a constitution allocating powers between the national and local levels.

The Commission therefore recommends that

Aboriginal Nations and Self-Government **2.3.7**

All governments in Canada recognize that the right of self-government is vested in Aboriginal nations rather than small local communities.

Territorial and Communal Forms of Government

2.3.13

All governments in Canada support Aboriginal peoples' desire to exercise both territorial and communal forms of jurisdiction, and co-operate with and assist them in achieving these objectives through negotiated self-government agreements.

Establishing Governments

2.3.14

In establishing and structuring their governments, Aboriginal peoples give consideration to three models of Aboriginal government – nation government, public government and community of interest government – while recognizing that changes to these models can be made to reflect particular aspirations, customs, culture, traditions and values.

2.3.15

When Aboriginal people establish governments that reflect either a nation or a public government approach, the laws of these governments be recognized as applicable to all residents within the territorial jurisdictions of the government unless otherwise provided by that government.

2.3.16

When Aboriginal people choose to establish nation governments,

(a) The rights and interests of residents on the nation's territory who are not citizens or members of the nation be protected.

(b) That such protection take the form of representation in the decision-making structures and processes of the nation.

Regarding Aboriginal peoples and citizenship,
the Commission concludes that

19. Under section 35 of the *Constitution Act, 1982,* an Aboriginal nation has the right to determine which individuals belong to the nation as members and citizens. However, this right is subject to two basic limitations. First, it cannot be exercised in a manner that discriminates between men and women. Second, it cannot specify a minimum blood quantum as a general prerequisite for citizenship. Modern Aboriginal nations, like other nations in the world today, represent a mixture of genetic heritages. Their identity lies in their collective life, their history, ancestry, culture, values, traditions and ties to the land, rather than in their race as such.

The Commission therefore recommends that

Aboriginal **2.3.8**
Citizenship The government of Canada recognize Aboriginal people in Canada as enjoying a unique form of dual citizenship, that is, as citizens of an Aboriginal nation and citizens of Canada.

2.3.9
The government of Canada take steps to ensure that the Canadian passports of Aboriginal citizens
  (a) explicitly recognize this dual citizenship; and
  (b) identify the Aboriginal nation citizenship of individual Aboriginal persons.

2.3.10
Aboriginal nations, in exercising the right to determine citizenship, and in establishing rules and processes for this purpose, adopt citizenship criteria that
  (a) are consistent with section 35(4) of the *Constitution Act, 1982;*
  (b) reflect Aboriginal nations as political and cultural entities rather than as racial groups, and therefore do not make blood quantum a general prerequisite for citizenship determination; and
  (c) may include elements such as self-identification, community or nation acceptance, cultural and linguistic knowledge, marriage, adoption, residency, birthplace, descent and ancestry among the different ways to establish citizenship.

2.3.11
As part of their citizenship rules, Aboriginal nations establish mechanisms for resolving disputes concerning the nation's citizenship rules generally, or individual applications specifically. These mechanisms are to be
  (a) characterized by fairness, openness and impartiality;
  (b) structured at arm's length from the central decision-making bodies of the Aboriginal government; and
  (c) operated in accordance with the *Canadian Charter of Rights and Freedoms* and with international norms and standards concerning human rights.

With regard to Aboriginal governments as one of three distinct orders of government in Canada, the Commission concludes that

20. The enactment of section 35 of the *Constitution Act, 1982* has had far-reaching significance. It serves to confirm the status of Aboriginal peoples as equal partners in the complex federal arrangements that make up Canada. It provides the basis for recognizing Aboriginal governments as one of three distinct orders of government in Canada: Aboriginal, provincial and federal. The governments making up these three orders are sovereign within their several spheres and hold their powers by virtue of their inherent or constitutional status rather than by delegation. They share the sovereign powers of Canada as a whole, powers that represent a pooling of existing sovereignties.

21. Aboriginal peoples also have a special relationship with the Canadian Crown, which the courts have described as *sui generis* or one of a kind. This relationship traces its origins to the treaties and other links formed over the centuries and to the inter-societal law and custom that underpinned them. By virtue of this relationship, the Crown acts as the protector of the sovereignty of Aboriginal peoples within Canada and as guarantor of their Aboriginal and treaty rights. This fiduciary relationship is a fundamental feature of the constitution of Canada.

22. Nevertheless, there is a profound need for a process that will afford Aboriginal peoples the opportunity to restructure existing governmental institutions and participate as partners in the Canadian federation on terms they freely accept. The existing right of self-government under section 35 of the *Constitution Act, 1982* is no substitute for a just process that implements the basic right of self-determination by means of freely negotiated treaties between Aboriginal nations and the Crown.

The Commission therefore recommends that

Jurisdiction and Orders of Government

2.3.12

All governments in Canada recognize that
  (a) section 35 of the *Constitution Act* provides the basis for an Aboriginal order of government that coexists within the framework of Canada along with the federal and provincial orders of government; and that
  (b) each order of government operates within its own distinct sovereign sphere, as defined by the Canadian constitution, and exercises authority within spheres of jurisdiction having both overlapping and exclusive components.

With respect to Aboriginal governments and the Canadian Charter of Rights and Freedoms, *the Commission concludes that*

17. The *Canadian Charter of Rights and Freedoms* applies to Aboriginal governments and regulates relations with individuals falling within their jurisdiction. However, under section 25, the Charter must be given a flexible interpretation that takes account of the distinctive philosophies, traditions and cultural practices of Aboriginal peoples. Moreover, under section 33, Aboriginal nations can pass notwithstanding clauses that suspend the operation of certain Charter sections for a period. Nevertheless, by virtue of sections 28 and 35(4) of the *Constitution Act, 1982*, Aboriginal women and men are in all cases guaranteed equal access to the inherent right of self-government and are entitled to equal treatment by their governments.

With regard to financing Aboriginal governments, the Commission recommends that

New Fiscal Arrangements
2.3.17
Aboriginal governments established under a renewed relationship have fundamentally new fiscal arrangements, not adaptation or modification of existing fiscal arrangements for *Indian Act* band governments.

Expenditure Needs
2.3.18
The financing mechanism used for equalization purposes be based not only on revenue-raising capacity, but also take into account differences in the *expenditure needs* of the Aboriginal governments they are designed to support, as is done with the fiscal arrangements for the territorial governments, and that the tax effort that Aboriginal governments make be taken into consideration in the design of these fiscal arrangements.

Own-Source Revenues
2.3.19
Financial arrangements provide greater fiscal autonomy for Aboriginal governments by increasing access to independent own-source revenues through a fair and just redistribution of lands and resources for Aboriginal peoples, and through the recognition of the right of Aboriginal governments to develop their own systems of taxation.

Income Taxes
2.3.20
Aboriginal citizens living on their territory pay personal income tax to their Aboriginal governments; for Aboriginal citizens

living off the territory, taxes continue to be paid to the federal and relevant provincial government; for non-Aboriginal residents on Aboriginal lands, several options exist:

(a) all personal income taxes could be paid to the Aboriginal government, provided that the level of taxation applied does not create a tax haven for non-Aboriginal people;

(b) all personal income taxes could be paid to the Aboriginal government, with any difference between the Aboriginal personal income tax and the combined federal and provincial personal income tax going to the federal government (in effect, providing tax abatements for taxes paid to Aboriginal governments); or

(c) provincial personal income tax could go to the Aboriginal government and the federal personal income tax to the federal government in circumstances where the Aboriginal government decides to adopt the existing federal/provincial tax rate.

2.3.21

Aboriginal governments reimburse provincial governments for services the latter continue to provide, thereby forgoing the requirement for provincial taxes to be paid by their residents.

Non-Aboriginal **2.3.22**
Representation Non-Aboriginal residents be represented effectively in the decision-making processes of Aboriginal nation governments.

Specific Claims **2.3.23**
Settlements Revenues arising from specific claims settlements not be considered a direct source of funding for Aboriginal governments and therefore not be included as own-source funding for purposes of calculating fiscal transfers.

Financial **2.3.24**
Settlements Financial settlements arising from comprehensive land claims and treaty land entitlements not be considered a direct source of funding for Aboriginal governments.

Investment **2.3.25**
Income Investment income arising from Aboriginal government decisions to invest monies associated with a financial settlement – either directly or through a corporation established for this purpose – be treated as own-source revenue for purposes of calculating intergovernmental fiscal transfers unless it is used to

repay loans advanced to finance the negotiations, to offset the effect of inflation on the original financial settlements, thereby preserving the value of the principal, or to finance charitable activities or community works.

Canada-Wide **2.3.26**
Framework Federal and provincial governments and national Aboriginal organizations negotiate

(a) a Canada-wide framework to guide the fiscal relationship among the three orders of government; and

(b) interim fiscal arrangements for those Aboriginal nations that achieve recognition and begin to govern in their core areas of jurisdiction on existing Aboriginal lands.

With regard to a legal framework for recognizing Aboriginal governments, the Commission recommends that

Aboriginal Nations **2.3.27**
Recognition and The Parliament of Canada enact an Aboriginal Nations
Government Act Recognition and Government Act to

(a) establish the process whereby the government of Canada can recognize the accession of an Aboriginal group or groups to nation status and its assumption of authority as an Aboriginal government to exercise its inherent self-governing jurisdiction;

(b) establish criteria for the recognition of Aboriginal nations, including

(i) evidence among the communities concerned of common ties of language, history, culture and of willingness to associate, coupled with sufficient size to support the exercise of a broad, self-governing mandate;

(ii) evidence of a fair and open process for obtaining the agreement of its citizens and member communities to embark on a nation recognition process;

(iii) completion of a citizenship code that is consistent with international norms of human rights and with the *Canadian Charter of Rights and Freedoms*;

(iv) evidence that an impartial appeal process had been established by the nation to hear disputes about individuals' eligibility for citizenship;

(v) evidence that a fundamental law or constitution has been drawn up through wide consultation with its citizens; and

(vi) evidence that all citizens of the nation were permitted, through a fair means of expressing their opinion, to ratify the proposed constitution;

(c) authorize the creation of recognition panels under the aegis of the proposed Aboriginal Lands and Treaties Tribunal to advise the government of Canada on whether a group meets recognition criteria;

(d) enable the federal government to vacate its legislative authority under section 91(24) of the *Constitution Act, 1867* with respect to core powers deemed needed by Aboriginal nations and to specify which additional areas of federal jurisdiction the Parliament of Canada is prepared to acknowledge as being core powers to be exercised by Aboriginal governments; and

(e) provide enhanced financial resources to enable recognized Aboriginal nations to exercise expanded governing powers for an increased population base in the period between recognition and the conclusion or reaffirmation of comprehensive treaties.

With regard to creating a Canada-wide framework agreement to guide treaty negotiations, the Commission recommends that

Canada-Wide Framework Agreement

2.3.28

The government of Canada convene a meeting of premiers, territorial leaders and national Aboriginal leaders to create a forum charged with drawing up a Canada-wide framework agreement. The purpose of this agreement would be to establish common principles and directions to guide the negotiation of treaties with recognized Aboriginal nations. This forum should have a mandate to conclude agreements on

(a) the areas of jurisdiction to be exercisable by Aboriginal nations and the application of the doctrine of paramountcy in the case of concurrent jurisdiction;

(b) fiscal arrangements to finance the operations of Aboriginal governments and the provision of services to their citizens;

(c) principles to govern the allocation of lands and resources to Aboriginal nations and for the exercise of co-jurisdiction on lands shared with other governments;

(d) principles to guide the negotiation of agreements for interim relief to govern the development of territories subject to claims, before the conclusion of treaties; and

(e) an interim agreement to set out the core powers that Canadian governments are prepared to acknowledge Aboriginal nations can exercise once they are recognized but before treaties are renegotiated.

With respect to rebuilding Aboriginal nations and reclaiming nationhood, the Commission recommends that

2.3.29
Aboriginal peoples develop and implement their own strategies for rebuilding Aboriginal nations and reclaiming Aboriginal nationhood. These strategies may
(a) include cultural revitalization and healing processes;
(b) include political processes for building consensus on the basic composition of the Aboriginal nation and its political structures; and
(c) be undertaken by individual communities and by groups of communities that may share Aboriginal nationhood.

Aboriginal **2.3.30**
Government The federal government, in co-operation with national
Transition Centre Aboriginal organizations, establish an Aboriginal government transition centre with a mandate to
(a) research, develop and co-ordinate, with other institutions, initiatives and studies to assist Aboriginal peoples throughout the transition to Aboriginal self-government on topics such as citizenship codes, constitutions and institutions of government, as well as processes for nation rebuilding and citizen participation;
(b) develop and deliver, through appropriate means, training and skills development programs for community leaders, community facilitators and field workers, as well as community groups that have assumed responsibility for animating processes to rebuild Aboriginal nations; and
(c) facilitate information sharing and exchange among community facilitators, leaders and others involved in nation rebuilding processes.

2.3.31
The federal government provide the centre with operational funding as well as financial resources to undertake research and design and implement programs to assist transition to self-government, with a financial commitment for five years, renewable for a further five years.

2.3.32

The centre be governed by a predominantly Aboriginal board, with seats assigned to organizations representing Aboriginal peoples and governments, the federal government, and associated institutions and organizations.

2.3.33

In all regions of Canada, universities and other post-secondary education facilities, research institutes, and other organizations, in association with the proposed centre, initiate programs, projects and other activities to assist Aboriginal peoples throughout the transition to Aboriginal self-government.

2.3.34

The Aboriginal government transition centre support Aboriginal nations in creating their constitutions by promoting, co-ordinating and funding, as appropriate, associated institutions and organizations for initiatives that

(a) provide professional, technical and advisory support services in key areas of Aboriginal constitutional development, such as
  • citizenship and membership;
  • political institutions and leadership;
  • decision-making processes; and
  • identification of territory;

(b) provide training programs to the leaders and staff of Aboriginal nation political structures who are centrally involved in organizing, co-ordinating, managing and facilitating constitution-building processes;

(c) provide assistance to Aboriginal nations in designing and implementing community education and consultation strategies;

(d) assist Aboriginal nations in preparing for, organizing and carrying out nation-wide referenda on Aboriginal nation constitutions; and

(e) facilitate information sharing among Aboriginal nations on constitutional development processes and experiences.

2.3.35

The Aboriginal government transition centre promote, co-ordinate and fund, as appropriate, in collaboration with associated institutions and organizations, the following types of initiatives:

(a) special training programs for Aboriginal negotiators to increase their negotiating skills and their knowledge of issues that will be addressed through negotiations; and

(b) training programs of short duration for Aboriginal government leaders

- to enhance Aboriginal leadership capacities in negotiation; and
- to increase the capacity of Aboriginal leaders to support and mandate negotiators and negotiation activities, as well as nation-level education, consultation and communication strategies.

2.3.36

Early in the process of planning for self-government agreements, whether in treaties or other agreements, provisions be drafted to

(a) recognize education and training as a vital component in the transition to Aboriginal government and implement these activities well before self-government takes effect; and

(b) include provisions for the transfer of resources to support the design, development and implementation of education and training strategies.

2.3.37

To assist Aboriginal nations in developing their governance capacities, the Aboriginal government transition centre promote, co-ordinate and fund, as appropriate, in collaboration with associated education institutions initiatives that

- promote and support excellence in Aboriginal management;
- reflect Aboriginal traditions; and
- enhance management skills in areas central to Aboriginal government activities and responsibilities.

2.3.38

A partnership program be established to twin Aboriginal governments with Canadian governments of similar size and scope of operations.

In regard to establishing and maintaining accountability in governments, the Commission recommends that

2.3.39

Aboriginal governments develop and institute strategies for accountability and responsibility in government to maintain integrity in government and public confidence in Aboriginal government leaders, officials and administrations.

2.3.40
Aboriginal governments take the following steps to address accountability:
(a) Formalize codes of conduct for public officials.
(b) Establish conflict of interest laws, policies or guidelines.
(c) Establish independent structures or agencies responsible for upholding and promoting the public interest and the integrity of Aboriginal governments.
(d) Establish informal accountability mechanisms to ensure widespread and continuing understanding of Aboriginal government goals, priorities, procedures and activities, administrative decision making and reporting systems.

2.3.41
To the extent deemed appropriate by the Aboriginal people concerned, strategies for accountability and responsibility in Aboriginal government reflect and build upon Aboriginal peoples' own customs, traditions and values.

Regarding the acquisition of information and information management systems, the Commission recommends that

Data Collection   **2.3.42**
Statistics Canada take the following steps to improve its data collection:
(a) continue its efforts to consult Aboriginal governments and organizations to improve understanding of their data requirements;
(b) establish an external Aboriginal advisory committee, with adequate representation from national Aboriginal organizations and other relevant Aboriginal experts, to discuss
  • Aboriginal statistical data requirements; and
  • the design and implementation of surveys to gather data on Aboriginal people;
(c) continue the post-census survey on Aboriginal people and ensure that it becomes a regular data-collection vehicle maintained by Statistics Canada;
(d) include appropriate questions in all future censuses to enable a post-census survey of Aboriginal people to be conducted;

(e) in view of the large numbers of Aboriginal people living in non-reserve urban and rural areas, extend sampling sizes off-reserve to permit the statistical profiling of a larger number of communities than was possible in 1991;

(f) test questions that are acceptable to Aboriginal people and are more appropriate to obtaining information relevant to the needs of emerging forms of Aboriginal government;

(g) test a representative sample of Aboriginal people in post-census surveys;

(h) include the Metis Settlements of Alberta in standard geographic coding and give each community the status of a census subdivision;

(i) review other communities in the mid-north, which are not Indian reserves or Crown land settlements, to see whether they should have a special area flag on the census database; and

(j) consider applying a specific nation identifier to Indian reserves and settlements on the geographic files to allow data for these communities to be aggregated by nation affiliation as well as allowing individuals to identify with their nation affiliation.

Future Censuses **2.3.43**

The federal government take the following action with respect to future censuses:

(a) continue its policy of establishing bilateral agreements with representative Aboriginal governments and their communities, as appropriate, for future census and post-census survey operations;

(b) in light of the issues raised in this report and the need for detailed and accurate information on Aboriginal peoples, the decision not to engage in a post-census survey, in conjunction with the 1996 census, be reversed; and

(c) make special efforts to establish such agreements in those regions of Canada where participation was low in the 1991 census.

Information **2.3.44**
Systems

Governments provide for the implementation of information management systems in support of self-government, which include

(a) financial support of technologies and equipment proportional to the scope of an Aboriginal government's operations; and

(b) training and skills development, including apprenticeships
and executive exchanges with Statistics Canada, to facilitate compatibility between Aboriginal government systems and Statistics Canada.

With regard to restructuring federal institutions,
the Commission recommends that

2.3.45

The government of Canada present legislation to abolish the
Department of Indian Affairs and Northern Development and
to replace it by two new departments: a Department of
Aboriginal Relations and a Department of Indian and Inuit
Services.

2.3.46

The prime minister appoint in a new senior cabinet position a
minister of Aboriginal relations, to be responsible for

• guiding all federal actions associated with fully developing and
implementing the new federal/Aboriginal relationship, which
forms the core of this Commission's recommendations;
• allocating funds from the federal government's total
Aboriginal expenditures across the government; and
• the activity of the chief Crown negotiator responsible for the
negotiation of treaties, claims and self-government accords.

2.3.47

The prime minister appoint a new minister of Indian and Inuit
services to

• act under the fiscal and policy guidance of the minister of
Aboriginal relations; and
• be responsible for delivery of the government's remaining
obligations to status Indians and reserve communities under
the *Indian Act* as well as to Inuit.

2.3.48

The prime minister establish a new permanent cabinet committee on Aboriginal relations that

• is chaired by the minister of Aboriginal relations;
• is cabinet's working forum to deliberate on its collective
responsibilities for Aboriginal matters; and
• takes the lead for cabinet in joint planning initiatives with
Aboriginal nations and their governments.

2.3.49

The government of Canada make a major effort to hire qualified Aboriginal staff to play central roles in
- the two new departments;
- other federal departments with specific policy or program responsibilities affecting Aboriginal people; and
- the central agencies of government.

2.3.50

The government of Canada implement these changes within a year of the publication of this report. Complying with this deadline sends a clear signal that the government of Canada not only intends to reform its fundamental relationship with Aboriginal peoples but is taking the first practical steps to do so.

An Aboriginal **2.3.51**
Parliament
The federal government, following extensive consultations with Aboriginal peoples, establish an Aboriginal parliament whose main function is to provide advice to the House of Commons and the Senate on legislation and constitutional matters relating to Aboriginal peoples.

2.3.52

The Aboriginal parliament be developed in the following manner:
- (a) the federal government, in partnership with representatives of national Aboriginal peoples' organizations, first establish a consultation process to develop an Aboriginal parliament; major decisions respecting the design, structure and functions of the Aboriginal parliament would rest with the Aboriginal peoples' representatives; and
- (b) following agreement among the parties, legislation be introduced in the Parliament of Canada before the next federal election, pursuant to section 91(24) of the *Constitution Act, 1867*, to create an Aboriginal parliament.

Elections to **2.3.53**
Aboriginal
Parliament
- (a) Aboriginal parliamentarians be elected by their nations or peoples; and
- (b) elections for the Aboriginal parliament take place at the same time as federal government elections to encourage Aboriginal people to participate and to add legitimacy to the process.

Enumeration **2.3.54**

The enumeration of Aboriginal voters take place during the general enumeration for the next federal election.

Regarding the fulfilment of Canada's international responsibilities with respect to Aboriginal peoples, the Commission recommends that

Self-Determination **2.3.1**
and International
Law
The government of Canada take the following actions:

(a) enact legislation affirming the obligations it has assumed under international human rights instruments to which it is a signatory in so far as these obligations pertain to the Aboriginal peoples of Canada;

(b) recognize that its fiduciary relationship with Aboriginal peoples requires it to enact legislation to give Aboriginal peoples access to a remedy in Canadian courts for breach of Canada's international commitments to them;

(c) expressly provide in such legislation that resort may be had in Canada's courts to international human rights instruments as an aid to the interpretation of the *Canadian Charter of Rights and Freedoms* and other Canadian law affecting Aboriginal peoples;

(d) commence consultations with provincial governments with the objective of ratifying and implementing International Labour Organisation Convention No. 169 on Indigenous Peoples, which came into force in 1991;

(e) support the Draft Declaration of the Rights of Indigenous Peoples of 1993, as it is being considered by the United Nations;

(f) immediately initiate planning, with Aboriginal peoples, to celebrate the International Decade of Indigenous Peoples and, as part of the events, initiate a program for international exchanges between Indigenous peoples in Canada and elsewhere.

Chapter 4 Lands and Resources

With respect to principles and policies governing the negotiation of a land base for each Aboriginal nation, the Commission recommends that

Principles Related **2.4.1**
to Land and
Aboriginal Title
Federal policy and all treaty-related processes (treaty making, implementation and renewal) conform to these general principles:

(a) Aboriginal title is a real interest in land that contemplates a range of rights with respect to lands and resources.

(b) Aboriginal title is recognized and affirmed by section 35(1) of the *Constitution Act, 1982.*

(c) The Crown has a special fiduciary obligation to protect the interests of Aboriginal people, including Aboriginal title.

(d) The Crown has an obligation to protect rights concerning lands and resources that underlie Aboriginal economies and the cultural and spiritual life of Aboriginal peoples.

(e) The Crown has an obligation to reconcile the interests of the public with Aboriginal title.

(f) Lands and resources issues will be included in negotiations for self-government.

(g) Aboriginal rights, including rights of self-government, recognized by an agreement are 'treaty rights' within the meaning of section 35(1) of the *Constitution Act, 1982.*

(h) Negotiations between the parties are premised on reaching agreements that recognize an inherent right of self-government.

(i) Blanket extinguishment of Aboriginal land rights will not be sought in exchange for other rights or benefits contained in an agreement.

(j) Partial extinguishment of Aboriginal land rights will not be a precondition for negotiations and will be agreed to by the parties only after a careful and exhaustive analysis of other options and the existence of clear, unpressured consent by the Aboriginal party.

(k) Agreements will be subject to periodic review and renewal.

(l) Agreements will contain dispute resolution mechanisms tailored to the circumstances of the parties.

(m) Agreements will provide for intergovernmental agreements to harmonize the powers of federal, provincial, territorial and Aboriginal governments without unduly limiting any.

Territory for Self-Reliance and Political Autonomy

2.4.2

Federal, provincial and territorial governments, through negotiation, provide Aboriginal nations with lands that are sufficient in size and quality to foster Aboriginal economic self-reliance and cultural and political autonomy.

Resources

2.4.3

The goal of negotiations be to ensure that Aboriginal nations, within their traditional territories, have

(a) exclusive or preferential access to certain renewable and non-renewable resources, including water, or to a guaranteed share of them;

(b) a guaranteed share of the revenues flowing from resources development; and

(c) specified preferential guarantees or priorities to the economic benefits and opportunities flowing from development projects (for example, negotiated community benefits packages and rights of first refusal).

Financial Transfers **2.4.4**

Aboriginal nations, through negotiation, receive, in addition to land, financial transfers, calculated on the basis of two criteria:

(a) *developmental needs* (capital to help the nation meet its future needs, especially relating to community and economic development); and

(b) *compensation* (partial restitution for past and present exploitation of the nation's traditional territory, including removal of resources as well as disruption of Aboriginal livelihood).

Determining **2.4.5**
Amount of Land

Negotiations on the amount and quality of additional lands, and access to resources, be guided by the

(a) size of the territory that the Aboriginal nation traditionally occupied, controlled, enjoyed, and used;

(b) nature and type of renewable and non-renewable resources, including water, that the Aboriginal nation traditionally had access to and used;

(c) current and projected Aboriginal population;

(d) current and projected economic needs of that population;

(e) current and projected cultural needs of that population;

(f) amount of reserve or settlement land now held by the Aboriginal nation;

(g) productivity and value of the lands and resources and the likely level of return from exploitation for a given purpose;

(h) amount of Crown land available in the treaty area; and

(i) nature and extent of third-party interests.

Land Selection **2.4.6**
Principles

In land selection negotiations, federal, provincial and territorial governments follow these principles:

(a) No unnecessary or arbitrary limits should be placed on lands for selection, such as

(i)   the exclusion of coastlines, shorelines, beds of water (including marine areas), potential hydroelectric power sites, or resource-rich areas;

(ii) arbitrary limits on size, shape or contiguity of lands; or

(iii) arbitrary limits on the ability of the Aboriginal nation to purchase land in order to expand its territory.

(b) Additional lands to be provided from existing Crown lands within the territory in question.

(c) Where parties are seeking to renew an historical treaty, land selection not be limited by existing treaty boundaries (for example, the metes and bounds descriptions contained in the post-Confederation numbered treaties).

(d) Provincial or territorial borders not constrain selection negotiations unduly.

(e) Where Crown lands are not available in sufficient quantity, financial resources be provided to enable land to be purchased from willing third parties.

Policy Principles **2.4.7**

The government of Canada adopt the principles outlined in recommendations 2.4.1 to 2.4.6 as policy to guide its interaction with Aboriginal peoples on matters of lands and resources allocation with respect to current and future negotiations and litigation.

2.4.8

The government of Canada propose these principles for adoption by provincial and territorial governments as well as national Aboriginal organizations during the development of the Canada-wide framework agreement.

2.4.9

Following such consultations, the government of Canada propose to Parliament that these principles, appropriately revised as a result of the consultations, be incorporated in an amendment to the legislation establishing the treaty processes.

Regarding categories of land ownership that result from negotiations and the determination of jurisdiction over them, the Commission recommends that

Three Categories **2.4.10**
of Lands Negotiations aim to describe the territory in question in terms of three categories of land. Using these three categories will help to identify, as thoroughly and precisely as possible, the rights of each of the parties with respect to lands, resources and governance.

Category I Lands   **2.4.11**

With respect to Category I lands,

(a) The Aboriginal nation has full rights of ownership and primary jurisdiction in relation to lands and renewable and non-renewable resources, including water, in accordance with the traditions of land tenure and governance of the nation in question.

(b) Category I lands comprise any existing reserve and settlement lands currently held by the Aboriginal nation, as well as additional lands necessary to foster economic and cultural self-reliance and political autonomy selected in accordance with the factors listed in recommendation 2.4.5.

Category II Lands   **2.4.12**

With respect to Category II lands,

(a) Category II lands would form a portion of the traditional territory of the Aboriginal nation, that portion being determined by the degree to which Category I lands foster Aboriginal self-reliance.

(b) A number of Aboriginal and Crown rights with respect to lands and resources would be recognized by the agreement, and rights of governance and jurisdiction could be shared among the parties.

Category III Lands   **2.4.13**

With respect to Category III lands, a complete set of Crown rights with respect to lands and governance would be recognized by the agreement, subject to residual Aboriginal rights of access to historical and sacred sites and hunting, fishing and trapping grounds, participation in national and civic ceremonies and events, and symbolic representation in certain institutions.

Legislative Authority   **2.4.14**

Aboriginal nations exercise legislative authority as follows:

(a) primary and paramount legislative authority on Category I lands;

(b) shared legislative authority on Category II lands; and

(c) limited, negotiated authority exercisable in respect of citizens of the nation living on Category III lands and elsewhere and in respect of access to historical and sacred sites, participation in national and civic ceremonies and events, and symbolic representation in certain institutions.

Protecting Third-Party Rights and Interests

2.4.15

As a general principle, lands currently held at common law in fee simple or, in Quebec, that are owned not be converted into Category I lands, unless purchased from willing sellers.

2.4.16

In exceptional cases where the Aboriginal nation's interests clearly outweigh the third party's rights and interests in a specific parcel, the Crown expropriate the land at fair market value on behalf of the Aboriginal party to convert it into Category I lands. This would be justified, for example, where

(a) a successful claim for the land might have been made under the existing specific claims policy based on the fact that reserve lands were unlawfully or fraudulently surrendered in the past; or

(b) the land is of outstanding traditional significance to the Aboriginal party (such as an Aboriginal cemetery or spiritual site or a place of substantial cultural significance).

2.4.17

Lands that at common law are held in fee simple or that in Quebec are owned can be included within Category II lands.

Lesser Interests on and Rights Less than Ownership in or in Relation to Crown Lands

2.4.18

Lands affected at common law by third-party interests less than fee simple or under the civil law by third-party rights of enjoyment other than ownership may be selected as Category I lands. If such lands are selected, the Aboriginal nation is to respect the original terms of all common law tenures and all civil law dismemberments of ownership and personal rights of enjoyment.

2.4.19

In exceptional circumstances, where Aboriginal interests significantly outweigh third-party rights and interests, the Crown revoke the common law tenure or the civil law dismemberment of ownership or personal right of enjoyment at fair market value on behalf of the Aboriginal party to convert it into Category I lands. Examples of when this would be justified are where

(a) a successful claim for the land might have been made under the existing specific claims policy (such as reserve lands unlawfully or fraudulently surrendered in the past); or

(b) the land is of outstanding traditional significance to the Aboriginal party (such as an Aboriginal cemetery or spiritual site or a place of substantial cultural significance.

2.4.20

Lands affected at common law by interests less than fee simple or under the civil law by rights of enjoyment other than ownership can be selected as Category II lands.

Parks and
Protected Areas

2.4.21

Existing parks and protected areas not be selected as Category I lands, except in exceptional cases where the Aboriginal nation's interests clearly outweigh the Crown's interests in a specific parcel. Examples of when this would be justified are where

(a) a successful claim for all or part of the park or protected area might have been made under the existing specific claims policy (such as reserve lands unlawfully or fraudulently surrendered in the past);

(b) all or part of the park or protected area is of outstanding traditional significance to the Aboriginal party (such as an Aboriginal cemetery or spiritual site); or

(c) a park occupies a substantial portion of a nation's territory.

2.4.22

Existing parks and protected areas, as well as lands being considered for protected area or park status, may be selected as Category II lands.

Public Interests on
Crown Land

2.4.23

Crown lands to which the public has access be available for selection as Category I or II lands.

Role of Provincial
Governments

2.4.26

Provincial governments establish policies parallel to the processes and reforms proposed in recommendations 2.4.1 to 2.4.22.

2.4.27

Provincial governments participate fully in the treaty-making and treaty implementation and renewal processes and in negotiations on interim relief agreements.

2.4.28

In addition to provisions made available under recommendations 2.4.2 to 2.4.5, provincial governments make Crown land available to an Aboriginal nation where traditional Aboriginal territory became provincial Crown land as the result of a breach of Crown duty.

With respect to measures to provide interim relief pending the resolution of
land negotiations, the Commission recommends that

Interim Relief **2.4.24**
Agreements Federal and provincial governments recognize, in the Canada-
wide framework agreement, the critical role of interim relief
agreements and agree on principles and procedures to govern
these agreements, providing for
(a) the partial withdrawal of lands that are the subject of
claims in a specific claims treaty process;
(b) Aboriginal participation and consent in the use or development of withdrawn lands; and
(c) revenues from royalties or taxation of resource developments on the withdrawn lands to be held in trust pending
the outcome of the negotiation.

2.4.25
In relation to treaties, the companion legislation to the proposed
royal proclamation state that the parties have a duty to make
reasonable efforts to reach an interim relief agreement.

Regarding the jurisdiction and operation of the Aboriginal Lands
and Treaties Tribunal, the Commission recommends that

Aboriginal Lands **2.4.29**
and Treaties Federal companion legislation to the royal proclamation pro-
Tribunal vide for the establishment of an independent administrative tribunal, to be called the Aboriginal Lands and Treaties Tribunal.

Jurisdiction of the **2.4.30**
Tribunal Parliament, and provincial legislatures when they are ready,
confer on the tribunal the necessary authority to enable it to dis-
charge its statutory mandate pertaining to both federal and
provincial spheres of jurisdiction.

2.4.31
Even without provincial delegation of powers to the tribunal,
Parliament confer on the tribunal jurisdiction to the full extent
of federal constitutional competence in respect of "Indians,
and Lands reserved for the Indians", including the power to
issue orders binding provincial governments and others, when
they relate essentially to this head of federal competence.

2.4.32

The tribunal be established by federal statute operative in two areas:
  (a) settlement of specific claims, including those removed by the Aboriginal party from the broader treaty-making, implementation and renewal processes; and
  (b) treaty-making, implementation and renewal processes.

2.4.33

In respect of specific claims, the tribunal's jurisdiction include
  (a) reviewing the adequacy of federal funding provided to claimants;
  (b) monitoring the good faith of the bargaining process and making binding orders on those in breach; and
  (c) adjudicating claims, or parts of claims, referred to it by Aboriginal claimants and providing an appropriate remedy where called for.

2.4.34

In respect of the longer-term treaty-making, implementation and renewal processes, the tribunal's jurisdiction include
  (a) reviewing the adequacy of federal funding to Aboriginal parties;
  (b) supervising the negotiation, implementation, and conclusion of interim relief agreements, imposing interim relief agreements in the event of a breach of the duty to bargain in good faith, and granting interim relief pending successful negotiations of a new or renewed treaty, with respect to federal lands and on provincial lands where provincial powers have been so delegated;
  (c) arbitrating any issues referred to it by the parties by mutual consent;
  (d) monitoring the good faith of the bargaining process;
  (e) adjudicating, on request of an Aboriginal party, questions of any Aboriginal or treaty rights that are related to the negotiations and justiciable in a court of law;
  (f) investigating a complaint of non-compliance with a treaty undertaking, adjudicating the dispute and awarding an appropriate remedy when so empowered by the treaty parties; and
  (g) recommending to the federal government, through panels established for the purpose, whether a group asserting the right of self-governance should be recognized as an Aboriginal nation.

2.4.35

The enabling legislation direct the tribunal to adopt a broad and progressive interpretation of the treaties, not limiting itself to technical rules of evidence, and to take into account the fiduciary obligations of the Crown, Aboriginal customary and property law, and the relevant history of the parties' relations.

2.4.36

The Aboriginal Lands and Treaties Tribunal replace the Indian Claims Commission.

Concurrent Jurisdiction

2.4.37

The tribunal's jurisdiction to determine specific claims be concurrent with the jurisdiction of the superior courts of the provinces.

Representation on Tribunal

2.4.38

The membership and staff of the tribunal
- (a) reflect parity between Aboriginal and non-Aboriginal nominees and staff at every level, including the co-chairs of the tribunal; and
- (b) be representative of the provinces and regions.

2.4.39

The process for appointing full-time and part-time members to the tribunal be as follows:
- (a) the appointment process be open;
- (b) nomination be by Aboriginal people, nations, or organizations, the federal government, and provinces that delegate powers to the tribunal;
- (c) nominees approved by a screening committee be qualified and fit to serve on the tribunal;
- (d) members be appointed by the federal government on the joint recommendation of the minister of justice and the proposed minister of Aboriginal relations; and
- (e) the terms of appointment of the co-chairs and members provide that, during their period of office, they be dismissable only for cause.

Structure and Procedure

2.4.40

The tribunal operate as follows:
- (a) emphasize informal procedures, respect the oral and cultural traditions of Aboriginal nations, and encourage direct participation by the parties;

(b) take an active role in ensuring the just and prompt resolution of disputes;

(c) maintain a small central research and legal staff and provide a registry for disputes; and

(d) hold hearings as close as is convenient to the site of the dispute, with panels comprising members from the region or province in question.

Judicial Review **2.4.41**

Decisions of the tribunal be final and binding and not subject to review by the courts, except on constitutional grounds and for jurisdictional error or breach of the duty of fairness under paragraphs 18.1(4)(a) and (b) of the *Federal Court Act.*

Concerning interim steps to expand First Nations' land base, the Commission recommends that

Interim Protocol on Specific Claims **2.4.43**

The federal government enter into an interim specific claims protocol with the Assembly of First Nations embodying, at a minimum, the following changes to current policy:

(a) the scope of the specific claims policy be expanded to include treaty-based claims;

(b) the definition of 'lawful obligation' and the compensation guidelines contained in the policy embody fiduciary principles, in keeping with Supreme Court decisions on government's obligations to Aboriginal peoples;

(c) where a claim involves the loss of land, the government of Canada use all efforts to provide equivalent land in compensation; only if restitution is impossible, or not desired by the First Nation, should claims be settled in cash;

(d) to expedite claims, the government of Canada provide significant additional resources for funding, negotiation and resolution of claims;

(e) the government of Canada improve access to the Indian Claims Commission and other dispute resolution mechanisms as a means of addressing interpretations of the specific claims policy, including submission to mediation and arbitration if requested by claimants; and

(f) the government of Canada respond to recommendations of the Indian Claims Commission within 90 days of receipt, and where it disagrees with such a recommendation, give specific written reasons.

Treaty Land **2.4.44**
Entitlements

The treaty land entitlement process be conducted as follows:

(a) the amount of land owing under treaty be calculated on the basis of population figures as of the date new negotiations begin;

(b) those population figures include urban residents, Bill C-31 beneficiaries and non-status Indians; and

(c) the federal government negotiate agreements with the provinces stipulating that a full range of land (including lands of value) be available for treaty land entitlement selection.

Purchase of Land **2.4.45**

Land purchases be conducted as follows:

(a) the federal government set up a land acquisition fund to enable all Aboriginal peoples (First Nations, Inuit and Métis) to purchase land on the open market;

(b) the basic principles of 'willing seller, willing buyer' apply to all land purchases;

(c) joint committees, with representatives from municipalities and neighbouring Aboriginal governments, be formed to deal with issues of common concern;

(d) the federal government do its utmost to encourage the creation of such committees;

(e) the federal government clarify the 1991 additions to reserves policy to ensure that the process of consultation with municipalities does not give them a veto over whether purchased lands are given reserve status; and

(f) the federal government compensate municipalities for the loss of tax assessment for a fixed sum or specific term (not an indefinite period), if the municipality can show that such loss would result from the transfer of the purchased lands to reserve status.

Unsold **2.4.46**
Surrendered Lands

Unsold surrendered lands be dealt with as follows:

(a) the Department of Indian Affairs and Northern Development compile an inventory of all remaining unsold surrendered lands in the departmental land registry;

(b) unsold surrendered lands be returned to the community that originally surrendered them;

(c) First Nations have the option of accepting alternative lands or financial compensation instead of the lands originally surrendered but not be compelled to accept either; and

(d) governments negotiate protection of third-party interests affected by the return of unsold surrendered lands, such as continued use of waterways and rights of access to private lands.

Return of Expropriated Lands

2.4.47

If reserve or community lands were expropriated by or surrendered to the Crown for a public purpose and the original purpose no longer exists, the lands be dealt with as follows:

(a) the land revert to the First Nations communities in question;

(b) if the expropriation was for the benefit of a third party (for example, a railway), the First Nations communities have the right of first refusal on such lands;

(c) any costs of acquisition of these lands be negotiated between the Crown and the First Nation, depending on the compensation given the First Nation community when the land was first acquired;

(d) if the land was held by the Crown, the costs associated with clean-up and environmental monitoring be borne by the government department or agency that controlled the lands;

(e) if the land was held by a third party, the costs associated with clean-up and environmental monitoring be borne jointly by the Crown and the third party;

(f) if an Aboriginal community does not wish the return of expropriated lands because of environmental damage or other reasons, they receive other lands in compensation or financial compensation equivalent to fair market value; and

(g) the content of such compensation package be determined by negotiation or, failing that, by the Aboriginal Lands and Treaties Tribunal.

Regarding interim measures to improve Aboriginal peoples'
access to resource-based economic opportunities,
the Commission recommends that

Access to Natural Resources

2.4.48

With respect to the general issue of improving Aboriginal access to natural resources on Crown land:

(a) the federal government seek the co-operation of provincial and territorial governments in drafting a national code of principles to recognize and affirm the continued exercise of traditional Aboriginal activities (hunting, fishing, trapping and gathering of medicinal and other plants) on Crown lands; and

(b) the provinces and territories amend relevant legislation to incorporate such a code.

On-Reserve Forest Resources **2.4.49**

With respect to forest resources on reserves, the federal government take the following steps:

(a) immediately provide adequate funding to complete forest inventories, management plans and reforestation of Indian lands;

(b) ensure that adequate forest management expertise is available to First Nations;

(c) consult with Aboriginal governments to develop a joint policy statement delineating their respective responsibilities in relation to Indian reserve forests;

(d) develop an operating plan to implement its own responsibilities as defined through the joint policy development process;

(e) continue the Indian forest lands program, but modify its objectives to reflect and integrate traditional knowledge and the resource values of First Nations communities with objectives of timber production; and

(f) in keeping with the goal of Aboriginal nation building, provide for the delivery of the Indian forest lands program by First Nations organizations (as has been the case with the Treaty 3 region of northwestern Ontario).

Crown Forests **2.4.50**

The following steps be taken with respect to Aboriginal access to forest resources on Crown lands:

(a) the federal government work with the provinces, the territories and Aboriginal communities to improve Aboriginal access to forest resources on Crown lands;

(b) the federal government, as part of its obligation to protect traditional Aboriginal activities on provincial Crown lands, actively promote Aboriginal involvement in provincial forest management and planning; as with the model forest program, this would include bearing part of the costs;

(c) the federal government, in keeping with the goal of Aboriginal nation building, give continuing financial and logistical support to Aboriginal peoples' regional and national forest resources associations;

(d) the provinces encourage their large timber licensees to provide for forest management partnerships with Aboriginal firms within the traditional territories of Aboriginal communities;

(e) the provinces encourage partnerships or joint ventures between Aboriginal forest operating companies and other firms that already have wood processing facilities;

(f) the provinces give Aboriginal people the right of first refusal on unallocated Crown timber close to reserves or Aboriginal communities;

(g) the provinces, to promote greater harmony with generally less intensive Aboriginal forest management practices and traditional land-use activities, show greater flexibility in their timber management policies and guidelines; this might include reducing annual allowable cut requirements and experimenting with lower harvesting rates, smaller logging areas and longer maintenance of areas left unlogged;

(h) provincial and territorial governments make provision for a special role for Aboriginal governments in reviewing forest management and operating plans within their traditional territories; and

(i) provincial and territorial governments make Aboriginal land-use studies a requirement of all forest management plans.

Mining, Oil and Natural Gas Resources on Reserves

2.4.51

In keeping with its fiduciary obligation to Aboriginal peoples, the federal government renegotiate existing agreements with the provinces (for example, the 1924 agreement with Ontario and the 1930 natural resource transfer agreements in the prairie provinces) to ensure that First Nations obtain the full beneficial interest in minerals, oil and natural gas located on reserves.

2.4.52

The federal government amend the Indian mining regulations to conform to the Indian oil and gas regulations and require companies operating on reserves to employ First Nations residents.

2.4.53

The federal government work with First Nations and the mining industry (and if necessary amend the Indian mining regulations and the Indian oil and gas regulations) to ensure the development of management experience among Aboriginal people and the transfer to them of industry knowledge and expertise.

Resources on Crown Lands **2.4.54**

The provinces require companies, as part of their operating licence, to develop Aboriginal land use plans to

(a) protect traditional harvesting and other areas (for example, sacred sites); and

(b) compensate those adversely affected by mining or drilling (for example, Aboriginal hunters, trappers and fishers).

2.4.55

Land use plans be developed in consultation with affected Aboriginal communities as follows:

(a) Aboriginal communities receive intervener funding to carry out the consultation process;

(b) intervener funding be delivered through a body at arm's length from the company and the respective provincial ministry responsible for the respective natural resource; and

(c) funding for this body come from licence fees and from provincial or federal government departments responsible for the environment.

2.4.56

The provinces require that a compensation fund be set up and that contributions to it be part of licence fees. Alternatively, governments could consider this an allowable operating expense for corporate tax purposes.

2.4.57

The federal government work with the provinces and with Aboriginal communities to ensure that the steps we recommend are carried out. Federal participation could include cost-sharing arrangements with the provinces.

Wildlife Harvesting **2.4.62**

The principles enunciated by the Supreme Court of Canada in the *Sparrow* decision be implemented as follows:

(a) provincial and territorial governments ensure that their regulatory and management regimes acknowledge the priority of Aboriginal subsistence harvesting;

(b) for the purposes of the *Sparrow* priorities, the definition of 'conservation' not be established by government officials, but be negotiated with Aboriginal governments and incorporate respect for traditional ecological knowledge and Aboriginal principles of resource management; and

(c) the subsistence needs of non-Aboriginal people living in remote regions of Canada (that is, long-standing residents of remote areas, not transients) be ranked next in the *Sparrow* order of priority after those of Aboriginal people and ahead of all commercial or recreational fish and wildlife harvesting.

Fishing **2.4.63**

All provinces follow the example set by Canada and certain provinces (for example, Ontario and British Columbia) in buying up and turning over commercial fishing quotas to Aboriginal people. This would constitute partial restitution for historical inequities in commercial allocations.

2.4.64

The size of Aboriginal commercial fishing allocations be based on measurable criteria that

(a) are developed by negotiation rather than developed and imposed unilaterally by government;

(b) are not based, for example, on a community's aggregate subsistence needs alone; and

(c) recognize the fact that resources are essential for building Aboriginal economies and that Aboriginal people must be able to make a profit from their commercial fisheries.

2.4.65

Canada and the provinces apply the priorities set out in the *Sparrow* decision to Aboriginal commercial fisheries so that these fisheries in times of scarcity

(a) have greater priority than non-Aboriginal commercial interests and sport fishing; and

(b) remain ranked below conservation and Aboriginal (and, in remote areas, non-Aboriginal) domestic food fishing.

2.4.66

The federal government ensure effective Aboriginal representation on the Canadian commission set up under the 1985 Pacific Salmon Treaty with the United States.

2.4.67

To establish adequate baseline data for assessing the relative impact of the Aboriginal and non-Aboriginal harvest, and to assist in determining quotas to be allocated in accordance with the principles set out in the *Sparrow* decision, federal and provincial governments improve their data gathering on the non-Aboriginal harvest of fish and wildlife.

2.4.68

Federal and provincial governments carry out joint studies with Aboriginal people to determine the size of the Aboriginal harvest and the respective effects of Aboriginal and non-Aboriginal harvesting methods on stocks.

2.4.69

Public education form a major component of government fisheries policy. This will require joint strategies to inform the public about Aboriginal perspectives on fishing, to resolve differences and to overcome fears that Aboriginal entry into fisheries will mean overfishing, loss of control, or loss of property.

Hunting **2.4.70**

Provincial and territorial governments take the following action with respect to hunting:

(a) acknowledge that treaty harvesting rights apply throughout the entire area covered by treaty, even if that area includes more than one province or territory;

(b) leave it to Aboriginal governments to work out the kinds of reciprocal arrangements necessary for Aboriginal harvesting across treaty boundaries; and

(c) introduce specific big game quotas or seasons for local non-Aboriginal residents in the mid- and far north.

Outfitting **2.4.71**

Provincial and territorial governments take the following action with respect to outfitting:

(a) increase their allocation of tourist outfitters' licences or leases to Aboriginal people, for example,

(i) by including exclusive allocations in certain geographical areas, as Ontario now does north of the 50th parallel;

(ii) by giving priority of access for a defined period to all new licences; and

(iii) by giving Aboriginal people the right of first refusal on licences or leases that are being given up.

(b) not impose one particular style of outfitting business (lodge-based fly-in hunting and fishing) as the only model; and

(c) encourage Aboriginal people to develop outfitting businesses based on their own cultural values.

Trapping **2.4.72**

By agreement, and subject to local capacity, provincial and territorial governments devolve trapline management to Aboriginal governments.

2.4.73

In Quebec, where exclusive Aboriginal trapping preserves have existed for many decades, the provincial government devolve trapline management of these territories to Aboriginal governments and share overall management responsibilities with them.

Water Resources **2.4.74**

Unless already dealt with in a comprehensive land claims agreement, revenues from commercial water developments (hydroelectric dams and commercial irrigation projects) that already exist and operate within the traditional land use areas of Aboriginal communities be directed to the communities affected as follows:

(a) they receive a continuous portion of the revenues derived from the development for the life of the project; and

(b) the amount of revenues be the subject of negotiations between the Aboriginal community(ies) and either the hydroelectric utility or the province.

Socio-Economic **2.4.75**
Agreements
If potential hydroelectric development sites exist within the traditional territory(ies) of the Aboriginal community(ies), the community have the right of first refusal to acquire the water rights for hydro development.

2.4.76

If a Crown utility or non-utility company already has the right to develop a hydro site within the traditional territory of an Aboriginal community, the provinces require these companies to develop socio-economic agreements (training, employment, business contracts, joint venture, equity partnerships) with the affected Aboriginal community as part of their operating licence or procedures.

Shared
Management of
Water Resources

2.4.77

Federal and provincial governments revise their water management policy and legislation to accommodate Aboriginal participation in existing management processes as follows:

(a) the federal government amend the *Canada Water Act* to provide for guaranteed Aboriginal representation on existing interjurisdictional management boards (for example, the Lake of the Woods Control Board) and establish federal/provincial/Aboriginal arrangements where none currently exist; and

(b) provincial governments amend their water resource legislation to provide for Aboriginal participation in water resource planning and for the establishment of co-management boards on their traditional lands.

With regard to measures to implement co-jurisdiction or co-management of lands and resources, the Commission recommends that

Co-management
and Jurisdiction

2.4.78

The following action be taken with respect to co-management and co-jurisdiction:

(a) the federal government work with provincial and territorial governments and Aboriginal governments in creating co-management or co-jurisdiction arrangements for the traditional territories of Aboriginal nations;

(b) such co-management arrangements serve as interim measures until the conclusion of treaty negotiations with the Aboriginal party concerned;

(c) co-management bodies be based on relative parity of membership between Aboriginal nations and government representatives;

(d) co-management bodies respect and incorporate the traditional knowledge of Aboriginal people; and

(e) provincial and territorial governments provide secure long-term funding for co-management bodies to ensure stability and enable them to build the necessary management skills and expertise (which would involve cost sharing on the part of the federal government).

Regarding the ownership and management of cultural and historic sites,
the Commission recommends that

Cultural Heritage **2.4.58**
Federal, provincial and territorial governments enact legislation
to establish a process aimed at recognizing
(a) Aboriginal peoples as the owners of cultural sites, archaeological resources, religious and spiritual objects, and sacred
and burial sites located within their traditional territories;
(b) Aboriginal people as having sole jurisdiction over sacred,
ceremonial, spiritual and burial sites within their traditional territories, whether these sites are located on unoccupied Crown land or on occupied Crown lands (such as
on lands under forest tenure or parks);
(c) Aboriginal people as having at least shared jurisdiction
over all other sites (such as historical camps or villages, fur
trade posts or fishing stations); and
(d) Aboriginal people as being entitled to issue permits and
levy (or share in) the fees charged for access to, or use of,
such sites.

2.4.59
In the case of heritage sites located on private land, the federal
government negotiate with landowners to acknowledge
Aboriginal jurisdiction and rights of access or to purchase these
sites if there is a willing seller, so that they can be turned over
to the appropriate Aboriginal government.

2.4.60
The federal government amend the *National Parks Act* to permit
traditional Aboriginal activity in national parks and, where
appropriate, Aboriginal ownership of national parks, on the
Australian model. Parks could then be leased back to the Crown
and managed jointly by federal and Aboriginal governments.

2.4.61
Federal, provincial and territorial governments develop legislation and policies to protect and manage Aboriginal heritage
resources in accordance with criteria set by negotiation with
Aboriginal governments. These might include
(a) detailed heritage impact assessment and protection guidelines for operations involving such activities as forestry,

mining, aggregate extraction, road building, tourism and recreation;

(b) funding and undertaking heritage resource inventories, documentation and related research, and archaeological and other scientific survey, in partnership with Aboriginal governments; and

(c) carrying out salvage excavation or mitigative measures at sites threatened by development, looting, resource extraction or natural causes such as erosion, and providing for Aboriginal monitoring of archaeological excavations.

With respect to public involvement in lands negotiations, the Commission recommends that

Public Education **2.4.42**

Public education be a major part of treaty processes and of the mandates of the treaty commissions and Aboriginal Lands and Treaties Tribunal, in keeping with the following principles:

(a) federal and provincial governments keep the public fully informed about the nature and scope of negotiations with Aboriginal peoples and not unduly restrict the release of internal reports and other research material;

(b) Aboriginal parties participate in educating the general public and ensure that their members fully understand the nature and scope of their negotiations with provincial and federal governments;

(c) the federal government ensure that negotiation processes have sufficient funding for public education; and

(d) treaties and similar documents be written in clear and understandable language.

Chapter 5 Economic Development

With respect to co-operative arrangements between Aboriginal and other governments in Canada to promote economic development, the Commission recommends that

Economic Development Agreements **2.5.1**

Federal, provincial and territorial governments enter into long-term economic development agreements with Aboriginal nations, or institutions representing several nations, to provide multi-year funding to support economic development.

2.5.2

Economic development agreements have the following characteristics:

(a) the goals and principles for Aboriginal economic development be agreed upon by the parties;

(b) resources from all government agencies and departments with an economic development-related mandate be channelled through the agreement;

(c) policies and instruments to achieve the goals be designed by the Aboriginal party;

(d) development activities include, but not necessarily be limited to, training, economic planning, provision of business services, equity funding, and loans and loan guarantees;

(e) performance under the agreement be monitored every two years against agreed criteria; and

(f) funds available for each agreement be determined on the basis of need, capacity to use the resources, and progress of the Aboriginal entity toward self-reliance.

2.5.3

Aboriginal nations that have negotiated modern treaties encompassing full self-government have full jurisdiction over their economic development programs, which should be funded through their treaty settlements, fiscal transfers and their own revenue sources, and that businesses on these territories continue to be eligible for regional, business or trade development programs administered by Canadian governments for businesses generally.

2.5.5

Aboriginal nations receive financial and technical support to establish and develop economic institutions through the federal funding we propose be made available for the reconstruction of Aboriginal nations and their institutions (see recommendations in Chapter 3 of this volume).

With regard to building capacity within Aboriginal nations to pursue economic development, the Commission recommends that

Building Economic Institutions

2.5.4

Aboriginal nations give high priority to establishing and developing economic institutions that

• reflect the nation's underlying values;

- are designed to be accountable to the nation; and
- are protected from inappropriate political interference.

Nation and Community Levels

2.5.6

Responsibility for economic development be divided between the nation and community governments so that policy capacity, specialist services and major investment responsibility reside with the nation's institutions, which would then interact with community economic development personnel at the community level.

Research Capacity

2.5.7

The recommended Aboriginal Peoples' International University establish a Canada-wide research and development capacity in Aboriginal economic development with close links to the developing network of Aboriginally controlled education and training institutions.

Beneficial Relationships

2.5.8

Leaders of municipalities, counties and larger regional bodies and their Aboriginal counterparts consider how to reduce the isolation between them and develop a mutually beneficial relationship.

Recognizing the importance of lands and resources to Aboriginal economic development, the Commission recommends that

Lands and Resources for Self-Reliance

2.5.12

Federal and provincial governments promote Aboriginal economic development by recognizing that lands and resources are a major factor in enabling Aboriginal nations and their communities to become self-reliant.

Private Sector Initiatives

2.5.9

Until self-government and co-jurisdiction arrangements are made, federal and provincial governments require third parties that are renewing or obtaining new resource licences on traditional Aboriginal territories to provide significant benefits to Aboriginal communities, including
- preferential training and employment opportunities in all aspects of the resource operation;
- preferred access to supply contracts;
- respect for traditional uses of the territory; and
- acceptance of Aboriginal environmental standards.

2.5.10

The efforts of resource development companies, Aboriginal nations and communities, and governments be directed to expanding the range of benefits derived from resource development in traditional territories to achieve

- levels of training and employment above the entry level, including managerial;
- an equity position in resource development projects; and
- a share of economic rents derived from the projects.

2.5.11

Unions in these resource sectors participate in and co-operate with implementation of this policy, because of the extraordinary under-representation of Aboriginal people in these industries.

Developing Institutional Capacity

2.5.13

Aboriginal governments, with the financial and technical support of federal, provincial and territorial governments, undertake to strengthen their capacity to manage and develop lands and resources. This requires in particular

(a) establishing or strengthening, as appropriate, Aboriginal institutions for the management and development of Aboriginal lands and resources;

(b) identifying the knowledge and skills requirements needed to staff such institutions;

(c) undertaking urgent measures in education, training and work experience to prepare Aboriginal personnel in these areas;

(d) enlisting communities in dedicated efforts to support and sustain their people in acquiring the necessary education, training and work experience; and

(e) seconding personnel from other governments and agencies so that these institutions can exercise their mandates.

Regarding the role of agriculture in economic development, the Commission recommends that

Developing Aboriginal Agriculture

2.5.14

The government of Canada remove from Aboriginal economic development strategies such as CAEDS and related programs any limitations that impede equitable access to them by Métis farmers and Aboriginal owners of small farms generally.

2.5.15
The government of Canada restore the funding of Indian agricultural organizations and related programs and support similar organizations and services for Métis farmers.

2.5.16
Band councils, with the support of the federal government, undertake changes in patterns of land tenure and land use so that efficient, viable reserve farms or ranches can be established.

2.5.17
The government of Canada implement the recommendations of the Aboriginal Agriculture Industrial Adjustment Services Committee designed to advance the education and training of Aboriginal people in agriculture.

With respect to measures to promote business development, the Commission recommends that

Business Services **2.5.18**
Governments, as a high priority, improve their economic development programming by
(a) developing business advisory services that combine professional expertise with detailed knowledge of Aboriginal communities; and
(b) placing these advisory services within the emerging economic development institutions of Aboriginal nations.

Access to Markets **2.5.19**
The capacity for trade promotion be built into the sectoral and other economic development organizations of Aboriginal nations, as appropriate.

2.5.20
The international trade promotion agencies of the federal and provincial governments, in co-operation with Aboriginal producers and economic development institutions, actively seek out markets for Aboriginal goods and services abroad.

2.5.21
Provincial and territorial governments join the federal government in establishing effective set-aside programs to benefit Aboriginal businesses and that municipal governments with large proportions of Aboriginal residents also undertake these programs.

Regarding the financing of Aboriginal economic and business development, the Commission recommends that

Making Banking Services Available

2.5.22

Banks, trust companies and credit union federations (the caisses populaires in Quebec), with the regulatory and financial assistance of federal, provincial and territorial governments, take immediate and effective steps to make banking services available in or readily accessible to all Aboriginal communities in Canada.

Micro-Business Lending and Support Programs

2.5.23

Federal, provincial and territorial governments, as well as financial institutions, support the development of micro-lending programs as an important tool to develop very small businesses. Governments and institutions should make capital available to these programs and support the operating costs of the organizations that manage them.

Revolving Community Loan Funds

2.5.24

Revolving community loan funds be developed and that federal, provincial and territorial governments review their policies about the establishment and operation of such funds and remove administrative and other barriers.

Access to Equity Capital

2.5.25

Federal and Aboriginal governments ensure that programs to provide equity to Aboriginal entrepreneurs
- continue for at least 10 more years;
- have sufficient resources to operate at a level of business formation equivalent to the highest rate experienced in the last decade; and
- allow for a growth rate of a minimum 5 per cent a year from that level.

2.5.26

The contribution of equity capital from government programs always be conditional on the individual entrepreneur providing some of the equity required by the business from the entrepreneur's own funds.

2.5.27

Resources for economic development be an important element in treaty settlements.

2.5.28

Aboriginal nations that have entered into modern treaties, including comprehensive claims, fund their programs to provide equity contributions to entrepreneurs from their own revenue sources, with businesses retaining access to all government programs available to mainstream Canadian businesses.

2.5.29

Equity contribution programs funded by the federal government be administered as follows:

(a) Programs be administered wherever possible by Aboriginal institutions according to development arrangements set out above.

(b) Funds for this purpose be allocated to the nation concerned as part of a general economic development agreement.

(c) Programs be administered by federal officials only where Aboriginal institutions have not developed to serve the client base.

Aboriginal Capital Corporations **2.5.30**

The federal government strengthen the network of Aboriginal capital corporations (ACCs) through measures such as

- providing operating subsidies to well-managed ACCs to acknowledge their developmental role;
- enabling ACCs to administer Canada Mortgage and Housing Corporation and DIAND housing funds; and
- providing interest rate subsidies and loan guarantees on capital ACCs raise from the private sector.

2.5.31

Aboriginal capital corporations take appropriate measures, with the assistance of the federal government, to improve

•their administrative efficiency;

•their degree of collaboration with other ACCs; and

•their responsiveness to segments of the Aboriginal population that have not been well served in the past.

Venture Capital Corporations **2.5.32**

Federal and provincial governments assist in the formation of Aboriginal venture capital corporations by extending tax credits to investors in such corporations. These corporations should have a status similar to labour-sponsored venture capital corporations and should be subject to the same stringent performance requirements. Tax credits should be available to the extent that Aboriginal venture capital corporations invest in projects that benefit Aboriginal people.

National Aboriginal Development Bank

2.5.33

A national Aboriginal development bank be established, staffed and controlled by Aboriginal people, with capacity to
* provide equity and loan financing, and technical assistance to large-scale Aboriginal business projects; and
* offer development bonds and similar vehicles to raise capital from private individuals and corporations for Aboriginal economic development, with such investments being eligible for tax credits.

2.5.34

The process for establishing the bank be as follows:
* The federal government, with the appropriate Aboriginal organizations, undertakes the background studies required to establish a bank.
* Aboriginal governments develop the proposal to establish the bank and, along with private sources, provide the initial capital. The federal government should match that capital in the initial years, retiring its funding as the bank reaches an agreed level of growth. Earnings on the portion of the capital lent by the federal government would be available to increase the rate of return to private investors in the early years of the bank's operations.
* The federal government introduces the necessary legislation in Parliament.
* Highly experienced management is hired by the bank with a clear mandate to recruit and train outstanding Aboriginal individuals for leadership of the bank's future operations.

2.5.35

The board of directors of the bank have an Aboriginal majority and be chosen for their expertise.

With respect to employment development, the Commission recommends that

Special Employment and Training Initiative

2.5.36

Federal and provincial governments fund a major 10-year initiative for employment development and training that is

- aimed at preparing Aboriginal people for much greater participation in emerging employment opportunities;
- sponsored by Aboriginal nations or regionally based Aboriginal institutions;
- developed in collaboration with public and private sector employers and educational and training institutions; and
- mandatory for public sector employers.

2.5.37

This initiative include

- identification of future employment growth by sector;
- classroom and on-the-job training for emerging employment opportunities;
- term employment with participating employers; and
- permanent employment based on merit.

Employment Equity ### 2.5.38

Employment equity programs for Aboriginal people adopt a new long-term approach involving

- the forecasting by employers of labour force needs; and
- the development of strategies, in collaboration with Aboriginal employment services and other organizations, for training and qualifying Aboriginal people to fill positions in fields identified through forecasting.

2.5.39

These employment equity programs be strengthened by

- expanding the range of employers covered by federal, provincial and territorial legislation; and
- making the auditing, monitoring and enforcement mechanisms more effective.

Employment Services ### 2.5.40

Canadian governments provide the resources to enable Aboriginal employment service agencies to

(a) locate in all major urban areas;
(b) have stable, long-term financial support;
(c) play a lead role in the 10-year employment initiative, contribute to the effectiveness of employment equity, and offer the wide range of services required by a diverse clientele; and
(d) evolve from being a program of federal, provincial and territorial governments to being one of the services pro-

vided by Aboriginal institutions on behalf of Aboriginal governments where appropriate, with appropriate financial transfers to be negotiated.

Employment Opportunities in Aboriginal Communities

2.5.41

Aboriginal nations adopt policies whereby
- their members continue to assume positions in the public service within their communities;
- as much as possible, they buy goods and services from Aboriginal companies; and
- they provide opportunities for skills development, business growth and the recycling of spending within their communities.

Child Care

2.5.42

Aboriginal, federal, provincial and territorial governments enter into agreements to establish roles, policies and funding mechanisms to ensure that child care needs are met in all Aboriginal communities.

2.5.43

The federal government resume funding research and pilot projects, such as those funded under the Child Care Initiatives Fund, until alternative, stable funding arrangements for child care services can be established.

2.5.44

Aboriginal organizations and governments assign a high priority to the provision of child care services in conjunction with major employment and business development initiatives, encouraging an active role for community volunteers as well as using social assistance funding to meet these needs.

2.5.45

Provincial and territorial governments amend their legislation respecting the licensing and monitoring of child care services to provide more flexibility in the standards for certification and for facilities that take into account the special circumstances of Aboriginal peoples.

Education and Training

2.5.46

To rebuild Aboriginal economies, all governments pay particular attention to

- the importance of enrolment in education and training programs and of retention and graduation;
- strengthening the teaching of mathematics and the sciences at the elementary and secondary levels;
- improving access to and completion of mathematics and science-based programs at the post-secondary level; and
- making appropriate programs of study available in fields that are relevant to the economic development of Aboriginal communities (for example, business management, economic development and the management of lands and resources).

With respect to restructuring social assistance programs to support employment and social development, the Commission recommends that

Employment and Social Development

2.5.47

Social assistance funds be directed toward a more dynamic system of programming that supports employment and social development in Aboriginal communities, whether in rural or urban settings.

2.5.48

Governments providing financial support for social assistance encourage and support proposals from Aboriginal nations and communities to make innovative use of social assistance funds for employment and social development purposes and that Aboriginal nations and communities have the opportunity

(a) to pursue personal development, training and employment under an individual entitlement approach, and

(b) to pursue the improvement of community infrastructure and social and economic development under a community entitlement approach.

2.5.49

In their active use of social assistance and other income support funds, Aboriginal nations and communities not be restricted to promoting participation in the wage economy but also be encouraged to support continued participation in the traditional mixed economy through income support for hunters, trappers and fishers and through other projects aimed at improving community life.

Aboriginal Control of Programming

2.5.50

Aboriginal control over the design and administration of social assistance programs be the foundation of any reform of the social assistance system.

2.5.51

All governments support a holistic approach to social assistance programming for Aboriginal peoples that is
- rooted in Aboriginal society, its traditions and values;
- aimed at integrating social and economic development; and
- explicitly included in the design and operation of any new institutions or programs created to implement social assistance reform as it relates to Aboriginal people and communities.

2.5.52

Initiatives to reform the design and administration of social assistance encourage proposals from Aboriginal nations and tribal councils, acting on behalf of and in co-operation with their member communities.

VOLUME 3

GATHERING STRENGTH

Chapter 2 The Family

The Commission recommends that

Authority for Child Welfare

3.2.1

The government of Canada acknowledge a fiduciary responsibility to support Aboriginal nations and their communities in restoring Aboriginal families to a state of health and wholeness.

3.2.2

Aboriginal, provincial, territorial and federal governments promptly acknowledge that child welfare is a core area of self-government in which Aboriginal nations can undertake self-starting initiatives.

3.2.3

Aboriginal, provincial, territorial and federal governments promptly reach agreements on the authority of Aboriginal nations and their communities for child welfare, and its relation to provincial, territorial and federal laws respecting child welfare.

Funding Child
Welfare Agencies

3.2.4

Block funding be provided to child welfare agencies mandated by Aboriginal governments or communities to facilitate a shift in focus from alternative child care to family support.

Voluntary Agencies

3.2.5

Until community of interest governments are established in urban and non-reserve areas, voluntary agencies endorsed by substantial numbers of Aboriginal people resident in the areas be authorized under provincial or territorial law to act in the field of child welfare

(a) where numbers warrant; and

(b) with levels of funding comparable to those of agencies providing comparable services to the general population and sufficient to meet the service needs of Aboriginal people.

Leadership Stance

3.2.6

Aboriginal leaders take a firm, public stance in support of the right to freedom from violence of all members in the community, but particularly of women, children, elders, persons with disabilities and others who may be vulnerable, as well as in support of a policy of zero tolerance of actions that violate the physical or emotional safety of Aboriginal persons.

Breadth of
Representation

3.2.7

Aboriginal governments adopt the principle of including women, youth, elders and persons with disabilities in governing councils and decision-making bodies, the modes of representation and participation of these persons being whatever they find most agreeable.

Participation of
Women

3.2.8

The full and equal participation of women be ensured in decision-making bodies responsible for ensuring people's physical and emotional security, including justice committees and boards of directors of healing centres and lodges.

Community Codes
of Behaviour

3.2.9

Aboriginal leaders and agencies serving vulnerable people encourage communities, with the full participation of women, to formulate, promote and enforce community codes of behaviour that reflect ethical standards endorsed by the community and that state and reinforce the responsibility of all citizens to create and maintain safe communities and neighbourhoods.

Core Area of Self-Government **3.2.10**

Federal, provincial and territorial governments promptly acknowledge that the field of family law is generally a core area of Aboriginal self-governing jurisdiction, in which Aboriginal nations can undertake self-starting initiatives without prior federal, provincial or territorial agreements.

Validity of Customary Law **3.2.11**

Federal, provincial and territorial governments acknowledge the validity of Aboriginal customary law in areas of family law, such as marriage, divorce, child custody and adoption, and amend their legislation accordingly.

Consultation on Family Law **3.2.12**

Aboriginal nations or organizations consult with federal, provincial and territorial governments on areas of family law with a view to

(a) making possible legislative amendments to resolve anomalies in the application of family law to Aboriginal people and to fill current gaps;

(b) working out appropriate mechanisms of transition to Aboriginal control under self-government; and

(c) settling issues of mutual interest on the recognition and enforcement of the decisions of their respective adjudicative bodies.

Family Law Committees **3.2.13**

With a view to self-starting initiatives in the family law area or to self-government, Aboriginal nations or communities establish committees, with women as full participants, to study issues such as

(a) the interests of family members in family assets;

(b) the division of family assets on marriage breakdown;

(c) factors to be considered in relation to the best interests of the child, as the principle is applicable to Aboriginal custody and adoption;

(d) rights of inheritance pertaining to wills, estates or intestacy; and

(e) obligations of spousal and child support.

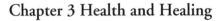

Chapter 3 Health and Healing

The Commission recommends that

Fundamental Principles

3.3.1

Aboriginal, federal, provincial and territorial governments, in developing policy to support health, acknowledge the common understanding of the determinants of health found in Aboriginal traditions and health sciences and endorse the fundamental importance of

- holism, that is, attention to whole persons in their total environment;
- equity, that is, equitable access to the means of achieving health and rough equality of outcomes in health status;
- control by Aboriginal people of the lifestyle choices, institutional services and environmental conditions that support health; and
- diversity, that is, accommodation of the cultures and histories of First Nations, Inuit and Métis people that make them distinctive within Canadian society and that distinguish them from one another.

Health: A Core Area of Self-Government

3.3.2

Governments recognize that the health of a people is a matter of vital concern to its life, welfare, identity and culture and is therefore a core area for the exercise of self-government by Aboriginal nations.

Action to Agree on Jurisdiction and Service Delivery

3.3.3

Governments act promptly to

(a) conclude agreements recognizing their respective jurisdictions in areas touching directly on Aboriginal health;

(b) agree on appropriate arrangements for funding health services under Aboriginal jurisdiction; and

(c) establish a framework, until institutions of Aboriginal self-government exist, whereby agencies mandated by Aboriginal governments or identified by Aboriginal organizations or communities can deliver health and social services operating under provincial or territorial jurisdiction.

Health Effects of Policy

3.3.4

Governments, in formulating policy in social, economic or political spheres, give foremost consideration to the impact of such policies on the physical, social, emotional and spiritual health of Aboriginal citizens, and on their capacity to participate in the life of their communities and Canadian society as a whole.

Four-Part Strategy 3.3.5

Governments and organizations collaborate in carrying out a comprehensive action plan on Aboriginal health and social conditions, consisting of the following components:

(a) development of a system of Aboriginal healing centres and healing lodges under Aboriginal control as the prime units of holistic and culture-based health and wellness services;

(b) development of Aboriginal human resources compatible with the new system, its values and assumptions;

(c) full and active support of mainstream health and social service authorities and providers in meeting the health and healing goals of Aboriginal people; and

(d) implementation of an Aboriginal community infrastructure development program to address the most immediate health threats in Aboriginal communities, including the provision of clean water, basic sanitation facilities, and safe housing.

Healing Centres and Lodges 3.3.6

Federal, provincial and territorial governments collaborate with Aboriginal nations, organizations or communities, as appropriate, to

(a) develop a system of healing centres to provide direct services, referral and access to specialist services;

(b) develop a network of healing lodges to provide residential services oriented to family and community healing;

(c) develop and operate healing centres and lodges under Aboriginal control;

(d) mandate healing centres and lodges to provide integrated health and social services in culturally appropriate forms; and

(e) make the service network available to First Nations, Inuit and Métis communities, in rural and urban settings, on an equitable basis.

Laws, Regulations and Funding to Support Integrated Services 3.3.7

Federal, provincial and territorial governments collaborate with Aboriginal nations, regional Aboriginal service agencies, community governments and Aboriginal organizations, as appropriate, to adapt legislation, regulations and funding to promote

(a) integrated service delivery that transcends restricted service mandates of separate ministries and departments;

(b) collaboration and shared effort between federal, provincial/territorial and local governments; and

(c) the pooling of resources flowing from federal, provincial, territorial, municipal or Aboriginal sources.

Transform Current Services

3.3.8

Aboriginal organizations, regional planning and administrative bodies and community governments currently administering health and social services transform current programs and services into more holistic delivery systems that integrate or co-ordinate separate services.

Planning and Needs Assessment

3.3.9

Federal, provincial and territorial governments, in consultation with Aboriginal nations and urban communities of interest, co-operate to establish procedures and funding to support needs assessment and planning initiatives by Métis and other Aboriginal collectivities, in rural and urban settings, to

(a) form interim planning groups for rural settlements with a minimum of 250 Aboriginal residents, or catchment areas, whether urban or rural, with a minimum of 1,000 residents;

(b) compile an inventory of existing services, organizations and networks directed to meet Aboriginal needs, from which to build on existing strengths and ensure continuity of effort; and

(c) prepare plans to develop, operate and house healing centres, considering the goal of equitable access by Aboriginal people wherever they reside, the historical pattern of distinct Métis and treaty nation development in the prairie provinces, the availability and adaptability of municipal and provincial services, and the cost and efficiency of services.

Regional Healing Lodges

3.3.10

Aboriginal, federal, provincial and territorial governments, as appropriate, collaborate on regional initiatives to develop healing lodges providing residential services oriented to family and community healing, with priority being given to

(a) needs assessment and planning that reflect regional Aboriginal initiative and responsiveness to the diversity of cultures and communities;

(b) services broadly inclusive of all Aboriginal people resident in a region or associated with the nations of the region;

(c) institutions that collaborate with and complement other Aboriginal institutions and services, particularly healing centres delivering integrated health and social services; and

(d) governance structures consistent with emerging forms of Aboriginal self-government in the region.

Capital and Operating Budgets

3.3.11

Aboriginal, federal, provincial and territorial governments incorporate in funding agreements plans for capital development and operating costs of a network of healing lodges.

Regional Planning Bodies

3.3.12

Federal, provincial and territorial governments, and Aboriginal governments and organizations, support the assumption of responsibility for planning health and social services by regional Aboriginal agencies and councils where these now operate, and the formation of regional Aboriginal planning bodies in new areas, to promote

(a) equitable access to appropriate services by all Aboriginal people;

(b) strategic deployment of regional resources; and

(c) co-operative effort between Aboriginal communities and communities of interest, consistent with the emergence of nation governments and confederacies.

Canada-Wide Human Resources Strategy

3.3.13

The government of Canada provide funds to the national Aboriginal organizations, including national Aboriginal women's organizations, to permit them to prepare a comprehensive human resources development strategy in health and social services that

(a) facilitates and draws upon regional initiatives, integrates information from diverse sources, and is structured to incorporate regular updating;

(b) builds an inventory of Aboriginal human resources currently available in health and social services, identifying where, in what field and at what level Aboriginal personnel are currently practising;

(c) assesses current and future Aboriginal human resources needs and identifies the actions needed on the part of governments, educational institutions and others to address these needs;

(d) assesses requirements for direct service personnel as well as for planners, researchers and administrators;

(e) collates an inventory and available evaluative data on training and education options;

(f) explores recruitment, training and retention issues;

(g) examines the personal and professional supports required to encourage Aboriginal professionals to practise in Aboriginal communities;

(h) develops proposals for a system to monitor the status of Aboriginal human resources; and

(i) develops an analysis of how, to the maximum extent possible, Aboriginal human resources development can be brought under Aboriginal control.

Commitment to Train 10,000 Professionals

3.3.14

Federal, provincial and territorial governments commit themselves to providing the necessary funding, consistent with their jurisdictional responsibilities,

(a) to implement a co-ordinated and comprehensive human resources development strategy;

(b) to train 10,000 Aboriginal professionals over a 10-year period in health and social services, including medicine, nursing, mental health, psychology, social work, dentistry, nutrition, addictions, gerontology, public health, community development, planning, health administration, and other priority areas identified by Aboriginal people;

(c) to support program development in educational institutions providing professional training, with preference given to Aboriginal institutions; and

(d) to ensure that student support through post-secondary educational assistance, scholarships, paid leave and other means is adequate to achieve the target.

Adaptation of Current Programs

3.3.15

Federal, provincial and territorial governments and national Aboriginal organizations, including Aboriginal women's organizations, explore how training approaches and personnel complements of current health and social services, including the community health representative and drug and alcohol abuse programs, can contribute to a more comprehensive, holistic and integrated system of services, while helping to maintain continuity and adequacy of Aboriginal community services.

Increase Number of Graduates

3.3.16

Post-secondary educational institutions providing programs of study leading to professional certification in health or social services collaborate with Aboriginal organizations to examine how they can

(a) increase the number of Aboriginal students participating in and graduating from their programs;

(b) provide support for students to promote completion of programs;

(c) develop or expand specialized programs; and

(d) modify the curriculum of programs leading to certification so as to increase the cultural appropriateness and effectiveness of training provided to Aboriginal and non-Aboriginal students who will be providing services to Aboriginal people.

Continuing Professional Education

3.3.17

Post-secondary educational institutions and professional associations collaborate with Aboriginal organizations to ensure that professionals already in the field have access to programs of continuing professional education that emphasize cultural issues associated with the provision of health and social services.

Recognize Aboriginal Knowledge

3.3.18

Post-secondary educational institutions involved in the training of health and social services professionals, and professional associations involved in regulating and licensing these professions, collaborate with Aboriginal organizations and governments to develop a more effective approach to training and licensing that recognizes the importance and legitimacy of Aboriginal knowledge and experience.

AUCC and CAUT Provide Leadership

3.3.19

The Association of Universities and Colleges of Canada and the Canadian Association of University Teachers encourage their members to implement the Commission's recommendations with respect to professional training of Aboriginal people for health and social services, and that these organizations provide leadership to help ensure that the recommendations are implemented.

Support for Community Participation

3.3.20

Federal, provincial and territorial governments, in collaboration with Aboriginal organizations and governments, allocate funds to support Aboriginal community participation in planning, program development, training, and promoting community awareness in relation to human resources development in health and social services.

Protect and Extend Traditional Healing

3.3.21

Governments, health authorities and traditional practitioners co-operate to protect and extend the practices of traditional healing and explore their application to contemporary Aboriginal health and healing problems.

Dialogue Between Aboriginal and Bio-Medical Practitioners

3.3.22

Aboriginal traditional healers and bio-medical practitioners strive actively to enhance mutual respect through dialogue and that they explore areas of possible sharing and collaboration.

Educational Institutions Respect Traditional Practices

3.3.23

Non-Aboriginal educational institutions and professional associations involved in the health and social services fields sensitize practitioners to the existence of traditional medicine and healing practices, the possibilities for co-operation and collaboration, and the importance of recognizing, affirming and respecting traditional practices and practitioners.

Action Plans of Mainstream Institutions and Voluntary Organizations

3.3.24

Non-Aboriginal service agencies and institutions involved in the delivery of health or social services to Aboriginal people, and professional associations, unions, and other organizations in a position to influence the delivery of health or social services to Aboriginal people

(a) undertake a systematic examination to determine how they can encourage and support the development of Aboriginal health and social service systems, and improve the appropriateness and effectiveness of mainstream services to Aboriginal people;

(b) engage representatives of Aboriginal communities and organizations in conducting such an examination;

(c) make public an action plan appropriate to the institution or organization involved, outlining measurable objectives and a timetable for achieving them; and

(d) establish means to monitor and evaluate implementation of the plan by the institution or organization itself and by Aboriginal representatives.

Enforcement of **3.3.25**
Service Standards
Governments responsible for funding and professional bodies responsible for accrediting non-Aboriginal institutions and agencies engaged in the delivery of Aboriginal health and social services

(a) establish as a criterion for continuing funding and accreditation the preparation and implementation of goals and standards for services to Aboriginal people; and

(b) require that Aboriginal people, communities and nations affected by such services be fully involved in the development, implementation and evaluation of such goals and standards of practice.

Chapter 4 Housing

The Commission recommends that

Commitment to **3.4.1**
Adequate Housing
Federal and provincial governments address Aboriginal housing and community services on the basis of the following policy principles:

(a) Governments have an obligation to ensure that Aboriginal people have adequate shelter, water and sanitation services.

(b) Governments have a responsibility to restore an economic base to Aboriginal people that enables them to meet their needs.

(c) Aboriginal people, individually and collectively, are responsible for meeting their housing needs according to their ability to pay or contribute in kind.

(d) Governments must supplement the resources available to Aboriginal people so that their housing needs are fully met.

(e) Aboriginal nations should assume authority over all housing matters as a core area of self-government jurisdiction.

(f) Acute risks to health and safety should be treated as an emergency and targeted for immediate action.

3.4.2
The government of Canada clarify with treaty nations a modern understanding of existing treaty terms regarding housing.

3.4.3
The government of Canada make resources available over the next 10 years to ensure that housing for Aboriginal people on-reserve is fully adequate in quantity and quality and engage the governments of the provinces and territories to reach the same goal in rural and northern communities and in urban areas.

Water and Sewage **3.4.4**
Systems The government of Canada provide additional resources for construction, upgrading and operation of water and sewage systems to ensure that adequate facilities and operating systems are in place in all First Nations communities within five years.

3.4.5
The government of Canada provide funding and technical support to First Nations governments to operate and maintain community water and sewer systems and to establish technical support institutions as required.

Housing in First **3.4.6**
Nations The government of Canada and First Nations governments
Communities and people undertake to meet the need of First Nations people for adequate housing within 10 years.

3.4.7
The government of Canada complement the resources supplied by First Nations people in a two-to-one ratio or as necessary to achieve adequate housing in 10 years by
- providing capital subsidies and committing to loan subsidies for construction of new homes and renovations;
- providing funds for property insurance and regular maintenance for home occupants receiving social assistance or with low earned incomes;
- paying rental subsidies for those receiving social assistance or with low earned incomes in amounts that are equitable compared to off-reserve programs; and
- offering financial incentives for private home ownership.

3.4.8

First Nations governments and people make every effort to marshall more resources for housing and community services, through financial contributions from residents in the form of maintenance fees, rents or mortgage payments, and contributions in kind, such as sweat equity and local materials.

3.4.9

First Nations governments assume jurisdiction over housing at the earliest opportunity, enact clear laws regarding housing tenure, and pursue authority to adjust other programs such as social assistance with a view to marshalling more resources for housing.

3.4.10

First Nations governments develop institutions at the nation level or through inter-nation agreements to administer housing and tenure regimes and deliver housing programs with financial and technical support from the government of Canada.

3.4.11

The government of Canada support the efforts of First Nations communities to develop and implement their own tenure systems and housing programs, innovative uses of social assistance to stimulate contributions to housing, and institutions above the community level.

Housing in Non-Reserve Communities

3.4.12

The government of Canada and the governments of the provinces and territories undertake to meet fully, in co-operation with Aboriginal people and within 10 years, the need for adequate housing of Aboriginal people not living on reserves.

3.4.13

Aboriginal people not living on reserves make every effort to marshall more resources for housing in a variety of ways, through contributions in kind, use of local materials, and effective housing organizations.

3.4.14

The government of Canada engage the provincial and territorial governments in a strategy to meet the housing needs of Aboriginal people living in non-reserve communities by

- reinstating and increasing funding for new social housing and mortgage subsidies under the Aboriginal off-reserve programs of the Canada Mortgage and Housing Corporation (CMHC);
- providing greater autonomy and flexibility to Aboriginal organizations delivering the program in rural areas and to urban social housing corporations; and
- providing rental subsidies as a cost-effective option where rental markets exist.

Economic
Development

3.4.15

The government of Canada help Aboriginal people exploit the economic development opportunities arising from an increase in construction, repair and maintenance of dwellings for Aboriginal people

- by providing funding and support through training and business development programs; and
- by actively expanding the involvement of Aboriginal financial institutions in mortgage financing as agents of CMHC and as mortgage lenders.

Chapter 5 Education

The Commission recommends that

Education and
Self-Government

3.5.1

Federal, provincial and territorial governments act promptly to acknowledge that education is a core area for the exercise of Aboriginal self-government.

Transitional
Control of
Education

3.5.2

Federal, provincial and territorial governments collaborate with Aboriginal governments, organizations or education authorities, as appropriate, to support the development of Aboriginally controlled education systems by

(a) introducing, adapting or ensuring the flexible application of legislation to facilitate self-starting initiatives by Aboriginal nations and their communities in the field of education;

(b) mandating voluntary organizations that are endorsed by substantial numbers of Aboriginal people to act in the field of education in urban and non-reserve areas where numbers warrant until such time as Aboriginal governments are established; and

(c) providing funding commensurate with the responsibilities assumed by Aboriginal nations and their communities, or voluntary organizations, given the requirements of institutional and program development, costs of serving small or dispersed communities, and special needs accruing from past failures of education services.

Early Childhood Education Support

3.5.3

Federal, provincial, and territorial governments co-operate to support an integrated early childhood education funding strategy that

(a) extends early childhood education services to *all* Aboriginal children regardless of residence;

(b) encourages programs that foster the physical, social, intellectual and spiritual development of children, reducing distinctions between child care, prevention and education;

(c) maximizes Aboriginal control over service design and administration;

(d) offers one-stop accessible funding; and

(e) promotes parental involvement and choice in early childhood education options.

Transfer Between Education Systems

3.5.4

Aboriginal, provincial and territorial governments act promptly to reach agreements for mutual recognition of programs provided by their respective educational institutions so as to facilitate the transfer of students between educational systems while protecting the integrity of cultural dimensions of Aboriginal education

Curriculum Development

3.5.5

Federal, provincial and territorial governments collaborate with Aboriginal governments, organizations and educators to develop or continue developing innovative curricula that reflect Aboriginal cultures and community realities, for delivery

(a) at all grade levels of elementary and secondary schools;

(b) in schools operating under Aboriginal control; and

(c) in schools under provincial or territorial jurisdiction.

Priority of Aboriginal Language Education

3.5.6

Aboriginal language education be assigned priority in Aboriginal, provincial and territorial education systems to complement and support language preservation efforts in local communities through

(a) first- or second-language instruction or immersion programs where parents desire it and numbers warrant;

(b) recognition of Aboriginal language competence for second-language academic credit whether competence is acquired through classroom or out-of-school instruction;

(c) involving elders and fluent Aboriginal speakers in programs to enhance Aboriginal language acquisition and fluency;

(d) developing instructional materials; and

(e) encouraging and rewarding language teaching as a career path and language research in lexical elaboration, structural analysis and cultural contexts as professional and academic specializations.

Involvement in Decision Making

3.5.7

Where Aboriginal children attend provincial and territorial schools, provincial and territorial governments take immediate steps to ensure that Aboriginal people are involved fully in the decision-making processes that affect the education of their children. Aboriginal control of education and parental involvement should be implemented through a variety of actions:

(a) legislation to guarantee Aboriginal representation on school boards where population numbers warrant;

(b) recognition of Aboriginally controlled schools under the jurisdiction of Aboriginal community of interest governments;

(c) establishment of Aboriginally governed schools affiliated with school districts, if requested by Aboriginal people; and

(d) creation of Aboriginal advisory committees to school boards.

Involvement in School Activities

3.5.8

All schools serving Aboriginal children adopt policies that welcome the involvement of Aboriginal parents, elders and families in the life of the school, for example, by establishing advisory or parents committees, introducing teaching by elders in the classroom, and involving parents in school activities

Required School Board Strategy

3.5.9

Provincial and territorial ministries require school boards serving Aboriginal students to implement a comprehensive

Aboriginal education strategy, developed with Aboriginal parents, elders and educators, including

(a) goals and objectives to be accomplished during the International Decade of Indigenous Peoples;

(b) hiring of Aboriginal teachers at the elementary and secondary school level, with negotiated target levels, to teach in all areas of school programs, not just Aboriginal programs;

(c) hiring of Aboriginal people in administrative and leadership positions;

(d) hiring of Aboriginal support workers, such as counsellors, community liaison workers, psychologists and speech therapists;

(e) curriculum, in all subject areas, that includes the perspectives, traditions, beliefs and world view of Aboriginal peoples;

(f) involvement of Aboriginal elders in teaching Aboriginal and non-Aboriginal students;

(g) language classes in Aboriginal languages, as determined by the Aboriginal community;

(h) family and community involvement mechanisms;

(i) education programs that combat stereotypes, racism, prejudice and biases;

(j) accountability indicators tied to board or district funding; and

(k) public reports of results by the end of the International Decade of Indigenous Peoples in the year 2004.

Youth **3.5.10**
Empowerment
Aboriginally controlled, provincial, and territorial schools serving Aboriginal youth develop and implement comprehensive Aboriginal youth empowerment strategies with elements elaborated in collaboration with youth, including

(a) cultural education in classroom and informal settings;

(b) acknowledgement of spiritual, ethical and intuitive dimensions of learning;

(c) education to support critical analysis of Aboriginal experience;

(d) learning as a means of healing from the effects of trauma, abuse and racism;

(e) academic skills development and support;

(f) sports and outdoor education;

(g) leadership development; and

(h) youth exchanges between Aboriginal nations, across Canada and internationally.

Community High School Programs

3.5.11

High school programs be extended to communities, using cost-effective options agreed upon by parents and families, including

(a) complete school facilities for local high school delivery;

(b) regional high schools in Aboriginal communities;

(c) culturally appropriate, interactive distance education; and

(d) seasonal institutes.

Secondary Study Re-entry

3.5.12

Aboriginal authorities and all provincial and territorial ministries of education fund programs for Aboriginal youth who have left secondary school before graduation to enable them to resume their studies with appropriate curriculum, scheduling, academic and social support.

Co-op Education

3.5.13

Federal, provincial and territorial governments encourage co-op initiatives by offering funding inducements to secondary schools that develop active co-op education programs for Aboriginal young people.

Expanded Teacher Education Programs

3.5.14

Federal, provincial and territorial governments expand financial support to post-secondary institutions for existing and new Aboriginal teacher education programs, contingent on

(a) evidence of Aboriginal support for the program;

(b) Aboriginal participation in the governance of the program;

(c) the incorporation of Aboriginal content and pedagogy into the program; and

(d) periodic evaluations that indicate that the quality of teacher education conforms to standards of excellence expected by Aboriginal people.

Aboriginal Secondary School Teachers

3.5.15

Canadian governments, Aboriginal education authorities, post-secondary institutions and teacher education programs adopt multiple strategies to increase substantially the number of Aboriginal secondary school teachers, including

(a) promoting secondary school teaching careers for Aboriginal people;

(b) increasing access to professional training in secondary education, for example, community-based delivery of courses and concurrent programs; and

(c) offering financial incentives to students.

Teacher Education Accessible in Communities 3.5.16

Federal, provincial and territorial governments provide support to increase the number of Aboriginal people trained as teachers by

(a) expanding the number of teacher education programs delivered directly in communities; and

(b) ensuring that students in each province and territory have access to such programs.

Career Paths 3.5.17

Teacher education programs, in collaboration with Aboriginal organizations and government agencies that sponsor professional and para-professional training, adopt a comprehensive approach to educator training, developing career paths from para-professional training to professional certification in education careers that

(a) prepare Aboriginal students for the variety of roles required to operate Aboriginal education systems; and

(b) open opportunities for careers in provincial education systems.

Aboriginal Component in All Teacher Education Programs 3.5.18

Provinces and territories require that teacher education programs

(a) in pre-service training leading to certification include at least one component on teaching Aboriginal subject matter to all students, both Aboriginal and non-Aboriginal;

(b) develop options for pre-service training and professional development of teachers, focused on teaching Aboriginal students and addressing Aboriginal education issues; and

(c) collaborate with Aboriginal organizations or community representatives in developing Aboriginal-specific components of their programs.

Aboriginal Delivery of Integrated Adult Training 3.5.19

Federal, provincial and territorial governments collaborate with Aboriginal governments and organizations to facilitate integrated delivery of adult literacy, basic education, academic upgrading and job training under the control of Aboriginal people through

(a) delegating responsibility for delivery of training under current jurisdictions by concluding agreements with Aboriginal governments, their mandated education authorities, or voluntary organizations representing Aboriginal communities of interest;

(b) supporting adaptation of program design, admission criteria, language of instruction, and internal allocation of funds by Aboriginal delivery agents, to accommodate Aboriginal culture and community needs;

(c) acting promptly to conclude agreements for multi-year block funding agreements to enable Aboriginal nation governments, during the transition to self-government, to assume primary responsibility for allocating funds to meet training needs through programs of Aboriginal design.

Treaty Promise of Education

3.5.20

The government of Canada recognize and fulfil its obligation to treaty nations by supporting a full range of education services, including post-secondary education, for members of treaty nations where a promise of education appears in treaty texts, related documents or oral histories of the parties involved.

Federal Support of Post-Secondary Students

3.5.21

The federal government continue to support the costs of post-secondary education for First Nations and Inuit post-secondary students and make additional resources available

(a) to mitigate the impact of increased costs as post-secondary institutions shift to a new policy environment in post-secondary education; and

(b) to meet the anticipated higher level of demand for post-secondary education services.

Métis and Aboriginal Scholarship Fund

3.5.22

A scholarship fund be established for Métis and other Aboriginal students who do not have access to financial support for post-secondary education under present policies, with

(a) lead financial support provided by federal and provincial governments and additional contributions from corporate and individual donors;

(b) a planning committee to be established immediately,

> (i)   composed of Métis and other Aboriginal representatives, students, and federal and provincial representatives in balanced numbers;
> (ii) given a maximum two-year mandate; and
> (iii) charged with determining the appropriate vehicle, level of capitalization, program criteria and administrative structure for initiation and administration of the fund; and

(c) provisions for evaluating demand on the fund, its adequacy and its impact on participation and completion rates of Métis and other Aboriginal students in post-secondary studies.

Aboriginal Languages Equivalent to Modern Languages

3.5.23

Canada's post-secondary institutions recognize Aboriginal languages on a basis equal to other modern languages, for the purpose of granting credits for entrance requirements, fulfilment of second language requirements, and general course credits.

Mainstream Post-Secondary Initiatives

3.5.24

Public post-secondary institutions in the provinces and territories undertake new initiatives or extend current ones to increase the participation, retention and graduation of Aboriginal students by introducing, encouraging or enhancing

(a) a welcoming environment for Aboriginal students;
(b) Aboriginal content and perspectives in course offerings across disciplines;
(c) Aboriginal studies and programs as part of the institution's regular program offerings and included in the institution's core budget;
(d) Aboriginal appointments to boards of governors;
(e) Aboriginal councils to advise the president of the institution;
(f) active recruitment of Aboriginal students;
(g) admission policies that encourage access by Aboriginal applicants;
(h) meeting spaces for Aboriginal students;
(i) Aboriginal student unions;
(j) recruitment of Aboriginal faculty members;
(k) support services with Aboriginal counsellors for academic and personal counselling; and
(l) cross-cultural sensitivity training for faculty and staff.

Residential University Colleges

3.5.25

Where there is Aboriginal support for an Aboriginal college within a university, and where numbers warrant, universities act to establish an Aboriginal college to serve as the focal point for the academic, residential, social and cultural lives of Aboriginal students on campus, and to promote Aboriginal scholarship.

Fund Aboriginal Post-Secondary Institutions

3.5.26

Federal, provincial and territorial governments collaborate with Aboriginal governments and organizations to establish and support post-secondary educational institutions controlled by Aboriginal people, with negotiated allocation of responsibility for

(a) core and program funding commensurate with the services they are expected to provide and comparable to the funding provided to provincial or territorial institutions delivering similar services;

(b) planning, capital and start-up costs of new colleges and institutes;

(c) improvement of facilities for community learning centres as required for new functions and development of new facilities where numbers warrant and the community establishes this as a priority; and

(d) fulfilment of obligations pursuant to treaties and modern agreements with respect to education.

Regional and National Aboriginal Boards

3.5.27

Aboriginally controlled post-secondary educational institutions collaborate to create regional boards and/or a Canada-wide board to

(a) establish standards for accrediting programs provided by Aboriginal post-secondary institutions;

(b) negotiate mutual recognition of course credits and credentials to facilitate student transfer between Aboriginal institutions and provincial and territorial post-secondary institutions;

(c) establish co-operative working relationships with mainstream accreditation bodies such as the Association of Universities and Colleges of Canada and professional associations such as the Canadian Association of University Teachers; and

(d) pursue other objectives related to the common interests of Aboriginal institutions.

Elders' Role in Education

3.5.28

Elders be reinstated to an active role in the education of Aboriginal children and youth in educational systems under Aboriginal control and in provincial and territorial schools.

Elders' Compensation

3.5.29

Elders be treated as professionals and compensated for their education contribution at a rate and in a manner that shows respect for their expertise, unique knowledge and skills.

Recognize Aboriginal Knowledge

3.5.30

Provincial and territorial education ministries, boards of education and educators recognize the value of elders' knowledge to all peoples' understanding of the universe by

(a) giving academic credits for traditional Aboriginal arts and knowledge whether acquired in the classroom or through non-formal means in cultural activities, camps and apprenticeships; and

(b) collaborating with elders to determine how traditional Aboriginal knowledge can be made accessible in the education of all students, whether Aboriginal or non-Aboriginal, in institutions under Aboriginal, provincial, or territorial control.

Exchanges Among Elders and with Academics

3.5.31

Educational institutions facilitate opportunities for elders to exchange traditional knowledge with one another and to share traditional knowledge with students and scholars, both Aboriginal and non-Aboriginal, in university settings.

Establish Aboriginal Peoples' International University

3.5.32

A university under Aboriginal control, which could be called the Aboriginal Peoples' International University, and with the capacity to function in all provinces and territories, be established to promote traditional knowledge, to pursue applied research in support of Aboriginal self-government, and to disseminate information essential to achieving broad Aboriginal development goals.

Steering Group to Plan APIU

3.5.33

First Nations, Inuit and Métis leaders in collaboration with the federal government establish a steering group funded by the federal government, with a three-year mandate

(a) to explore options, conduct consultations and prepare a plan to implement an Aboriginal Peoples' International University by the year 2000; and

(b) to collaborate with other working groups in determining the appropriate location of a documentation centre and archive, an electronic information clearinghouse, and statistical data bases.

Electronic Clearinghouse **3.5.34**

An electronic clearinghouse be established to facilitate the free flow of information among Aboriginal communities, education and self-government workers and individuals, the planning and development of this clearinghouse to be carried forward by a working group

(a) established in collaboration with First Nations, Inuit and Métis leaders;

(b) funded by the federal government and given a two-year mandate; and

(c) attentive to the need for Canada-wide and international communication as well as exchange in Aboriginal languages within linguistic communities.

Working Group for Statistical Clearinghouse **3.5.35**

First Nations, Inuit and Métis leaders establish a working group, funded by the federal government, with a two-year mandate to plan a statistical clearinghouse controlled by Aboriginal people to

(a) work in collaboration with Aboriginal governments and organizations to establish and update statistical data bases; and

(b) promote common strategies across nations and communities for collecting and analyzing data relevant to Aboriginal development goals.

Documentation Centre on Residential Schools and Relocations **3.5.36**

The federal government fund the establishment of a national documentation centre to research, collect, preserve and disseminate information related to residential schools, relocations and other aspects of Aboriginal historical experience, the planning and development of the centre to be carried forward by a working group

(a) established in collaboration with First Nations, Inuit and Métis leaders; and

(b) having a two-year mandate.

Education for Self-Government Funding

3.5.37

Federal, provincial and territorial governments establish funding programs to support education for self-government, to be available to

(a) public post-secondary institutions that have entered into partnerships with Aboriginal people to initiate or expand training and education in areas identified as priorities by Aboriginal governments, organizations and communities for the implementation of self-government; and

(b) Aboriginally controlled post-secondary institutions for program innovation to enhance capacity for self-government.

Youth Careers Campaign

3.5.38

Aboriginal governments and organizations collaborate to launch a Canada-wide campaign to make youth aware of the opportunities to serve their nations that will open up with the advent of self-government and of the tangible and intangible rewards that accompany public service.

Student Incentives for Self-Government Studies

3.5.39

The federal government make funds available to First Nation and Inuit governments and organizations to support incentives to encourage students to complete bachelor's and master's level studies and professional training in areas of priority to self-government, including such measures as

(a) employee release time for concurrent work and study;

(b) paid leave to pursue full-time study;

(c) scholarships in studies related to self-government;

(d) top-up of educational assistance for family needs, including exceptional housing costs; and

(e) student loans that are forgivable on completion of a period of employment in the service of self-government.

Co-op Placements in Business and Government

3.5.40

Canada's corporations, small businesses and governments become active partners in Aboriginal self-government education by identifying co-op placement and internship opportunities in their organizations, in consultation with Aboriginal people.

Executive Interchange

3.5.41

Canada's corporations and governments at all levels establish executive interchange opportunities in partnership with Aboriginal governments.

Professional **3.5.42**
Associations Professional associations and self-governing bodies in the pro-
Support fessions actively support the professional training of Aboriginal
Aboriginal people by
Training

    (a) entering into dialogue on such issues as credentials, recruit-
ment, mentoring, career paths linking para-professional
and professional training, education based on Aboriginal
culture, systemic discrimination and racism;

    (b) establishing scholarships for Aboriginal people;

    (c) encouraging their members to gain an understanding of
Aboriginal perspectives;

    (d) spearheading initiatives to introduce Aboriginal cultural
perspectives into professional training programs; and

    (e) providing leadership by encouraging implementation of the
recommendations in this report that are relevant to their
areas of expertise.

Support of **3.5.43**
Distance The federal government, media corporations, provincial and ter-
Education Models ritorial governments and private donors provide funding and/or
gifts in kind (for example, access to facilities and technology)
to establish a distance education model of professional training
suitable for Aboriginal people who wish to pursue post-secondary studies from their communities.

Canada-Wide **3.5.44**
Aboriginal Human The federal government provide funding for national Aboriginal
Resources organizations to co-ordinate establishment of a Canada-wide
Inventory Aboriginal human resources inventory that is amenable to reg-
ular updating.

Chapter 6 Arts and Heritage

The Commission recommends that

Inventory of **3.6.1**
Historical and Federal, provincial and territorial governments collaborate with
Sacred Sites Aboriginal organizations and communities to prepare a comprehensive inventory of historical and sacred sites, involving
elders as expert advisers, before negotiations on designation of
lands in accordance with our recommendations in Volume 2,
Chapter 4.

Urgent Protection of Threatened Sites

3.6.2

Federal, provincial and territorial governments review legislation affecting sacred and historical sites to ensure that Aboriginal organizations and communities have access to urgent remedies to prevent or arrest damage to significant heritage sites such as the Mnjikaning Fish Fence, whether they be threatened by human actions or natural processes.

Legislation on Historical Sites and Cultural Artifacts

3.6.3

Federal, provincial and territorial governments in collaboration with Aboriginal organizations review legislation affecting historical and sacred sites and the conservation and display of cultural artifacts to ensure that

(a) Aboriginal interests are recognized in designing, protecting, developing and managing sites significant to Aboriginal culture and heritage and in conserving, repatriating and displaying Aboriginal cultural artifacts;

(b) Aboriginal people are fully involved in planning and managing heritage activities relevant to their cultures; and

(c) Aboriginal people share the economic benefits that may accrue from appropriate development of relevant heritage sites and display of cultural artifacts.

Museums and Cultural Institutions Adopt Ethical Guidelines

3.6.4

Museums and cultural institutions adopt ethical guidelines governing all aspects of collection, disposition, display and interpretation of artifacts related to Aboriginal culture and heritage, including the following:

(a) involving Aboriginal people in drafting, endorsing and implementing the guidelines;

(b) creating inventories of relevant holdings and making such inventories freely accessible to Aboriginal people;

(c) cataloguing and designating appropriate use and display of relevant holdings;

(d) repatriating, on request, objects that are sacred or integral to the history and continuity of particular nations and communities;

(e) returning human remains to the family, community or nation of origin, on request, or consulting with Aboriginal advisers on appropriate disposition, where remains cannot be associated with a particular nation; and

(f) ensuring that Aboriginal people and communities have effective access to cultural education and training opportunities available through museums and cultural institutions.

Access to Cultural Education

3.6.5

Aboriginal, federal, provincial and territorial governments, in collaboration with Aboriginal elders, artists, educators and youth, develop and implement joint strategies to ensure that Aboriginal people have

(a) effective access to cultural and heritage education;

(b) resources to develop facilities for display of cultural artifacts; and

(c) means to participate in exchanges and joint undertakings with museums and cultural institutions.

Heritage Vocations a Part of Capacity Building

3.6.6

Aboriginal, federal, provincial and territorial governments include heritage research, conservation and presentation in the list of skills identified as priorities in building the capacity to implement self-government.

Protect Aboriginal Intellectual Property

3.6.7

The federal government, in collaboration with Aboriginal people, review its legislation on the protection of intellectual property to ensure that Aboriginal interests and perspectives, in particular collective interests, are adequately protected.

Determining Language Status a Core Power of Self-Government

3.6.8

Federal, provincial and territorial governments recognize promptly that determining Aboriginal language status and use is a core power in Aboriginal self-government, and that these governments affirm and support Aboriginal nations and their communities in using and promoting their languages and declaring them official languages within their nations, territories and communities where they choose to do so.

Nations Implement a Multi-Faceted Language Strategy

3.6.9

Each Aboriginal nation in the various stages of nation building, capacity building, negotiating and implementing self-government consult with its constituent communities to establish priorities and policies with respect to Aboriginal language conservation, revitalization and documentation, including

(a) assessing the current state of Aboriginal language use and vitality;

(b) determining priorities of communities for language conservation, revitalization and documentation;

(c) consulting on the most effective means of implementing priorities;

(d) facilitating initiatives to support Aboriginal language use in families and the broader community;

(e) incorporating their Aboriginal language in education policies and programs;

(f) enhancing co-operation among nations and communities of the same language group to promote research, curriculum development and language elaboration;

(g) using their Aboriginal language in public forums and Aboriginal government business; and

(h) declaring their Aboriginal language an official language on nation territory.

Endowed Aboriginal Languages Foundation

3.6.10

The federal government make a commitment to endow an Aboriginal Languages Foundation for the purpose of supporting Aboriginal initiatives in the conservation, revitalization and documentation of Aboriginal languages, the foundation to be

(a) capitalized by an annual federal grant of $10 million for five years, beginning in 1997;

(b) eligible to receive charitable contributions, to be matched by the federal government in a ratio of two dollars for each dollar contributed;

(c) established to support language initiatives undertaken or endorsed by Aboriginal nations and their communities;

(d) developed by a federally funded planning body, with a majority of First Nations, Inuit and Métis representatives and a two-year mandate; and

(e) directed in its operation by a board with a majority of First Nations, Inuit and Métis members.

Special Status of Aboriginal-Language Broadcasting

3.6.11

The government of Canada recognize the special status of Aboriginal-language broadcasting explicitly in federal legislation.

CRTC Require **3.6.12**
Representation of
Aboriginal   The Canadian Radio-Television and Telecommunications
Programming   Commission include in licence conditions for public and com-
mercial broadcasters, in regions with significant Aboriginal
population concentrations, requirements for fair representa-
tion and distribution of Aboriginal programming, including
Aboriginal language requirements.

Access to **3.6.13**
Aboriginal Media Public and private media outlets, in particular the Canadian
Products   Broadcasting Corporation, provide access to Aboriginal media
products for Aboriginal and non-Aboriginal Canadians by
(a) purchasing and broadcasting Aboriginal programming
from independent Aboriginal producers; and
(b) producing English and French versions of original Aboriginal
programs for regional and national redistribution.

Employment **3.6.14**
Equity in Public Public and private media outlets address the need for training
and Private Media and better representation of Aboriginal people in public communications by developing and implementing employment
equity plans.

Freedom of **3.6.15**
Expression for Governments, including Aboriginal governments, recognize
Aboriginal Media the critical role that independent Aboriginal print and broadcast media have in the pursuit of Aboriginal self-determination
and self-government, and that they support freedom of expression through
(a) policies on open access to information; and
(b) dedicated funding at arm's length from political bodies.

Aboriginal Access **3.6.16**
to Media Training Colleges and universities with programs in communications,
journalism and film co-operate to support access for Aboriginal
students by providing transition courses, scholarships and counselling services.

Fees and Joint **3.6.17**
Ventures to   The Canadian Radio-Television and Telecommunications
Finance Aboriginal Commission be mandated to establish fee structures and provisions
Media Products for joint ventures as part of licensing conditions to ensure a stable

financial base for the production and distribution of Aboriginal broadcast media products, particularly in southern Canada.

Core Funding and Incentives for Private Support

3.6.18

Federal, provincial, territorial and Aboriginal governments provide core funding for Aboriginal media that

(a) is accessible to all Aboriginal nations and communities;

(b) builds upon existing government programs and Aboriginal media organizations;

(c) results in long-term funding agreements that realistically reflect Aboriginal media requirements and promote self-financing; and

(d) encourages private and corporate support through tax incentives.

Aboriginal Arts Council

3.6.19

Federal, provincial, territorial and Aboriginal governments co-operate to establish and fund an Aboriginal Arts Council, with a minimum 20-year life span and an annual budget equivalent to five per cent of the Canada Council budget, to foster the revitalization and development of Aboriginal arts and literature.

Arts Granting Criteria Relevant to Aboriginal Arts

3.6.20

Governments, public agencies and private organizations that provide support for the visual and performing arts, in co-operation with Aboriginal artists and performers, review all aspects of their programs to ensure that

(a) criteria for grants and awards are relevant to Aboriginal arts and artists; and

(b) Aboriginal people and perspectives are adequately represented on decision-making bodies, juries, advisory committees and staff.

Arts Training and Facilities

3.6.21

Federal, provincial, territorial and Aboriginal governments, in co-operation with Aboriginal artists, writers and performers, support and promote the revitalization and development of Aboriginal literary, visual and performing arts through

(a) support of training programs in schools, cultural institutions and professional associations, and participation of Aboriginal students in professional studies in the arts; and

(b) accommodating requirements for appropriate display and performance of Aboriginal arts in the design of public facilities in Aboriginal communities and the community at large.

VOLUME 4
PERSPECTIVES
AND REALITIES

Chapter 2 Women's Perspectives

The Commission recommends that

Participation in **4.2.1**
Nation Building The government of Canada provide funding to Aboriginal women's organizations, including urban-based groups, to
(a) improve their research capacity and facilitate their participation in all stages of discussion leading to the design and development of self-government processes; and
(b) enable them to participate fully in all aspects of nation building, including developing criteria for citizenship and related appeal processes.

Participation in **4.2.2**
Health Institutions Aboriginal governments and organizations provide for the full and fair participation of Aboriginal women in the governing bodies of all Aboriginal health and healing institutions.

Inventory of **4.2.3**
Aboriginal Aboriginal governments and planning bodies with a mandate
Women's Groups to develop new structures for human services undertake, in collaboration with women's organizations, an inventory of existing services, organizations and networks with a view to building on existing strengths and ensuring continuity of effort.

Chapter 3 Elders' Perspectives

The Commission recommends that

Participation in **4.3.1**
Nation Building Aboriginal, federal, provincial and territorial governments acknowledge the essential role of Elders and the traditional knowledge that they have to contribute in rebuilding Aboriginal nations and reconstructing institutions to support Aboriginal self-determination and well-being. This acknowledgement should be expressed in practice by
(a) involving Elders in conceptualizing, planning and monitoring nation-building activities and institutional development;

(b) ensuring that the knowledge of both male and female Elders, as appropriate, is engaged in such activities;

(c) compensating Elders in a manner that conforms to cultural practices and recognizes their expertise and contribution;

(d) supporting gatherings and networks of Elders to share knowledge and experience with each other and to explore applications of traditional knowledge to contemporary issues; and

(e) modifying regulations in non-Aboriginal institutions that have the effect of excluding the participation of Elders on the basis of age.

Protection of Sacred Sites

4.3.2

Aboriginal Elders be involved in the formulation and implementation of policies for the preservation and protection of sacred sites. In co-management situations, Elders should be board members.

Access to Public Lands for Traditional Purposes

4.3.3

Federal, provincial and territorial governments

(a) recognize Aboriginal people's right of access to public lands for the purpose of gathering traditional herbs, plants and other traditional medicines where the exercise of the right is not incompatible with existing use; and

(b) consult with Aboriginal governments on guidelines to govern the implementation of this right.

Chapter 4 The Search for Belonging: Perspectives of Youth

The Commission recommends that

Cultural Centres for Youth

4.4.1

Youth centres be established on reserves and in communities, including urban communities, where there is a significant Aboriginal population. Where cultural centres exist they should develop a specific youth component, including cultural and recreational programs.

Cultural Camps for Youth

4.4.2

Federal, provincial and territorial governments provide funding for community initiatives to establish Aboriginal youth camps that would

(a) pursue cultural activities linking youth with elders through the development of traditional skills and knowledge;

(b) promote a healthy lifestyle (counselling, fitness and nutrition); and

(c) encourage positive social interaction between Aboriginal youth of different nations and between Aboriginal and non-Aboriginal youth.

Aboriginal Sports and Recreation Advisory Council

4.4.3

The federal government, through the Minister of State for Fitness and Amateur Sport, establish and fund an Aboriginal sports and recreation advisory council to advise – in consultation with regional, provincial and territorial sports and recreation organizations – federal, provincial, territorial and Aboriginal governments on how best to meet the sports and recreation needs of Aboriginal people (including those living in urban areas).

Sports and Recreation Initiatives

4.4.4

The proposed Aboriginal sports and recreation advisory council promote programs and initiatives that are

(a) community-driven, based on needs identified by the community, with programming developed or modified by the community to meet the community's needs;

(b) sustainable, as opposed to one-time tournaments or events; and

(c) capacity builders aimed at providing instruction in recreation programming, leadership development and coaching skills.

Intergovernmental Forum within 1 Year of Report

4.4.5

A meeting of ministers responsible for sports and recreation be convened within one year of the publication of this report to discuss the form and structure of the proposed Aboriginal sports and recreation advisory council, and that Aboriginal youth and Aboriginal experts in the field – recreation and sports programmers, co-ordinators, administrators and researchers – be invited to take part in this discussion.

Co-operative Home Construction

4.4.6

Co-operative home construction, based on the Habitat for Humanity model, be initiated in Aboriginal communities to provide housing, employment and construction skills for Aboriginal youth.

Canada-Wide Policy Framework

4.4.7

Federal, provincial and territorial governments develop and adopt, through the leadership of the Ministry of State for Youth, and in close consultation with Aboriginal youth and their representative organizations, a comprehensive Canada-wide policy framework to guide initiatives and programs directed to Aboriginal youth.

Key Program Areas

4.4.8

Key program areas for a Canada-wide Aboriginal youth policy be education, justice, health and healing, sports and recreation, and support programs for urban Aboriginal youth:

(a) Education in the broadest sense must be a priority, with greater efforts to develop a culturally appropriate curriculum that reinforces the value of Aboriginal culture. Transformative education – which uses students' personal experiences as a springboard for deeper analysis and understanding of the world around them – should be considered in developing initiatives in education.

(b) The justice and corrections system has a substantial impact on youth. New programs should be developed and existing programs modified to focus on reintegrating youth into the community through approaches that reflect Aboriginal culture.

(c) Health and healing must reflect the needs of Aboriginal youth, particularly in the areas of counselling and support.

(d) Sports and recreation must be treated as an integral part of Aboriginal youth policy. Increased resources for facilities and programming are needed, as are trained people to co-ordinate sports and recreation programs for Aboriginal youth. Also, the sports community – athletes and fans – must be seen as a way to build and strengthen relationships among Aboriginal and non-Aboriginal people.

(e) Aboriginal youth in urban areas need innovative programs to help them bridge the traditional and urban worlds and support their choices about where and how to live.

Developing and Implementing Youth Policy

4.4.9

All governments pursue the following goals in developing and implementing a Canada-wide Aboriginal youth policy: youth participation at all levels, leadership development, economic development and cultural rebirth, youth involvement in nation building, and cultural and spiritual development.

Monitoring **4.4.10**
Progress and
Setting Priorities The federal government provide funding for a biennial conference of Aboriginal youth delegates and invited representatives
from government and non-government organizations, the purpose of which would be to
(a) review progress over the preceding 24 months on goals established under the Canada-wide Aboriginal youth policy; and
(b) set priorities for new policies and programs where a need
is identified by delegates.

Chapter 5 Métis Perspectives

The Commission recommends that

Nation-to-Nation **4.5.1**
Approach Political negotiation on a nation-to-nation or analogous basis
be the primary method of resolving Métis issues.

Métis Identity **4.5.2**
Every person who
(a) identifies himself or herself as Métis, and
(b) is accepted as such by the nation of Métis people with
which that person wishes to be associated, on the basis of
criteria and procedures determined by that nation,
be recognized as a member of that nation for purposes of
nation-to-nation negotiations and as Métis for that purpose.

Section 91(24) **4.5.3**
Coverage The government of Canada either
(a) acknowledge that section 91(24) of the *Constitution Act,
1867* applies to Métis people and base its legislation, policies and programs on that recognition; or
(b) collaborate with appropriate provincial governments and
with Métis representatives in the formulation and enactment of a constitutional amendment specifying that section
91(24) applies to Métis people.
If it is unwilling to take either of these steps, the government
of Canada make a constitutional reference to the Supreme
Court of Canada, asking that court to decide whether section
91(24) of the *Constitution Act, 1867* applies to Métis people.

Constitutional **4.5.4**
Confirmation of
Alberta Metis The substance of the constitutional amendments relating to the
Settlements Metis Settlements of Alberta, referred to in section 55 of the
Charlottetown Accord and contained in sections 12 and 23 of

the Draft Legal Text of 9 October 1992, be enacted as soon as possible by joint action of the Parliament and government of Canada and the legislature and government of Alberta.

Education 4.5.5

When implementing this Commission's recommendations on education affecting Aboriginal persons, great care be exercised to ensure the preservation and propagation of distinct Métis cultures. Measures to achieve that goal might include, where appropriate,

(a) consultation with Métis elders when educational programs are being planned;

(b) establishment of and public funding support of separate Métis schools where numbers warrant;

(c) assisted access to post-secondary education for Métis persons;

(d) creation of a college or faculty of Métis studies and professorships, scholarships and programs of Métis studies; and

(e) provision of residential facilities in post-secondary educational institutions that will be congenial to Métis students.

Culture and Language 4.5.6

When implementing the recommendations made in Volume 3, all governments and relevant agencies bear in mind the distinct circumstances of Métis culture and languages.

Governments and private authorities and agencies should collaborate with authorized Métis representatives on measures to preserve, cultivate and study elements of Métis culture, including the following:

(a) Aboriginal languages: to encourage and assist Métis people to learn and use the Aboriginal languages with which their Métis ancestors were historically associated;

(b) Michif language: to implement, with Métis collaboration and public funding, special measures to save Michif from extinction and to encourage and assist Michif research and instruction;

(c) research and publications about Métis history and culture: to provide financial support for research and publications to disseminate information about Métis Nation history and culture by means of print, radio, television, film, theatre and other modes of expression;

(d) historical sites: to establish major Métis cultural history centres at historically significant sites such as Batoche and the Forks in Winnipeg, to be owned and operated by Métis representatives; and

(e) repatriation of artifacts: to repatriate major Métis artifacts from public and private collections to appropriate Métis-run locations.

Métis Land Bases 4.5.7

The governments of Canada and the relevant provinces and territories be prepared to make available, through negotiations with each recognized nation of Métis people, land bases sufficient in number, size, location and quality to permit the fulfilment of the nation's legitimate social, cultural, political and economic aspirations.

Métis Right to 4.5.8
Hunt and Fish for The governments of Manitoba, Saskatchewan and Alberta
Food
(a) recognize immediately that the right, under the *Constitution Act, 1930*, of "Indians" of those provinces to hunt, trap and fish for food in all seasons on unoccupied Crown land and other land to which they have a right of access applies to all Métis persons in those provinces;
(b) consult with leaders of the Métis Nation when determining who qualifies as a Métis person for that purpose;
(c) give the same right to non-status Indians residing in the prairie provinces after they have demonstrated their Aboriginal ancestry by some prescribed and fair method; and
(d) give the same right to Aboriginal persons residing outside the prairie provinces unless it has been extinguished by a legally binding extinguishment measure, and extend the right, where appropriate, to public waters.

Interim and 4.5.9
Permanent Land Federal, provincial and territorial governments
Use Agreements
(a) be prepared to enter into temporary land use agreements with Métis nations while land claims negotiations are pending or continuing; and
(b) be prepared, where appropriate, to consider longer-term land use agreements with Métis nations, perhaps in association with other interests, Aboriginal or private.

Negotiations on 4.5.10
Métis Self- The governments of Canada and of relevant provinces and territories
Government
(a) be prepared to negotiate immediately with appropriate Métis representatives (as well as, where appropriate, other Aboriginal governments) on the manner in which Métis self-government

will be recognized by and integrated with other governments and assisted to become financially self-sufficient; and

(b) pursue independently and swiftly those aspects of self-government that are not dependent upon land base considerations, although it will be appropriate for part of these negotiations to take place in the context of negotiations concerning the nation's land base.

Chapter 6 The North

The Commission recommends that

Nations and Public Territorial Government

4.6.1

Dene of Denendeh (Northwest Territories) be given the opportunity to come to future negotiations on new political arrangements in Denendeh as a nation.

4.6.2

A treaty commission be established at the request of Dene communities seeking a treaty process.

4.6.3

The treaty commission's deliberations be the means by which the governing authorities for Dene are determined within the new western territory in addition to the framework of public government for that territory as a whole.

4.6.4

Those charged with developing institutions for Denendeh recognize the leading role Aboriginal nation government will play across the territory and design a form of territorial government that exercises lead responsibility in relatively few areas and plays a co-ordinating role with other governments' activities where appropriate.

4.6.5

Communities that want to participate in a treaty implementation process rather than regional land claims be given the same range of flexibility in terms of subject matter and quantity of land as if they were participating in a land claims process.

High Cost of Government in the North

4.6.6

In Nunavut and in the remaining part of the Northwest Territories, future arrangements allocate clear responsibilities between Aboriginal nation governments and territorial institutions and be kept simple and focused, given the high cost of government across a widely dispersed population.

Public Education **4.6.7**
Public education materials be developed in co-operation with Aboriginal communications groups to explain the institutional changes taking place in Nunavut and the remaining part of the Northwest Territories.

Aboriginal People **4.6.8**
in Environmental The government of Canada recognize the contribution of
Stewardship Aboriginal traditional knowledge to environmental stewardship and support its development.

4.6.9
The government of Canada make provisions for the participation of Aboriginal governments and organizations in future international agreements concerning environmental stewardship.

4.6.10
The federal department of health continue the close monitoring of contamination of northern country food by atmospheric and other pollution and, given the importance of these foods to northern people, communicate the results of this work quickly and effectively to users of these renewable northern resources.

4.6.11
All governments in Canada support the development of co-management regimes along the lines of those already established in the North.

Redesign of **4.6.12**
Income Programs Federal and territorial governments establish a task force with strong Aboriginal representation to review all social assistance and income supplement programs across the territorial North with the goal of restructuring these programs to make them effective instruments in promoting a mixed economy and sustain viable, largely self-reliant communities.

4.6.13
Based on the work of the task force recommended in 4.6.12 and recognizing the fundamental changes under way in the structure and administration of social assistance programs across Canada, territorial governments take the initiative, in consultation with federal and provincial governments, to create a northern social policy

framework with sufficient flexibility to allow existing levels of social assistance spending to be used to fund community work creation and provide income supplements related to community employment or traditional production and harvesting.

4.6.14

Employment insurance and social assistance legislation be amended to take into account the specific differences in employment patterns, the high cost of living, the administrative delays that result from great distances between communities, and other factors unique to the northern economy.

Skilled
Management
Supports

4.6.15

Aboriginal, federal, provincial and territorial governments encourage innovative means of delivering skilled management support – including operations, financial and marketing expertise – to small enterprises through Aboriginal economic development corporations.

Research Program

4.6.16

Faculties of agriculture, forestry and business administration in Canadian universities, in collaboration with the proposed Aboriginal Peoples International University, develop a northern research program focused on the creation of employment and business opportunities through the use of the renewable resources sector, the exportation of traditional foods and food products, and the development of expertise to manage these resources at sustainable levels.

Hiring Criteria

4.6.17

All governments hiring personnel for northern and remote communities take into account skills acquired through life experience and the demonstrated capacity to develop new skills along with, and at times in place of, formal educational credentials.

Accommodating
the Traditional
Economy

4.6.18

Government employment policies accommodate the demands of traditional economic activities by increasing opportunities for job sharing, periodic leave and shift work.

Stable Funding for
Education and
Training

4.6.19

Governments provide stable multi-year funding to northern educational institutions that have the capacity to deliver the education and training needed for self-government and a diversified economy.

Education and Institutional Development **4.6.20**
The education and training of Aboriginal adults and young people form an integral part of all plans for institutional development in the North.

Support for Traditional Knowledge **4.6.21**
Governments provide continuing support for the development of institutes that gather and research traditional knowledge and apply it to contemporary issues.

4.6.22
Traditional knowledge be incorporated in all appropriate institutions, including cultural and research institutes, regulatory boards and the education and training system.

Chapter 7 Urban Perspectives

The Commission recommends that

Cultural Identity **4.7.1**
Aboriginal cultural identity be supported and enhanced in urban areas by
(a) Aboriginal, municipal, territorial, provincial and federal governments initiating programs to increase opportunities to promote Aboriginal culture in urban communities, including means to increase access to Aboriginal elders;
(b) municipal governments and institutions and Aboriginal elders co-operating to find ways of facilitating Aboriginal spiritual practices in the urban environment; and
(c) all governments co-operating to set aside land in urban areas dedicated to Aboriginal cultural and spiritual needs.

Financing Social Programs **4.7.2**
The federal government be responsible for
(a) the costs associated with developing, implementing and operating Aboriginal self-government initiatives on and off a land base through program funding and fiscal arrangements;
(b) programs, services and treaty entitlements for Aboriginal people living on reserves or extended Aboriginal territories;
(c) treaty entitlements or agreed upon social programs such as financial assistance for post-secondary education and unin-

sured health benefits for Indian people living off-reserve, to the extent that these exceed the programs or services provided to other residents by the province or territory in which they reside; and

(d) the cost of services for Métis people agreed to in treaty negotiations, once they have achieved self-government and a land base, including additional payments to Métis people living off their land base to cover benefits agreed to by treaty where those exceed benefits normally available to other provincial residents.

4.7.3
Provincial and territorial governments be responsible for

(a) providing and financing the programs and services that are available to residents in general, to all Aboriginal people residing in the province or territory, except those resident on-reserve, in Inuit communities or on extended Aboriginal territory; and

(b) providing programs and services for Aboriginal people that are culturally appropriate where numbers warrant.

Financing
Affirmative Action
Programs

4.7.4
The cost of affirmative action programs and services to address economic and social disadvantage affecting urban Aboriginal people be shared by the federal, provincial and territorial governments on the basis of a formula basis that reflects provincial/territorial fiscal capacity.

Aboriginal Service
Institutions

4.7.5
Provincial, territorial and municipal governments give priority to making the existing Aboriginal service delivery system more comprehensive as the most effective means of meeting the immediate needs of urban Aboriginal people.

4.7.6
Federal, provincial and territorial governments ensure that existing and new Aboriginal service institutions have a stable and secure funding base by

(a) making contribution and grant agreements with Aboriginal service institutions for periods of at least five years; and

(b) adjusting funding for existing and new Aboriginal and non-Aboriginal agencies to reflect actual services provided and caseloads.

Non-Aboriginal Service Agencies

4.7.7

Aboriginal people and organizations be directly involved in the design, development, delivery and evaluation of all services provided to Aboriginal clients by non-Aboriginal agencies.

4.7.8

Staff of non-Aboriginal service agencies directly involved in Aboriginal service delivery be given cross-cultural training delivered by Aboriginal people and organizations and that government funding agreements reflect this obligation.

Status-Blind versus Separate Institutions

4.7.9

Services to Aboriginal people in urban areas generally be delivered without regard to legal or treaty status.

4.7.10

Government policies on service delivery take into account the history and tradition of separate institutional development for Métis and treaty people in Manitoba, Saskatchewan and Alberta as well as local cultural, political and economic conditions.

Youth Services

4.7.11

Aboriginal governments and organizations accord higher priority to youth programming, particularly leadership development, sport and recreation.

4.7.12

Municipal, provincial, territorial and federal governments support, fund and actively provide services and programs for urban Aboriginal youth.

4.7.13

Aboriginal youth be closely involved in the design, development and delivery of youth services.

Support for Disabilities Organization

4.7.14

The federal government provide funding for a national organization to represent and speak on behalf of Aboriginal people with disabilities.

National Friendship Centre Program

4.7.15

The federal government devolve the administration of the National Aboriginal Friendship Centre program to the National Association of Friendship Centres.

Urban Cultural
Education
Program

4.7.16

The federal government establish and fund a national urban
Aboriginal cultural education program designed for Aboriginal
and non-Aboriginal people in large urban centres across
Canada, to be generally administered by friendship centres.

Aboriginal Women
in Urban Areas

4.7.17

Aboriginal women give Aboriginal and non-Aboriginal service
agencies direction and guidance in formulating policy and
developing services that may be used by Aboriginal women
and children and participate fully in the delivery of programs
and services established specifically to meet the needs of urban
Aboriginal women.

4.7.18

In addition to cross-cultural training, non-Aboriginal individuals and organizations whose work or responsibilities directly
affect urban Aboriginal women's lives receive comprehensive
information and education on the situation of urban Aboriginal
women.

Representation of
Urban Aboriginal
People

4.7.19

Positions be designated for Aboriginal representatives on local
boards and commissions responsible for services and the boards
of institutions in which Aboriginal people have a significant
interest.

4.7.20

Municipal councils and school boards in municipalities with a
large Aboriginal population establish Aboriginal affairs committees to provide advice and guidance on Aboriginal issues.

4.7.21

Municipal, provincial, territorial and federal governments seek
opportunities for co-management arrangements that would
involve Aboriginal people in establishing, managing and operating urban institutions, programs and services in which they
have an interest.

Urban
Community of
Interest
Approaches

4.7.22

Where urban Aboriginal residents wish to pursue self-government based on an urban community of interest, whether
involved in multiple government functions or acting through
a single institution,

(a) municipal, provincial and federal governments foster and support community building, including, where appropriate, developing the community of interest's governance initiative; and

(b) municipal, provincial and federal governments participate in negotiations to establish urban community of interest governments and assist them in operating institutions and services for members of the community of interest.

Nation-Based Approaches 4.7.23

Nation-based urban governance initiatives be pursued by nations when they have sufficient capacity to assume governance responsibility for the needs and interests of urban Aboriginal citizens.

4.7.24

The urban citizens of Aboriginal nations be fully consulted and participate in decisions concerning urban governance initiatives pursued by nations.

4.7.25

Aboriginal nations ensure that their urban citizens' needs and interests are recognized and that mechanisms are instituted to ensure they are represented in the political structures and decision-making processes of the nation.

4.7.26

Federal, provincial, territorial and municipal governments give full support to Aboriginal nations when they develop and implement urban governance initiatives.

VOLUME 5
RENEWAL:
A TWENTY-YEAR COMMITMENT

Chapter 1 Laying the Foundations of a Renewed Relationship

The Commission recommends that

First Ministers Meeting 5.1.1

First Ministers, territorial leaders and leaders of the national Aboriginal organizations meet within six months of the release of this report to

(a) review its principal recommendations;

(b) begin consultations on the drafting and enactment of a Royal Proclamation redefining the nature of the relationship between Aboriginal nations and Canadian governments; and

(c) establish a forum to create a Canada-Wide Framework Agreement.

Aboriginal Peoples Review Commission

5.1.2

The government of Canada introduce legislation to establish an Aboriginal Peoples Review Commission that is independent of government, reports to Parliament and is headed by an Aboriginal chief commissioner.

5.1.3

The Aboriginal Peoples Review Commission regularly monitor progress being made

(a) by governments to honour and implement existing treaties;

(b) in achieving self-government and providing an adequate lands and resource base for Aboriginal peoples;

(c) in improving the social and economic well-being of Aboriginal people; and

(d) in honouring governments' commitments and implementing the recommendations of the Royal Commission on Aboriginal Peoples.

5.1.4

The Aboriginal Peoples Review Commission report annually to Parliament and that Parliament use the occasion of the annual report to address Aboriginal issues in committee hearings and debate.

5.1.5

Provincial and territorial governments co-operate with the commission in fulfilling its mandate and respond in their legislatures to the commission's annual assessment of progress.

5.1.6

Federal and provincial first ministers and territorial leaders meet at regular intervals with national Aboriginal representatives to assess implementation of reform measures and to raise public awareness of Aboriginal concerns.

Chapter 4 Public Education: Building Awareness and Understanding

The Commission recommends that

Principles for Public Education

5.4.1

Public education on Aboriginal issues be based on the following principles:

(a) Building public awareness and understanding should become an integral and continuing part of every endeavour and every initiative in which Aboriginal people, their organizations and governments are involved and in which non-Aboriginal governments and stakeholders have a part.

(b) Public education should involve both the sharing of information and a process of interaction, leading in time to a shared sense of advocacy and of public support.

(c) Non-Aboriginal organizations and corporations should establish internal mechanisms to make themselves aware of the distinctive needs of Aboriginal people whom they serve or employ and to ensure that they respond to those needs.

Cross-Cultural Understanding

5.4.2

Bodies that represent or serve both Aboriginal and non-Aboriginal people

(a) be proactive and innovative in promoting understanding of Aboriginal issues; and

(b) review their own activities to ensure that they contribute to cross-cultural understanding and enhance relations with Aboriginal people.

Role for Aboriginal Organizations

5.4.3

Aboriginal people and organizations participate in the process of public education through direct involvement, by creating opportunities for interpersonal contact and by acting as agents of change in Canadian society.

5.4.4

Aboriginal organizations and governments include their own members and citizens in efforts to build greater public understanding of Aboriginal issues and the changes now affecting Aboriginal communities.

Aboriginal
Presence in the
Media

5.4.5

Canadian media reflect the growing presence of Aboriginal people in their audience or readership by hiring Aboriginal journalists and broadcasters and by giving greater priority to coverage of Aboriginal issues and communities.

5.4.6

Aboriginal radio and television programming be available to all Canadians via cable TV, building on the service of TV Northern Canada and the radio services of Aboriginal communications societies.

Symbols and
Occasions

5.4.7

Parliament and the national Aboriginal organizations jointly designate a national First Peoples Day to coincide with the issuing of a new Royal Proclamation and to be celebrated annually across Canada.

5.4.8

Special events such as Aboriginal Awareness Weeks be organized under joint Aboriginal and non-Aboriginal direction in all municipalities with a substantial Aboriginal population.

5.4.9

The commemoration of important occurrences in Aboriginal history through events such as treaty days and Louis Riel Day be expanded as a means of building solidarity and a vehicle for public education.

Use of Symbols,
Place Names and
Ceremonies

5.4.10

Canadian governments recognize Aboriginal people's contribution to Canada through much greater use of Aboriginal place names, languages, ceremonies and exhibits and by honouring Aboriginal meeting places and historic sites.

Public Education
Integral to All
Programs

5.4.11

Federal, provincial and territorial governments make public education an integral part of all programs that affect Aboriginal people and ensure that it is delivered in collaboration with Aboriginal organizations.

5.4.12

The federal government ensure that the history and present circumstances of Aboriginal peoples are communicated to immigrants and to persons becoming Canadian citizens.

Immediate Steps **5.4.13**

The CD-ROM version of the Commission's final report, research studies and public hearings be distributed by the government of Canada free of charge to every Canadian high school, college and university library.

5.4.14

A task force be established by a coalition of interested organizations and funded in part by the federal government to promote understanding and wide public discussion of the findings and recommendations of the Royal Commission on Aboriginal Peoples for at least the first year following publication of this report.

Chapter 5 Constitutional Amendment: The Ultimate Challenge

The Commission recommends that

Constitutional Conference **5.5.1**

Representatives of Aboriginal peoples be included in all planning and preparations for any future constitutional conference convened by the government of Canada.

5.5.2

A role for Aboriginal peoples and their governments in the amending process, including a veto for Aboriginal people on changes to sections 25, 35, 35.1 of the *Constitution Act, 1982* and section 91(24) of the *Constitution Act, 1867,* be one matter for consideration at any future conference.

5.5.3

Other matters of concern to Aboriginal peoples, including, in particular, explicit recognition of the inherent right of self-government, treaty making and implementation, the inclusion of Métis people in section 91(24), entrenchment of the Alberta *Metis Settlements Act,* and alterations to section 91(24) to reflect the broad self-governing jurisdiction of Aboriginal nations, form part of the constitutional agenda.

Appendix B

Tables of Contents
Volumes 1-5

Volume I
Looking Forward,
Looking Back

VOLUME 2

RESTRUCTURING
THE RELATIONSHIP

PART ONE

VOLUME 3

GATHERING STRENGTH

1. New Directions in Social Policy 1

2. The Family 9

VOLUME 4
Perspectives and Realities

VOLUME 5

Renewal:
A Twenty-Year Commitment

Appendices

APPENDIX C

How We Fulfilled
Our Mandate

The mandate conferred on the Royal Commission on Aboriginal Peoples on 26 August 1991 was extremely broad – possibly the broadest in the history of Canadian royal commissions. We were asked to look at virtually every aspect of the lives of the First Nations, Inuit and Métis peoples of Canada – their history, health and education; their aspirations for self-government and relations with Canadian governments; their land claims, treaties, economies and cultures; their living conditions in the North as well as in cities; their relationship with the justice system; the state of their languages; their spiritual well-being and, more generally, their situation in Canada relative to that of non-Aboriginal Canadians.

As we discovered soon after embarking on our task, any one of the sixteen points in our mandate could have been the subject of a royal commission. Even so, we saw the breadth and scope of our mandate as an advantage. For the first time, the problems confronting Aboriginal people could be approached not as single issues, to be dealt with in isolation and treated to ad hoc solutions, by as interrelated issues requiring the holistic approach that is fundamental to the Aboriginal view of the world: the sense that the many facets of human life and the natural world are interconnected, that problems arise from interrelated causes, not just a single cause, and that solutions must therefore be holistic and multifaceted as well.

How did we tackle this broad mandate? Underpinning our approach was the partnership referred to by Chief Justice Brian Dickson in his report to the government recommending the Commission's mandate and membership: Aboriginal and non-Aboriginal people working together to re-establish the association of equals that once characterized the relationship between Indigenous peoples and newcomers in North America. The composition of the Commission – four Aboriginal and three non-Aboriginal members – was echoed in our staff, in our consultation and research activities, and in the way we conducted the business of the Commission. It was represented graphically by our logo, designed by Joseph Sagutch, an Ojibwa artist living in Toronto. Four individuals are seated in a circle representing the Métis, Inuit, First Nations and non-Aboriginal peoples of Canada. The circular design conveys harmony, mirrors the shape of Mother Earth, and stands for the continuous journey of life. The bear paw centred in the circle symbolizes healing energy.

Bringing to the table their knowledge, experience and good faith, Commissioners faced the task of developing recommendations based on a large body of evidence accumulated by the Commission and by the various inquiries that had preceded ours. The information, advice and analysis that nurtured our policy development process came from two general sources: our program of consultations, including our public hearings and briefs from organizations and individuals, and our research program.

Consultations

We recognized from the outset that consultation would be a cornerstone of our process. In November and December 1991 we held informal meetings with regional, provincial and territorial Aboriginal leaders, representing some 100 Aboriginal organizations, with provincial premiers, and with federal and provincial ministers responsible for Aboriginal matters. The purpose of the meetings was fourfold: to introduce Commissioners to the individuals and organizations that would play a role in the future relationship between Aboriginal and non-Aboriginal people in Canada, to talk about issues within the Commission's mandate, to explain how the we intended to approach our mandate, and to encourage participation in our public consultation processes.

Public consultation played a significant role in our process. The Commission's work was concerned largely with *people* – their lives, their goals and their dreams – so we wanted to pay particular attention to the voices and ideas of the people concerned. We wanted to hear what they had to say about everything in our mandate and made a deliberate choice not to set limits on the issues that could be raised.

To the greatest degree possible, we went wherever we were invited, recognizing the need to meet with as broad a cross-section of Canadians as possible. We also reached out to people in a variety of ways: through advertisements in the media; with a video, *Forging a New Relationship*, encouraging people to participate in our public hearings; through invitations to submit opinions and ideas in writing; and with toll-free telephone lines where Canadians could make their views known in one of five languages (Inuktitut, Cree, Ojibwa, French and English).

Our public hearings opened in Winnipeg on 21 April 1992. The location was chosen for several reasons. Winnipeg is the geographic centre of Canada and of Turtle Island, the name by which many Aboriginal people know North America. Before Europeans moved into the west, the location now called Winnipeg was a traditional gathering place for trade and commerce among Aboriginal people, and today it has one of the largest urban Aboriginal populations in Canada. Winnipeg is also the capital city of a province that joined Confederation largely through the efforts of the Métis leader, Louis Riel. Joining us at the formal opening of the hearings were representatives of all the circles we hoped to touch through our work – youth and elders, women and men, Inuit, Métis and First Nations, Aboriginal and non-Aboriginal people from across the country.

To keep the process as open as possible, we began by listening to what people at the grassroots had to say. We felt that options and solutions had to emerge from consensus among Aboriginal people if our eventual recommendations were to command broad support and acceptance.

There followed another 18 months of crisscrossing the country from south to north and west to east and holding hearings in communities large and small between April 1992 and December 1993. Working in three teams to cover the largest possible number of locations, we visited northern and remote communities and urban centres. Over the four rounds of hearings, we listened to Canadians – Aboriginal and non-Aboriginal alike – in friendship centres, community halls, penitentiaries, band council offices, traditional long houses, schools, women's shelters, and hockey rinks, as well as in hotels and conference centres.

In many places, we hired a local person recommended by the community to prepare for our visit by identifying the main issues of interest to the community and to seek out presenters. These community and regional representatives acted as ambassadors, preparing communities for the hearings and briefing Commissioners about each community we visited – what some of the main concerns were, who the presenters would be, and any special circumstances that might prevail in the community.

At each hearing, we invited an elder or community leader to join the panel as a Commissioner for that day, to introduce presenters and Commissioners to each other, and to help us understand the background and complexity of the issues being presented. These respected community members played the essential role of catalyst to the interaction between presenters and Commissioners. They put presenters at ease – making informal what could have been a daunting experience. They encouraged them to speak in their own language, and many did – we heard Inuktitut, Cree, Montagnais, Saulteaux and Ojibwa, among other languages – and drew out information from them in a way that a stranger to the community might not have been able to do in the limited time available. As the hearings progressed, we encouraged these Commissioners of the day to play a more active role, asking questions and clarifying points as they felt necessary. In some cases elders also gave the opening and closing prayers at each hearing.

By the end of the fourth round, in December 1993, we had visited 96 communities (some of them more than once), held 178 days of hearings, heard briefs or statements from some 2,067 people representing organizations, communities or associations or speaking on their own behalf, and generated 75,000 pages of transcribed testimony. At the conclusion of each round of hearings we published an overview that was widely circulated to Aboriginal communities. We also received close to 1,000 written submissions from presenters and other members of the public.

All this took a significant amount of time and energy – not only in terms of the organizational and logistical challenge for the Commission's staff, but also the time and effort put in by organizations and individuals preparing presentations to us. But if our work results in positive change in the lives of Aboriginal people and in their communities, it was time well spent.

Our approach to consultation also involved reaching out to the various communities of experts – those with specialized knowledge and experience in fields such as health and healing, economic development, justice and urban issues. For example, close to the beginning of our mandate we sought advice to help us achieve a holistic approach to the issues by holding two brainstorming sessions with 20 distinguished Aboriginal and non-Aboriginal thinkers. Each contributed a think piece to focus discussions during those sessions.

Many of the challenging aspects of the relationship between Aboriginal and non-Aboriginal Canadians have counterparts for Indigenous peoples elsewhere in the world. Chief Justice Dickson advised that we should consider the experiences of Indigenous peoples in other countries. We decided to visit the Dineh (Navaho), Apache and Pueblo territories in the southwestern United States to learn about their experience with a separate justice system. With passage of the act to create the new northern territory of Nunavut, we decided also to visit Greenland, where home rule has been in effect since 1979. We also attended the Dakota-Lakota Summit in Rapid City, South Dakota, to learn about the process of rebuilding in which the Dakota-Lakota-Nakota Nation (which now spans both sides of the Canada-U.S. border) is engaged.

We also held a series of round tables in 1992 and 1993: on health and social issues, education, justice, urban issues, and economic development. The goal of each was to focus expert discussion on practical solutions and the steps necessary to produce positive change in the policies, programs and conditions affecting Aboriginal lives and communities.

In a similar vein, we held a special consultation with the Métis National Council and its affiliates and one with other Métis organizations recently affiliated in the Metis Confederacy, to examine and debate the history, current conditions and aspirations of the diverse Métis population of Canada.

Throughout our mandate we maintained close contact with Aboriginal organizations and provincial governments. This was particularly helpful during our initial consultations to identify key issues and to plan consultations. For example, senior staff met numerous times with their counterparts at the Assembly of First Nations, Inuit Tapirisat of Canada, the Métis National Council, Pauktuutit (the Inuit Women's Association), the Congress of Aboriginal Peoples (formerly the Native Council of Canada), and the Native Women's Association of Canada. We also maintained contact with provincial governments and with the federal government through the liaison office established by the Department of Indian Affairs and Northern Development, which provided assistance on many occasions.

To facilitate participation in our work, the federal government set up an Intervenor Participation Program to help groups and organizations prepare well researched briefs, which they presented during our last two rounds of hearings. This program recognized that many Aboriginal groups did not have the resources needed to research and articulate their positions. The Honourable David Crombie administered the program, reviewing and approving all funding applications at arm's length from the Commission. In all, 241 projects were funded, and we received 228 completed research reports.[1] Recipients of this funding included national, provincial and territorial Aboriginal political organizations, Aboriginal women's groups, associations of friendship centres, social service associations, elders' and youth associations, associations of people with disabilities, and non-Aboriginal national, provincial and territorial professional and voluntary organizations.

Finally, we held several special consultations on subjects raised at the hearings that seemed to warrant further, more focused attention. These special consultations concerned the relocation of Inuit from Inukjuak in northern Quebec and Pond Inlet on Baffin Island to the High Arctic in the 1950s; residential schools for Aboriginal children (including a consultation between the Commission and the historical mission churches); and the pressing issue of suicide among Aboriginal people (two formal consultations with community leaders and other experts on the issue of suicide in Aboriginal communities).

The second major source of information and advice for our deliberations on policy and recommendations was our research program.

Research

The Commission's wide-ranging research program encompassed more than 350 research projects (see Appendix D). To focus our research agenda, Commissioners and the Commission's research directors met with some 150 of Canada's most distinguished scholars in two brainstorming sessions that identified major issue areas. We also identified where reliable research had already been conducted and where gaps needed to be filled by policy-oriented research in the various areas of our mandate.[2] The Commission's research program concentrated on these areas.

We chose four major research themes – governance, lands and economy, social and cultural matters, and the North – cross-cut by the particular perspectives of history, women, youth and Aboriginal people living in urban areas. We organized our research around themes rather than traditional academic disciplines; this allowed us to conduct research on the sixteen points of our mandate while also developing an integrated picture of all the issues on which to base recommendations that take account of the interconnections between and among the issues and the need for a holistic approach to policy.

We recognized from the outset that one of the problems with much of the existing research was the difficulty of representing Aboriginal reality authentically. To ensure that all research sponsored by the Commission gave appropriate respect to the cultures, languages, knowledge and values of Aboriginal peoples and to the standards used by Aboriginal peoples to legitimate knowledge, we developed ethical guidelines to be followed by researchers under contract with the Commission. These guidelines were a significant step forward in encouraging culturally based approaches to research and stimulating research that represents Aboriginal experience, society and history in ways that are authenticated by Aboriginal people themselves (see Appendix E).

We used several criteria to decide what research to commission. The research had to be relevant for policy making, leading to policy advice and recommendations. It had to be completed in a timely way, since the results had to be available within a certain time frame if they were to influence the final report. Research had to be forward-looking and directed to shaping the future, although the historical perspective was also reflected in the research program. Finally, we sought a mix of scholarly studies and case studies at the community level, of university-based research and research examining initiatives in Aboriginal communities in such areas as justice and policing systems, education and economic development. To monitor progress on the integrated research plan, we established a Research Advisory Committee composed of Aboriginal and non-Aboriginal scholars and two commissioners (see Appendix F).

We sought a balance of Aboriginal people and non-Aboriginal people not only to conduct research but also to develop, plan and manage the research program, again in keeping with our desire to ensure that Aboriginal peoples' perspectives and understandings – derived from distinctive cultures and histories and embodied in Aboriginal languages – were reflected in research on the Aboriginal experience. Development of the research program also involved extensive consultation with Aboriginal peoples and governments. Again, these efforts took time, but it is time we judged essential to do justice to our mandate and to the peoples encompassed by it.

We are confident that our research activities have made a significant contribution to advancing the state of scholarship in Aboriginal affairs. Our research contributed to the development of our recommendations for restructuring the relationship between Aboriginal and non-Aboriginal people in Canada and added significant new dimensions to the existing body of knowledge on Aboriginal affairs and culture.

In the area of treaties, for example, where the oral tradition has predominated in the Aboriginal experience, research conducted for us has added a new dimension to our understanding of this area of our history and the present relationship between Aboriginal peoples and governments in Canada. We accorded respect to oral sources that have frequently been neglected. Our understanding of the diverse governance systems of Aboriginal communities has been enhanced by the 20 community studies on governance. Ten three-generation life histories of First Nations, Inuit and Métis families have enriched our understanding of Aboriginal cultural values.

By the time the research program was completed, we had some 330 studies in hand. These represented the efforts of about 365 researchers from most Canadian and a number of foreign universities and involving more than 100 communities and some 30 Aboriginal organizations across the country. This research legacy will be available to future generations of Canadians in the form of a CD-ROM, published studies, archival materials and other documents.

Keeping Canadians Informed

Throughout the process the Commission placed ideas, suggestions and principles before the people of Canada for their reaction. We did not propose solutions based on theory or academic study; instead we developed discussion documents based on what we had heard at the public hearings. These documents served two purposes: they made sure that we had listened well and grasped the messages presented to us in communities across Canada by parents, teachers, health care workers, counsellors, elders, school children and many others. They also enabled us to begin the process of testing the solutions that were starting to emerge, helping to ensure that our final recommendations were firmly grounded in the realities of Aboriginal peoples' lives and reflected their aspirations and visions for the future.

The first round of public hearings was a listening phase, when Canadians from many different backgrounds and cultures had an opportunity to speak about their varied experiences, interests, needs and desires. As the rounds of hearings progressed, certain issues and questions began to emerge that we wanted to see explored more fully, and we began to look for people's ideas not just about problems but about possible solutions. In each successive round of hearings we encouraged interveners to focus their comments in these areas – or to challenge the Commission's interpretation of what the important issues were. In some locations, community and regional representatives and Commission staff worked with communities and organizations to support their efforts to develop solutions and recommendations for presentation. We also made available four documents summarizing what we had heard at each of the four rounds – *Framing the Issues, Focusing the Dialogue, Exploring the Options* and *Toward Reconciliation,* in some cases with accompanying videos, designed to identify the kinds of contributions the Commission was looking for in the next round.

Other publications – discussion papers, summaries of round table proceedings, and research reports (see Appendix G) – disseminate the results of our work and add to the body of resource materials on Aboriginal affairs.

At various points during our mandate we were asked to express opinions on or to draw public attention to matters of urgency, with the goal of launching or focusing national debate. We released two constitutional commentaries, *The Right of Aboriginal Self-Government and the Constitution* (February 1992) and *Partners in Confederation: Aboriginal Peoples, Self-Government, and the*

Constitution (August 1993), to contribute to the public debate on the Aboriginal right of self-government during and after negotiations on the Charlottetown Accord.

As a result of the special consultations we held, we published several reports with recommendations to the government, beginning in the summer of 1994: *The High Arctic Relocation: A Report on the 1953-55 Relocation; Choosing Life, A Special Report on Suicide among Aboriginal people; Treaty Making in the Spirit of Co-Existence: An Alternative to Extinguishment;* and *Bridging the Cultural Divide: A Report on Aboriginal People and Criminal Justice in Canada.* Each concerned a subject that requires urgent attention and is pivotal to establishing a new basis for relations between Aboriginal and non-Aboriginal people in Canada.

Governments were not our only audience, however. The Commission took its public education role seriously and recognized the importance of talking to today's youth about the future of relations between Aboriginal and non-Aboriginal people in Canada. To reach these audiences, we produced a number of video tapes. One, *A Time for Action,* reflected on the issues raised at the round table on justice. Another, a music video entitled *Let's Make a Difference* and co-sponsored by the Bank of Montreal, was targeted to the youth of the country. In addition, the National Film Board produced a one-hour television documentary on issues put before the Commission during its public hearings, for broadcast around the time our report is released.

At the close of our work, a CD-ROM containing a large part of the evidence we considered will be available: the public hearing transcripts, this report and other special reports, discussion papers and much of the research conducted for us. The CD-ROM will include a guide for use by teachers in secondary schools and adult learning programs.

Formulating our Recommendations

Finally, in the fall of 1993, we launched a policy process to prepare this report. We created a policy directorate to guide the process and struck 14 policy teams composed of Aboriginal and non-Aboriginal staff and sector specialists from outside the Commission. There was great diversity in the personnel on each of these teams, to ensure that a wide range of perspectives, knowledge and practical experience was brought to bear on the policy analysis and formulation of recommendations.

The first challenge we faced was to bring about a satisfactory integration of the enormous amount of evidence and research that had been collected through oral testimony and written submissions, round table discussions and special consultations, and the research studies. After identifying the issues under each theme and perspective, we began to develop a framework showing how the issues could be resolved in an interrelated fashion.

Our initial hope was to return to test our ideas with the communities we originally visited. There would no doubt have been much to learn through such a process, but it did not prove feasible with the time and resources available. We were able to use our community-based research, however, to gain a perspective on the types of recommendations that would be workable at the community level.

Drafting of the final report began in the fall of 1994. This proved to be an intense and interactive process between the 14 policy teams and the Commissioners. Staff prepared background papers on the critical issues in each area of the mandate. These led to conceptual outlines of chapters, which gave Commissioners an opportunity to provide policy direction early in the drafting process. As the shape of the volumes began to take form, staff returned with drafts and redrafts, always seeking to move beyond analysis of the problem to solutions that would address their underlying causes. As chapters were developed, Commissioners and staff addressed the linkages between issues and proposed integrated solutions for a range of problems in a holistic fashion.

Commissioners finished their collective work on this report in late August 1995. What remained was to review the report volume by volume, to ensure that the positions developed in the various areas of our mandate contained no internal conflict or inconsistency. As each volume was reviewed, it was sent off to the team of editors and translators whose work readied it for printing.

Staffing the Commission

To organize this massive undertaking, we assembled a staff that reflected exceptional diversity in background, life experiences, culture, and regional origin. They organized hearings, round tables and special consultations; figured out the logistics of transporting and housing three teams of Commissioners, staff and technical support in cities and remote communities in all kinds of weather conditions (travelling by jet, small charter plane, boat, skidoo, dogsled, bus and pick-up truck). Under the Commissioners' direction, staff planned and managed research, collated and analyzed information, developed options and drafted issue papers, chapters and recommendations, and ran the Commission's internal administrative functions.

We received more than 3,500 applications for employment from interested and qualified individuals. In hiring, we strove to achieve a balance between Aboriginal and non-Aboriginal people, between men and women, among regions, and among First Nations, Inuit and Métis. We were fortunate in being able to offer some summer employment to qualified students. More than 90 per cent of these positions were filled by Aboriginal young people from across the country. A list of commission staff appears in Appendix H and a breakdown of expenditures in Appendix I.

They came together from across the country for a common purpose, developed a sense of community and a spirit of teamwork. The nature of the issues and the importance of the Commission's conclusions and recommendations, particularly to Aboriginal staff, coupled with the diverse backgrounds and experiences that staff and Commissioners brought to these tasks, aroused strong feelings and conflicting views. On many occasions staff met in a circle to speak openly about their views, feelings and expectations; sometimes Commissioners joined them. These sessions did not always produce consensus but they always restored respect and built bonds of understanding. Along with the prayers that opened and closed every Commission meeting, these circles became the spiritual underpinnings that proved to be a vital aspect of the Commission's work.

A Final Word

As we look back over the times since the Commission was appointed late in the summer of 1991, Chief Justice Brian Dickson's recommendations for our mandate stand out like *inuksuit,* the Inuit stone landmarks that have guided travellers through the ages. They indicated the direction we were to travel, though perhaps not all the peaks and valleys we would encounter along the way. As we embarked on this voyage of discovery, we were guided by a vision of the renewed relationship that is possible between Aboriginal and non-Aboriginal people in Canada, and this is what we hope will continue to guide Canadians as they read our report, digest our recommendations, and decide on how best to forge our common future together.

NOTES

1. Intervenor Participation Program, *Final Report* (August 1994).

2. See Royal Commission on Aboriginal Peoples, *Public Policy and Aboriginal Peoples, 1965-1992,* 4 volumes (Ottawa: Supply and Services, 1993-1996).

Appendix D

Research Studies Prepared for the Commission

Studies are listed alphabetically by author, followed by the author's affiliation (in parentheses) where applicable and the title or subject of the research study. Where there is more than one study by an author or authors, entries are separated by a semi-colon. Where there is more than one author, the other authors' names are cross-referenced to the main entry. Studies marked with an asterisk may have been quoted or cited in other volumes of this report under another title. Titles listed here are for authors' final versions, after peer review and editing; titles cited earlier in the report may have been for previous drafts.

Abel, Alizette, *see* Lutra Associates Ltd.

Absolon, Kathleen E., and Anthony R. Winchester, Urban Perspectives/Cultural Identity Project/Victoria Report/Case Studies of 'Sonny' and 'Emma'; Cultural Identity For Urban Aboriginal Peoples, Learning Circles Synthesis Report

Ahenakew, Freda, et al. (Cree Language Consulting), Aboriginal Language Policy and Planning in Canada

Alfred, Gerald R., A Review and Analysis of the Major Challenges and Concerns of Aboriginal Youth in Canada

Alfred, Gerald R., and Nadine S. Huggins, Learning from the International Experience: A Comparative Review of State Policies for Indigenous Youth

Alfred, Gerald R. (Mohawk Council of Kahnawake), The Meaning of Self-Government in Kahnawake

Allard, Yvon, Georg Lithman, John O'Neil and Moneca Sinclaire, Winnipeg Case Study of Health and Social Services: Final Report

Anaquod, Del C., Aboriginal Economic, Training, Education and Employment; Urban Institutional Development – Case Study, Regina

Anaquod, Del C., and Vikas Khaladkar, Case Study – The First Nations Economy in the City of Regina

Anaya, S. James, Richard Falk, and Donat Pharand, Canada's Fiduciary Obligation to Aboriginal Peoples in the Context of Accession to Sovereignty by Quebec, Volume 1 – International Dimensions

Anderson, Margaret, *see* Tammy Blumhagen

Apamuwek Institute, *see* Russel Lawrence Barsh

Apikan Ltd., *see* Simon Brascoupé

Aronson, Stephen, and Ronald C. Maguire, Federal Treaty Policy Study

Arrison, Sonia, *see* Roger Gibbins

Arctic Institute of North America, *see* Wanda Wuttunee; Ellen Bielawski

Ashlee, Jette Elisabeth, Four Generations of an Arctic Family

ATII Training Inc., Northern Education and Training Systems for Inuit: A Strategic Analysis

Aucoin, Peter, and Violet Paul, Canadian Governments and Aboriginal Peoples Project/Province of Nova Scotia

Augustine, Stephen J., Tammy Augustine, Beatrice Francis, Richard M. Lacasse, Berthe A. Lambert and Darlene Sock, Economic Profile of Big Cove – Case Study Analysis; Social Profile of Big Cove – Case Study Analysis

Augustine, Tammy, see Stephen Augustine

Baird, Peter, see Conexus Research Group Inc.

Barham, Vicky, and Robin Boadway, Financing Aboriginal Self-Government

Barsh, Russel Lawrence, Aboriginal Self-Government in the United States: A Qualitative Political Analysis; High Arctic Relocation – International Norms and Standards

Barsh, Russel Lawrence, and James Youngblood Henderson (Apamuwek Institute), International Context of Crown-Aboriginal Treaties in Canada

Bear Robe, Andrew (Siksika Nation), The Historical, Legal and Current Basis for Siksika Nation Governance, Including its Future Possibilities within Canada

Begley Consulting Ltd., Oil and Gas Sectoral Study

Belcourt, Tony, see Wolfwalker Communications

Bell, Emil, Urban Perspectives/Cultural Identity Project – Case Study of 'Walter'

Bell, Lucille (Old Massett Village Council), 1993 Youth Perspectives Report of Old Massett

Berry, John W. (Cross-Cultural/Multi-Cultural Association), Aboriginal Cultural Identity

Bielawski, Ellen (Arctic Institute of North America), Barney Masuzumu, and the Lutsel K'e Dene First Nation, The Desecration of Nánúlá Kúé: Impact of Taltson Hydroelectric Development on Dene Sonline

Bishop, Angela, Green Lake community study, Saskatchewan

Bissonnette, Alain, see Andrée Lajoie

Bissonnette, Alain, and André Patry, The Rights of Aboriginal Peoples: From the Past to the Future (TRANSLATION)

Blackduck, Alison, and Marina Devine, The Stanton Yellowknife Abortion Crisis: A Case Study in Aboriginal Women's Health Care, Phase One – Background and History of Events

Blondin, George, Dene Life in the Sahtu Region of the Northwest Territories: A Life History over Three Generations*

---

* Revised title; see introductory note at the beginning of this appendix (page 306).

Blumhagen, Tammy Anderson, and Margaret Seguin Anderson, Memories and Moments: Conversation and Recollections – Life History Project

Boadway, Robin, *see* Vicky Barham

Brascoupé, Simon, Cultural Centres and Cultural Revitalization; Kitigan Zibi Anishinabeg Economic Case Study

Brascoupé, Simon, Anita Tenasco and Mona Tolley (Apikan Ltd.), Kitigan Zibi Anishinabeg Education Case Study

Brice-Bennett, Carol (Labrador Institute of Northern Studies), Dispossessed: The Eviction of Inuit from Hebron, Labrador; Labrador Inuit Life Histories

Brisson, Jean-Maurice, *see* Andrée Lajoie

Brock, Kathy L., Relations with Canadian Domestic Governments – Manitoba

Brockman, Aggie, *see* Lutra Associates Ltd.

Brodbar, Jay, The Development of the Institutional Infrastructure of the Jewish Community of Greater Toronto

Brodhead, Dal, *see* New Economy Development Group

Brooke, Lorraine F., An Inventory of Mapping Projects in Connection with Aboriginal Land and Resource Use in Canada; The James Bay and Northern Quebec Agreement: Experiences of the Nunavik Inuit with Wildlife Management

Brown, Douglas M., and Alan Kari, Aboriginal Peoples and Canadian Federalism: An Overview

Brown, Douglas M., and Jonathan Rose, Exercising Aboriginal Self-Government: The Intergovernmental Transition

Brown, Leslie A., Community and the Administration of Aboriginal Governments

Cameron, David, and Jill Wherrett, New Relationship, New Challenges: Aboriginal Peoples and the Province of Ontario

Cardinal, Harold (Grand Council of Treaty 8 First Nations), Treaty 8 – A Case Study

Carens, Joseph H., Citizenship and Aboriginal Self-Government

Carleton University, Centre for Policy and Program Assessment, Public Policy and Aboriginal Peoples, 1965-1992 (4 volumes)

Caswell, Heather M., First Nations Taxation Exemption and Jurisdiction: The Legal Context and Policy Options

Catholique, Bertha, *see* Lutra Associates Ltd.

CESO Aboriginal Services, Lessons from the CESO Experience: Helping People to Help Themselves

Chamberlin, Ted, and Hugh Brody, Aboriginal History

Chambers, Cynthia, *see* Lutra Associates Ltd.

Champagne, Louise, *see* John Loxley

Chapeskie, Andrew, Land, Landscape, Culturescape: Aboriginal Relationships to Land and the Co-Management of Natural Resources

---

* Revised title; see introductory note at the beginning of this appendix (page 306).

Davis, Lynne, Electronic Classrooms, Electronic Highways: A Review of
    Aboriginal Distance Education in Canada

de Aguayo, Anna, Background Paper on Customary Adoption

de Montigny, Gerald A.J., The Assumptions of Non-Aboriginal Child and
    Family Services

Deer, Kevin, Mohawk of Kahnawake Community Study: A Narrative of a
    Future Beyond Disunity

Deh Cho Tribal Council (Rene Lamothe, Dene Nation), "It Was Only A
    Treaty": Treaty 11 According to the Dene of the Mackenzie Valley

Deiter-McArthur, Pat, Plains Cree Women

Delâge, Denys, Cultural Exchanges within the Franco-Amerindian Alliance,
    1600-1760 [TRANSLATION]

Delâge, Denys, Jean-Pierre Sawaya, Marc Jetten and Régent Sioui, Les sept
    feux, les alliances et les traités autochtones du Québec dans l'histoire*

Dene Cultural Institute, Dogrib Traditional Government

Dene Nation (Antoine Mountain and Susan Quirk), Dene Nation: An Analysis

Dene Nation (Susan Quirk), Yellowknife 1993: Aboriginal Peoples in the
    Capital of the Northwest Territories

Dene Nation, see also Deh Cho Tribal Council

Denhez, Marc, see Anne Noonan

Deom, Christine, Community Profile – Kahnawake

Depew, Robert C., Aboriginal Policing: A Research Perspective

DesBrisay, David, The Gaming Industry in Aboriginal Communities; The
    Impact of Major Resource Development Projects on Aboriginal
    Communities: A Review of the Literature

Descent, Danielle, Violence and Healing: Data on Family Violence and
    Healing among the Innuat of Uashat mak Mani-Utenam [TRANSLATION]

Despins, Daniel, see Insight Canada Research

Devine, Marina, see Alison Blackduck

Dialla, Andrew, see Praxis Research Associates

Dickerson, Mark O., and Robert Shotton, Northern Self-Government and
    Subsidiarity: Centralization vs. Community Empowerment

Dittburner, Carolyn and Allan M. Maslove, Making Finance Fit: Funding
    Arrangements for Aboriginal Governments

Doern, G. Bruce, The Politics of Slow Progress: Federal Aboriginal Policy
    Processes

Dore, Thomas, see Paul Dudgeon

Dorion, John, and Kuan R. Yang, Métis Post-Secondary Education: A Case
    Study on the Gabriel Dumont Institute

Dorion, Leah, see Frank Tough

---

* Revised title; see introductory note at the beginning of this appendix (page 306).

Fouillard, Camille, Gathering Voices: Discovering Our Past, Present and Future

Four Directions Consulting Group (Stewart Clatworthy, Jeremy Hull and Neil Loughran), Patterns of Employment, Unemployment and Poverty, Part One

Four Directions Consulting Group (Stewart Clatworthy), The Migration and Mobility Patterns of Canada's Aboriginal Population

Francis, Beatrice, see Stephen Augustine

Frederick H. Weihs Consulting (Sinaaq Enterprises Inc.), A Review and Assessment of the Economic Utilization and Potential of Country Food in the Northern Economy

Futura Consulting (J.P. Woods), Urban Treaty and Jurisdictional Mechanisms

Fulham, Richard Scott, A Historical Review of Metis Agriculture and its Current Status in Canada

Gardner, Ethel, First Nations House of Learning: A Continuity of Transformation

Gareau, Marcelle, and Heather Harris, Edmonton Social Service Agency: Case Study

Geddes, Carol, Tom Hill and Mary E. Jamieson, Aboriginal People and Arts Policies in Canada

General, Rowena, A Case Study of the Traditional Roles of Women in Collective Decision Making in the Mohawk Community of Ahkwesa'hsne

Gibbins, Roger, Sonia Arrison and Jennifer Stewart, Domestic Governments and Aboriginal Peoples: The Alberta Case

Gilchrist, Lauri, and R. Anthony Winchester, kāptītipis ē-pimohteyahk: Vancouver, Winnipeg, and Montreal

Gilmour, E. Ann, see Louise Mandell

Giokas, John, The Indian Act: Evolution, Overview and Options for Amendment and Transition

Giokas, John, see also Bradford W. Morse

Girard, Camil, Culture and Intercultural Dynamics, Volume 1 – The Life Stories of Three Men from Saguenay-Lac-Saint-Jean; Volume 2 – The Life Stories of Three Women from Saguenay-Lac-Saint-Jean [TRANSLATION]

Godin-Beers, Monique, Youth Perspectives Community Studies – Synthesis Paper

Godin-Beers, Monique, and Cinderina Williams, Report of the Spallumcheen Child Welfare Program

Goldsmith, Claire K., Training the Teachers of Aboriginal Children

Goodwill, Jean, Historical Overview of Social, Political, Cultural and Economic Aboriginal Women's Organizations in Canada

Goss Gilroy Inc., Federal, Territorial and Provincial Expenditures Relating to Aboriginal Peoples

Graham, Katherine A., et al., Report of the Urban Governance Working Group

---

[*] Revised title; see introductory note at the beginning of this appendix (page 306).

---

[*] Revised title; see introductory note at the beginning of this appendix (page 306).

Mandell, Louise, B.C. Issues; Urban Land Base

Mandell, Louise, and E. Ann Gilmour, Metis Land Rights in Canada

Manitoba Metis Federation, A Report on Metis Self-Government*

Manyfingers, Brenda, Treaty 7 Community Study: Family Violence and Community Stress

Maracle, Richard R., and Associates, Wildlife Sectoral Study

Marcotte, Giselle, "Métis, c'est ma nation. 'Your own people' comme on dit": Life Histories From Eva, Evelyn, Priscilla and Jennifer Richard

Marcus, Alan Rudolph, Inuit Relocation Policies in Canada and Other Circumpolar Countries, 1925-1960

Marshall, Murdena, The Role of Mi'kmaq Women in a Contemporary Society

Martin, Fred, see Don McMahon

Maslove, Allan M., see Carolyn Dittburner

Masty, Emily, Women's Three Generations: Life History Project in Whapmagoostui, Quebec

Masuzumu, Barney, see Ellen Bielawski

Matte, Rock J., Francophone Workshop Report on Cultural Identity [TRANSLATION]; Quebec City Case Study: An Urban Perspective on Cultural Identity

Matthews, Hans, see Price Waterhouse

Mauro, Jennifer, see JM Consulting

Metis Family and Community Justice Services Inc. (Clement Chartier), Governance Study: Metis Self-Government in Saskatchewan

Metis Nation of Alberta Association, Metis Nation of Alberta Association Final Report

Metis Settlements General Council, Aboriginal Governance Project: Metis Settlements General Council

Metis Society of Saskatchewan, see Metis Family and Community Justice Services

Mews Corporation (Stan Willox), Urban Aboriginal Housing Project: Case Study – Gabriel Housing Corporation

Milen, Robert A., Canadian Representation and Aboriginal Peoples: A Survey of the Issues

Miller, George W., Inuit Non-Profit Housing Corporation of Ottawa / A Case Study

Milne, David, The Case of New Brunswick/Aboriginal Relations

Milloy, J.S., "Suffer the Little Children..." A History of the Residential School System, 1830-1992*

Mitchell, Darcy A., and Paul Tennant, Government to Government: Aboriginal Peoples and British Columbia

---

* Revised title; see introductory note at the beginning of this appendix (page 306).

Penn, Alan, The James Bay and Northern Quebec Agreement: Natural Resources, Public Lands, and the Implementation of a Native Land Claim Settlement*

Petch, Virginia (Northern Lights Heritage Services), The Relocation of the Sayisi Dene of Tadoule Lake

Pharand, Donat, see S. James Anaya

Phillips, Henry, see H.P. Consultants

Pierce, Jon, and Robert Hornal, Aboriginal People and Mining in Nunavut, Nunavik and Northern Labrador; Uranium Exploration and Mining and Aboriginal Peoples in Northern Canada

Pinder, Leslie, see Louise Mandell

Pinkerton, Evelyn, Fred Fortier and Dave Moore, A Model for First Nation Leadership in Multi-Party Stewardship of Watersheds and their Fisheries

Pinkham, Delphine, see André LeDressay

Pompana, Yvonne, Cultural Identity Case Study; A Metis Woman Draft Case Study; Male Prisoner

Pratt, Alan, Discussion Paper Regarding the Natural Resources Transfer Agreements of the Prairie Provinces; The Numbered Treaties and Extinguishment: A Legal Analysis

Praxis Research Associates (Gwen D. Reimer and Andrew Dialla), A Case Study of the Inuit Economy: Pangnirtung, Northwest Territories

Price Waterhouse (Hans Matthews), Aboriginal Participation in the Minerals Industry

Prince, Michael J., and Gary Juniper, Public Power and the Public Purse: Governments, Budgets and Aboriginal Peoples in the Canadian North

Public Policy Nexus Group Inc. (J. Weinstein, L. Mandell, J. Magnet, D.N. Sprague, F. Tough and L. Dorion), Métis Land Rights – Legal and Historical Issues

Queen's University, Case Study of the Current Political and Financial Situation of the United Native Nations

Queen's University, see also Vicky Barham

Quirk, Susan, see Dene Nation

Rasmussen, Ken, The Case of Saskatchewan-Aboriginal Relations

Reaume, Denise G., et al., Education for Subordination: Redressing the Adverse Effects of Residential Schooling

Reed, Estelle, Citizenship

Reid, John D., see Bill Wicken

Reimer, Gwen, see Praxis Research Associates

Reporter, Cyrus, Literature Review of Alternatives to the *Indian Act* and the Department of Indian Affairs (Governance)

---

* Revised title; see introductory note at the beginning of this appendix (page 306).

Reynolds, Henry, Aboriginal Governance in Australia

Richard R. Maracle & Associates, *see* Richard R. Maracle

Roberts, Carol, International Models Relevant to Aboriginal Self-Government in Canada

Rose, Jonathan, *see* Douglas Brown

Rudnicki, Walter, Land, Identity and Survival: The Dislocation of Aboriginal Nations in Canada

Russell, Peter, and Roger Jones, Aboriginal Peoples and Constitutional Reform

Ryan, Ron, *see* Sinaaq Enterprises Inc.

Sanders, Douglas, Developing a Modern International Law on the Rights of Indigenous Peoples; Indigenous Peoples and Canada's Role on the International Stage; Tribal Self-Government in India

Sasakamoose, Eileen, Sharon Venne and Rene Lamothe, Comparative Analysis of Treaties and Comprehensive Claims – Dene Views on Treaty Making and Claims Settlement

Saskatchewan Indian Federated College, Aboriginal Post-Secondary Education: Indigenous Student Perceptions

SaskNative Economic Development Corporation (L. Heinemann), Metis Economic Development in Regina

Saulis, Conrad, Regional Overview of Aboriginal Child Care in Atlantic Canada

Sawaya, Jean-Pierre, The Seven Nations of Canada: The Alliance Tradition in the Northeast in the Eighteenth and Nineteenth Centuries [TRANSLATION]

Sawaya, Jean-Pierre, *see also* Denys Delâge

Scribe, Charles, *see* John Loxley

Serpent River First Nation, Anishnabe Niigaanziwin: Structures and Procedures of the Serpent River First Nation

Shotton, Robert, *see* Mark O. Dickerson

Siksika Nation, *see* Andrew Bear Robe

Sinaaq Enterprises Inc. (Robert Higgins, Ron Ryan and Fred Weihs), Community Economic Case Study: Nain, Labrador

Sinaaq Enterprises Inc., *see also* Frederick H. Weihs Consulting

Sinclair, Jeannette, A Case Study of the Métis in Slave Lake: The Traditional Role of Women in Collective Decision Making

Sinclaire, Moneca, *see* Yvon Allard

Sioui, Régent G., The Great Law of the Wampum: The Path of the Anishnabek [TRANSLATION]

Sioui, Régent G., *see also* Denys Delâge

Smith, Brian, Youth Perspectives: Wabaseemoong Community Case Study

Sock, Darlene, *see* Stephen Augustine

Spaulding, Richard, Doctrines of Dispossession: A Critical Analysis of Four
    Rationales for the Denial or Extinguishment of Aboriginal Rights in Canada*
Sprague, D.N., Administrative History of Metis Claims
Stanborough, Maria, *see* André LeDressay
Staples, Lindsay, The Inuvialiut Final Agreement: Implementing its Land,
    Resource and Environmental Regimes*
Statistics Canada, Canada's Aboriginal Population, 1981-1991; Literature
    Review on the Demography of the Aboriginal Population in Canada;
    Projections of the Aboriginal Identity Population in Canada, 1991-2016;
    Canada's Aboriginal Population, 1981-1991: A Summary Report
Stevenson, Marc G., Traditional Inuit Decision-Making Structures and the
    Administration of Nunavut
Stewart, Jennifer, *see* Roger Gibbins
Swimmer, Eugene, *see* David Hennes
Symes-Grehan, Marie, Ile a la Crosse Community Study
Tanner, Adrian, et al., Aboriginal Peoples and Governance in Newfoundland
    and Labrador
Tenasco, Anita, *see* Simon Brascoupé
Tennant, Paul, *see* Darcy A. Mitchell
Teslin Tlingit First Nation, Aboriginal Governments Case Study: Teslin
    Tlingit First Nation*
Thalassa Research, Nation to Nation: Indian Nation-Crown Relations in Canada
Timpson, Joyce, Aboriginal Families and Child Welfare: Challenges for First
    Nations and Family Services; Summary of Policy Implications of
    Community and Child Welfare Agency Studies
Tolley, Mona, *see* Simon Brascoupé
Tompkins, Gary N., La Loche Community Case Study
Tough, Frank, and Leah Dorion, "The claims of the Half-breeds...have been
    finally closed": A Study of Treaty Ten and Treaty Five Adhesion Scrip
Townley, Peter G.C., *see* L. Wade Locke
Townshend, Roger, *see* Morris/Rose/Ledgett
Turpel, Mary Ellen, Enhancing Integrity in Aboriginal Government: Ethics
    and Accountability for Good Governance
Turpel, Mary Ellen, *see also* Peter W. Hogg
Urban Representative Body of Aboriginal Nations, An Urban Model of Self-
    Government: Traditional, Flexible, Dynamic and Accessible
Usher, Peter J., Contemporary Aboriginal Land, Resource and Environment
    Regimes – Origins, Problems, and Prospects; Lands, Resources and
    Environment Regimes Research Project – Summary of Case Study
    Findings and Recommendations

---

* Revised title; see introductory note at the beginning of this appendix (page 306).

Van Bibber, Marilyn, Fetal Alcohol Syndrome in Aboriginal Communities in Canada: A Review of Existing Epidemiological Research and Current Preventive and Intervention Approaches

Venne, Sharon H., Treaty 6

Venne, Sharon H., *see also* Eileen Sasakamoose

Vermette, Kathy L., Issues of Pedagogy in Aboriginal Education

Vincelli, Maria, *see* Paul F. Wilkinson

von Rosen, Franziska, Three Generations of a Micmac Family – Stories and Conversations

Wachowich, Nancy, et al., Unikaavut: Our Lives / Stories from the Lives of Three Generations of Iglulik Inuit Women*

Wachowich, Nancy, Pond Inlet Inuit Women Speak About Power*

Walmark, Brian, The Ottertail Clan: A Three Generational Study of Healers in a Traditional Ojibwa Family in Northwestern Ontario

Warrior, Roxanne, Case Study of the Economy of the Peigan Nation

Wasteneys, Clare, Regional Overview of Aboriginal Child Care in Ontario and Quebec

Waterfall, Pauline (Hilistis), Traditional Roles of Heiltsuk Women in Collective Decision Making

Watts, Ronald L., Federal Systems and Accommodation of Distinct Groups: A Comparative Survey of Institutional Arrangements

Webster, Andrew, "They are Impossible People, Really": Social Administration and Aboriginal Social Welfare in the Territorial Norths, 1927-1993.

Webster, Andrew, *see also* Allan Moscovitch

Weihs, Frederick, A Review and Assessment of the Economic Utilization and Potential of Country Food in the Northern Economy

Weihs, Fred, *see also* Sinaaq Enterprises Inc.

Weinstein, Martin, The Ross River Dena: A Yukon Aboriginal Economy

Westcoast Development Group, Aboriginal Economic Development Institutions

Wherrett, Jill, *see* David Cameron

White, Graham, The Adaptation of Non-Aboriginal Institutions of Governance in the Northwest Territories

Whitecloud, Wendy J., The Role of Dakota Women in the Past and Today

Wicken, Bill, and John D. Reid, An Overview of the 18th Century Treaties Signed Between the Mi'kmaq and Wuastukwiuk Peoples and the English Crown, 1725-1928

Wilkinson, Paul F., and Maria Vincelli, The James Bay and Northern Quebec Agreement: An Evaluation of the Implementation of Environmental Regimes*

---

* Revised title; see introductory note at the beginning of this appendix (page 306).

Appendix E
Ethical Guidelines for Research

Purpose
- These guidelines have been developed to help ensure that, in all research sponsored by the Royal Commission on Aboriginal Peoples, appropriate respect is given to the cultures, languages, knowledge and values of Aboriginal peoples, and to the standards used by Aboriginal peoples to legitimate knowledge.
- These guidelines represent the standard of "best practice" adopted by the Commission.

Principles
- Aboriginal peoples have distinctive perspectives and understandings, deriving from their cultures and histories and embodied in Aboriginal languages. Research that has Aboriginal experience as its subject matter must reflect these perspectives and understandings.
- In the past, research concerning Aboriginal peoples has usually been initiated outside the Aboriginal community and carried out by non-Aboriginal personnel. Aboriginal people have had almost no opportunity to correct misinformation or to challenge ethnocentric and racist interpretations. Consequently, the existing body of research, which normally provides a reference point for new research, must be open to reassessment.
- Knowledge that is transmitted orally in the cultures of Aboriginal peoples must be acknowledged as a valuable research resource along with documentary and other sources. The means of validating knowledge in the particular traditions under study should normally be applied to establish authenticity of orally transmitted knowledge.
- In research portraying community life, the multiplicity of viewpoints present within Aboriginal communities should be represented fairly, including viewpoints specific to age and gender groups.
- Researchers have an obligation to understand and observe the protocol concerning communications within any Aboriginal community.
- Researchers have an obligation to observe ethical and professional practices relevant to their respective disciplines.
- The Commission and its researchers undertake to accord fair treatment to all persons participating in Commission research.

Guidelines

Aboriginal Knowledge

In all research sponsored by the Commission, researchers shall conscientiously address themselves to the following questions:

- Are there perspectives on the subject of inquiry that are distinctively Aboriginal?
- What Aboriginal sources are appropriate to shed light on those perspectives?
- Is proficiency in an Aboriginal language required to explore these perspectives and sources?
- Are there particular protocols or approaches required to access the relevant knowledge?
- Does Aboriginal knowledge challenge in any way assumptions brought to the subject from previous research?
- How will Aboriginal knowledge or perspectives portrayed in research products be validated?

Consent

- Informed consent shall be obtained from all persons and groups participating in research. Such consent may be given by individuals whose personal experience is being portrayed, by groups in assembly, or by authorized representatives of communities or organizations.
- Consent should ordinarily be obtained in writing. Where this is not practical, the procedures used in obtaining consent should be recorded.
- Individuals or groups participating in research shall be provided with information about the purpose and nature of the research activities, including expected benefits and risks.
- No pressure shall be applied to induce participation in research.
- Participants should be informed that they are free to withdraw from the research at any time.
- Participants should be informed of the degree of confidentiality that will be maintained in the study.
- Informed consent of parents or guardian and, where practical, of children should be obtained in research involving children.

Collaborative Research

- In studies located principally in Aboriginal communities, researchers shall establish collaborative procedures to enable community representatives to participate in the planning, execution and evaluation of research results.
- In studies that are carried out in the general community and that are likely to affect particular Aboriginal communities, consultation on planning, exe-

cution and evaluation of results shall be sought through appropriate Aboriginal bodies.

- In community-based studies, researchers shall ensure that a representative cross-section of community experiences and perceptions is included.
- The convening of advisory groups to provide guidance on the conduct of research shall not pre-empt the procedures laid down in this part but shall supplement them.

Review Procedures

- Review of research results shall be solicited both in the Aboriginal community and in the scholarly community prior to publication.

Access to Research Results

- The Commission shall maintain a policy of open public access to final reports of research activities. Reports may be circulated in draft form, where scholarly and Aboriginal community response at this stage is deemed useful for Commission purposes.
- Research reports or parts thereof shall not be published where there are reasonable grounds for thinking that publication will violate the privacy of individuals or cause significant harm to participating Aboriginal communities or organizations.
- Results of community research shall be distributed as widely as possible within participating communities, and reasonable efforts shall be made to present results in non-technical language and Aboriginal languages where appropriate.

Community Benefit

- In setting research priorities and objectives for community-based research, the Commission and the researchers it engages shall give serious and due consideration to the benefit of the community concerned.
- In assessing community benefit, regard shall be given to the widest possible range of community interests, whether the groups in question be Aboriginal or non-Aboriginal, and also to the impact of research at the local, regional or national level. Wherever possible, conflicts between interests within the community should be identified and resolved in advance of commencing the project. Researchers should be equipped to draw on a range of problem-solving strategies to resolve such conflicts as may arise in the course of research.
- Whenever possible research should support the transfer of skills to individuals and increase the capacity of the community to manage its own research.

Implementation

- These guidelines shall be included in all research contracts with individuals, groups, agencies, organizations and communities conducting research sponsored by the Commission.
- It shall be the responsibility, in the first instance, of all researchers to observe these guidelines conscientiously. It shall be the responsibility, in ascending order, of research managers, the Co-Directors of Research, and the Commission itself to monitor the implementation of the guidelines and to make decisions regarding their interpretation and application.
- Where, in the opinion of the researcher or the research manager, the nature of the research or local circumstances make these guidelines or any part of them inapplicable, such exception shall be reported to the Commission through the Co-Directors of Research, and the exception shall be noted in the research contract or contract amendments as well as in any publication resulting from the research.

APPENDIX F

RESEARCH ADVISORY COMMITTEE MEMBERS

Peter Russell (Chair)
Department of Political Science
University of Toronto

Antoine Lussier
Winnipeg, Manitoba

Brian Slattery
Osgoode Hall Law School
York University

Murdeena Marshall
Eskasoni, Nova Scotia

Harvey Feit
Department of Anthropology
McMaster University

Ken Coates
Vice-President (Academic)
University of Northern British
    Columbia

Robin W. Boadway
Department of Economics
Queen's University

Cecil King
Faculty of Education
Queen's University

Benoît Robitaille
Département de géographie
Université Laval

Beatrice Watts
Northwest River, Labrador

Dora Wilson
New Hazelton, British Columbia

Michael Asch
Department of Anthropology
University of Alberta

Harold Cardinal
LLM Student
Harvard University

Bertha Wilson
Commissioner
Royal Commission on
    Aboriginal Peoples

Paul L.A.H. Chartrand
Commissioner
Royal Commission on
    Aboriginal Peoples

Appendix G

Commission Publications

The Mandate (Background Documents, August 1991)
Bilingual (English/French)

Terms of Reference (Pamphlet)
English, French, Inuktitut, Cree, Ojibwa

The Circle (Newsletter)
Bilingual (English/French), Inuktitut

A Time to Talk, A Time to Listen (Poster)
English, French

Forging a New Relationship (Video)
English, French

The Right of Aboriginal Self-Government and the Constitution: A Commentary (February 1992)
English, French

Partners in Confederation: Aboriginal Peoples, Self-Government, and the Constitution (August 1993)
English, French

Speeches by Co-Chairs at the Official Launch of the Public Consultation Process (21 April 1992)
Bilingual (English/French), Inuktitut

Ethical Guidelines for Research (Pamphlet)
English, French, Inuktitut

Integrated Research Plan (January 1994)
English, French

Framing the Issues, Discussion Paper No. 1 (October 1992)
English, French

Focusing the Dialogue, Discussion Paper No. 2 (April 1993)
English, French

Overview of the First Round (October 1992)
English, French

Overview of the Second Round (April 1993)
English, French

Exploring the Options: Overview of the Third Round (November 1993)
English, French

Toward Reconciliation: Overview of the Fourth Round (April 1994)
English, French

Framing the Issues (Video)
English, French, Inuktitut

Focusing the Dialogue (Video)
English, French

Aboriginal Peoples in Urban Centres: Report of the National Round Table on Aboriginal Urban Issues (May 1993)
English, French

The Path to Healing: Report of the National Round Table on Aboriginal Health and Social Issues (October 1993)
English, French

Aboriginal Peoples and the Justice System: Report of the National Round Table on Aboriginal Justice Issues (June 1993)
English, French

A Time for Action: Aboriginal Peoples and the Justice System (Video)
English, French

Sharing the Harvest: The Road to Self-Reliance, Report of the National Round Table on Aboriginal Economic Development and Resources (December 1993)
English, French

Public Policy and Aboriginal Peoples, 1965-1992
Volume 1: Soliloquy and Dialogue: The Evolution of Public Policy Discourse on Aboriginal Issues since the Hawthorn Report
Volume 2: Summaries of Reports by Federal Bodies and Aboriginal Organizations
Volume 3: Summaries of Reports by Provincial and Territorial Bodies and Other Organizations
Volume 4: Bibliography
Volumes 1-3, English and French
Volume 4, Bilingual (English/French)

The High Arctic Relocation: A Report on the 1953-55 Relocation and *Summary of Supporting Information* (three volumes) (July 1994)
English, French

Choosing Life: Special Report on Suicide Among Aboriginal People (February 1995)
English, French

Treaty Making in the Spirit of Co-existence: An Alternative to Extinguishment (March 1995)
English, French

Let's Make a Difference Now (Music Video)
English/French/Cree/Inuktitut

Aboriginal Self-Government: Legal and Constitutional Issues (1995)
English, French

Canada's Fiduciary Obligation to Aboriginal Peoples in the Context of Accession to Sovereignty by Quebec (1995)
Volume 1: International Dimensions
Volume 2: Domestic Dimensions
English, French

Bridging the Cultural Divide: A Report on Aboriginal People and Criminal Justice in Canada (1996)
English, French

Copies of Commission publications can be ordered from the Canada Communication Group – Publishing, 45 Sacre-Coeur Boulevard, Hull, Quebec K1A 0S9, or by telephoning (819) 956-4800.

Transcripts of the Commission's public hearings and round tables are available in print and electronic form (diskette). Please state the precise location, date and name of the presenter when ordering. To order written transcripts, contact Stenotran, 1376 Kilborn Avenue, Ottawa, Ontario K1H 6L8, or telephone (613) 521-0703.

A CD-ROM containing the Commission's final report, hearings and round table transcripts, research studies, and many of the publications listed above is being produced by Libraxus Inc. (75 Sparks Street, Suite 400, Ottawa, Ontario K1P 5A5 (613) 567-2484) and will be available from the Canada Communication Group – Publishing at the address above.

Appendix H

Commission Staff and Advisers

Commissioners

Co-Chairs
René Dussault
Georges Erasmus

Allan Blakeney (September 1991 to April 1993)
Paul L.A.H. Chartrand
J. Peter Meekison (June 1993 to November 1996)
Viola Robinson
Mary Sillett
Bertha Wilson

Office of the Co-Chairs
Madeleine Cabana-Hay
Ava Hill
Danielle Labonté
Kelly Wood

Executive Director

Jean Fournier
    (August 1991 to April 1993)
H. Anthony Reynolds
    (April 1993 to November 1996)

*Office of the
Executive Director*
Jeanne d'Arc Arsenault
Roger Arsenault
Marie Dansereau
Louise Delisle
Pierre Gauthier
Marlene Lamarche
Richard Lynn

Senior Advisers
Peter Russell
Brian Slattery

Secretariat

Commission Secretary
Jerome Berthelette
    (October 1991 to May 1993)
Linda Jordan
    (August 1993 to September 1995)

Judy Bertrand L'Ecuyer
Myrtle Bush
Les Clayton
Karen Collins
Roger Farley
Violet Ford
Marceline Francis
Rhondda MacKay
Mel Maracle
Marie Mayer
Susan McLeod

---

* Some of the staff listed here served for limited periods during the Commission's mandate.

Bradley Michael
Kimberley Scott
Suzanne Schryer-Belair
Mona Virdi
Sheila Marie Cook

Public Participation

Director
Patrick Brascoupé
    (February 1992 to May 1992)
John Morrisseau
    (May 1992 to July 1993)

Kathryn Boissoneau
Nipisha Bracken
Dolores Comegan
Laurie Fenner
Sandra Germain
Ovilu Goo-Doyle
Eleanora Jarrett
Rhonda Kayakjuak
Luc Lainé
Michael Lazore
Rebecca Printup
Patricia Saulis
Tammy Saulis
Gordon Spence
Robert Tookoome
Bernard Wood
Charlene Wysote

Administration and Finance

Director
Nicole Viau

Comptroller
Mike McNamara

Neil Blaney
Josée Brascoupé
Pierre Brascoupé
Michel Collard

Darlene Commanda
Madeleine D'Argencourt
Janice Davison
Michel Dickner
Diann Franklin
Don Henry
David Herman
Drew Hightower
Laralee Isaac
Jeannette LaForte
Céline Lalonde
Hélène Leroux
Katherine Livingstone
Gilles Longpré
Françoise McNamee
Kenneth Meshake
Michèle Noël
Cindy Peltier
Donald Roach
Nancy Schnobb
Pamela Shaw
Patricia Steele
Tracy Tarnowski
Sylvie Trépanier
Jason Winters

Design and Publishing Services
Expression Communications Inc.
Michel Hénault
Kathryn Randle

Communications

Director
Dan Gaspé

Head
Allen Gabriel

James Compton
Sandra Dubé
Laralee Isaac
Don Kelly
Hugh McCullum

Verna Stevens
Mona Virdi

Research

Co-Directors
Marlene Brant Castellano
David Hawkes

Frances Abele
Daniel Arsenault
Michael Asch
Anik Aubin
Carole Blackburn
Jean-Pierre Bourdeau
Gail Bradshaw
Suzanne Bronner
François Cadieux
Colleen Cardillo
Mary-Jane Commanda
John Crump
Dara Culhane
Valerie Decontie
Leslie Donnelly
Lynn Farbotko
Katherine Fletcher
Joyce Ford
Violet Ford
Karen Ginsberg
Anita Gordon-Murdoch
Deborah Hanly
Karen Janelle
Alexandra Ker
Francine Lachapelle
Lorie Lafreniere
Louise Lahache
Leina Landriault
Dawn Lavergne-Brady
Sheila Lumsden
Christine Maracle
Beatrice Medicine
George Morin
Linda Paquette

Kenneth Paul
Bill Sainnawap
Andy Siggner
Liette Simard
Nancy-Ann Sutton
Rosalee Tizya
Dale Turner
Fred Wien
Jill Wherrett
Donavon Young

Policy

Co-Directors
James Bourque
Mary Simon
Bert Waslander

Peggy Blair
Shane Book
Carolanne Brewer
Clem Chartier
Larry Chartrand
David DesBrisay
Dirk deVos
Martin Dunn
Joyce Ford
Claudette Fortin
Jo Ann Gagnon
Patricia Hayward
Dwight Herperger
Karen Jacobs-Williams
Tanya King
Simeonie Kunnuk
Catherine Littlejohn
John Loxley
Joanne MacDonald
Phoebe Nahanni
Susan O'Donnell
Leslie Pal
Evelyn Peters
Joanne Pindera
Chris Printup

Sheila Robertson
Jonathan Robinson
Ian Robinson
Konrad Sioui
Jerome Slavik
Garth Wallbridge
Brenda Wattie
Beatrice Watts
Andrew Webster
Wanda Wuttunee

Policy Advisers and Writers

Frances Abele
Mary Alex
Gerald Alfred
Russel Barsh
Marie Battiste
Mary Brodhead
Michael Cassidy
David Crenna
Lynne Davis
Janet Davison
Mark Dockstator
Bruce Doern
Lynn Drapeau
John Evans
Dale Gibson
John Giokas
Katherine Graham
Karen Green
John Hylton
Michael Jackson
Linda Jordan
Lenore Keeshig-Tobias
Don Kelly
Alexandra Ker
Cecil King
Patrick Macklem
John Milloy
James Morrison
Allan Moscovitch
Beatrice Mosionier
David Nahwegahbow

David Newhouse
John O'Neil
Alan Pratt
Gwen Reimer
Jonathan Rudin
David Schneiderman
Nikol Schultz
Brian Slattery
Douglas Sprague
Judi Stevenson
Madeleine Dion Stout
George Tough
James Tully
Gail Valaskakis
Alex von Gernet
Terrance Wade
Jeremy Webber
Fred Wien
Donavon Young

Research Advisers

Harold Bhérer
Frank Cassidy
Michael Asch
Douglas Brown
Andrée Lajoie
Mary Ellen Turpel
Peter Usher
John Weinstein

Intervenor Participation Program

Chairman
David Crombie

Director
Celia Asselin

Richard Budgel
Richard Charles
Steven Horne
Sylvie Moreau
Linda Paquette